AFRICAN POLITICAL FACTS
SINCE 1945

AFRICAN POLITICAL FACTS SINCE 1945

Chris Cook and David Killingray

Facts On File, Inc.

460 Park Avenue South, New York, N.Y. 10016

First published in the United Kingdom in 1983 by
THE MACMILLAN PRESS LTD
London and Basingstoke

First published in the United States of America in 1983 by
FACTS ON FILE, INC.
New York

Library of Congress Cataloging in Publication Data

Cook, Chris, 1945–
   African political facts since 1945.

   Bibliography: p.257
   Includes index.
   1. Africa – Politics and government – 1945–1960 –
Handbooks, manuals, etc.
   2. Africa – Politics and government – 1960 –
Handbooks, manuals, etc.
   I. Killingray, David.   II. Title.
   DT30.C594   960'.32   81-17514
   ISBN 0-87196-381-7   AACR2

Printed in Hong Kong

092013

CONTENTS

PREFACE AND ACKNOWLEDGEMENTS

The aim of *African Political Facts Since 1945* has been to provide as many of the important facts and figures as possible, within a single volume, for the student and teacher of modern African history and politics. The book covers the history of Africa from 1945 to the birth of independent Zimbabwe in 1980. The whole of Africa – from Egypt to Namibia, from Mauritania to Madagascar – has been included. Inevitably, no medium-sized reference work can be entirely comprehensive. The compilers would welcome suggestions for material to be included in future editions of this book.

Among the people we must thank for their help in the compilation of this book are Stephen Brooks, Sheila Fairfield, Alison Johnson and Philip Jones.

London
June 1982

Chris Cook
David Killingray

1 CHRONOLOGY OF MAJOR EVENTS

1945   End of war in Europe
      Algerian nationalist demonstration at Sétif leads to riots; large numbers
        of people killed by French authorities
      African representatives elected to French Constituent Assembly in Paris
      United Nations formed; Egypt, Liberia, Ethiopia and South Africa
        founder-members
      Fifth Pan-African Congress held at Manchester
      Arab League founded in Cairo

1946   Mouvement pour le Triomphe des Libertés Démocratiques founded in
        Algeria by Messali Hadj
      New constitution for the Gold Coast, which becomes the first British
        colony to have an African majority in the legislative council
      Rassemblement Démocratique Africain (RDA) founded by Houphouët-
        Boigny
      Fonds d'Investissement pour le Développement Économique et Social
        (FIDES) set up by France for colonial development
      French abolish forced labour in colonies; by Loi Lamine Gueye French
        citizenship extended to all inhabitants of overseas territories

1947   New constitution for Nigeria with African majority on the legislature
      Groundnut scheme begun in Tanganyika
      Nationalist revolt in Madagascar against French rule
      United Gold Coast Convention founded by Dr J. B. Danquah
      East African High Commission formed

1948   Ibadan University College opened in Nigeria
      Boycott of European goods and riots in Gold Coast
      Union des Populations du Cameroun (UPC) formed
      Egypt at war with Israel (1948–9)
      National Party wins South African general election and begins to
        implement policy of apartheid
      Ethiopia reoccupies Ogaden

Bloc Démocratique Sénegalais founded by Léopold Senghor
General strike in Zanzibar
African–Indian riots in Durban

1949 University of Louvanium established in Belgian Congo
Convention People's Party (CPP) founded in Gold Coast by Kwame
Nkrumah
Victoria Falls Conference in favour of federation of Rhodesia and Nyasa-
land; African opposition to proposed federation
Industrial disturbances at Enugu colliery and riots in southern Nigeria
Makarere becomes a university college

1950 Britain returns Somalia to Italy as a United Nations trust territory for 10
years
Apartheid laws passed in South Africa: Immorality Act, Population
Registration Act, Suppression of Communism Act, Group Areas Act
International Court rules that South West Africa still under United
Nations trusteeship
Association des Bakongos (Abako) formed in Belgian Congo
Action Group formed in Nigeria
Sierra Leone People's Party (SLPP) founded by Milton Margai

1951 New constitutions for Nigeria and Gambia
CPP wins general election in Gold Coast and Nkrumah becomes 'leader
of government business'
Increased Egyptian pressure to force Britain to leave occupied Canal
Zone
British Government accepts idea of a federation of Rhodesia and
Nyasaland
Libya becomes an independent kingdom

1952 Kwame Nkrumah becomes Prime Minister of the Gold Coast
Increased opposition to French in Maghrib
Army coup in Egypt: committee of 'Free Officers' forces King Farouk to
abdicate; Gen. Neguib in power
Eritrea federated with Ethiopia
'Mau Mau' rising begins in Kenya; emergency proclaimed (to 1960)
All non-whites compelled to carry passes in South Africa; non-white
political organisations launch 'passive resistance' campaign against
apartheid

1953 Emergency powers introduced by the South African government against
passive resistance; new racial laws introduced: Reservation of Separate

Amenities Act, Public Safety Act, Criminal Law Amendment Act, Bantu Education Act

Egypt becomes a republic; Rally of National Liberation under Neguib as Egypt's sole political party

Jomo Kenyatta and five others convicted of managing 'Mau Mau' in Kenya

Albert Margai becomes Chief Minister of Sierra Leone

Julius Nyerere elected President of Tanganyika African Association

Central African Federation of Rhodesia and Nyasaland created (lasts till 1963)

France deposes the Sultan of Morocco

1954   Colonel Nasser seizes power in Egypt

Federal system of government formalised by Lyttleton constitution in Nigeria

CPP wins general election in Gold Coast and Britain promises independence

Start of Algerian war of independence (to 1962) led by the Front Libération Nationale (FLN)

British–Egyptian agreement on the evacuation of Suez Canal Zone

Tanganyika African National Union (TANU) formed with Julius Nyerere as President

1955   Bandung Conference in Indonesia attended by representatives of many African nationalist parties

State of emergency throughout Algeria

Moroccan 'Army of Liberation' attacks French posts in West Algeria

King Mohamed of Morocco restored to throne by French

Start of armed rebellion in South Sudan (to 1972)

UPC banned in Cameroon

South African Congress of the People adopts Freedom Charter

1956   Sudan becomes an independent republic

Oil discovered in southern Nigeria

Morocco and Tunisia become independent

Loi cadre in French overseas territories provides for local autonomy

Egypt nationalises the Suez Canal; Egypt–Israel war and British and French invasion of Egypt

African miners strike in Northern Rhodesian copperbelt; state of emergency declared

End of Cape Coloured voting rights in South Africa

Oil found in Algeria

Start of the Treason Trial in South Africa (lasts till 1961)

African Party for the Independence of Guinea and Cape Verde (PAIGC)

and the Popular Movement for the Liberation of Angola (MPLA)
founded

1957 Gold Coast becomes independent as Ghana
Houphouët-Boigny President of Grand Council of French West Africa
Eastern and Western regions of Nigeria become self-governing
SLPP wins general election in Sierra Leone
In South Africa laws passed to ban Africans from worshipping in 'white'
churches
Bey of Tunis deposed; Tunisia becomes a republic
Afro-Asian Solidarity Conference in Cairo

1958 French military raids into Tunisia
Togo becomes independent
Dr Hastings Banda returns to Nyasaland
General de Gaulle advocates a federation with internal autonomy for
French overseas territories as the French Community; at Brazzaville
he announces independence for French Africa
Algerian provisional government set up in Cairo
Guinea becomes independent with Sekou Touré as President; all other
French African territories remain within French Community
Military coup led by Gen. Abboud overthrows Sudanese government.

1959 State of Emergency declared in Nyasaland; Dr Banda imprisoned
Oil discovered in Libya
Northern Region of Nigeria becomes self-governing
Saniquelle Meeting of Presidents Nkrumah, Tubman and Touré to plan
union of free African states
Riots in Belgian Congo
United Nations condemns apartheid
Senegal and Sudan demand independence and bring about the end of the
French Community

1960 Harold Macmillan's 'wind of change' speech in Capetown
French atomic device exploded in the Sahara
Pan-African Congress organises demonstration at Sharpeville, fired on
by South African police; 67 Africans killed
African heads of state meet at Monrovia
Belgian Congo becomes independent; *Force publique* mutinies; United
Nations troops sent into Congo
Somalia becomes independent
Most member states of the French Community become independent
TANU wins election in Tanganyika and Julius Nyerere becomes Chief
Minister
Nigeria becomes an independent state within the Commonwealth

1961 Armed forces announce that they have taken over control of Algeria; OAS terrorism begins
Patrice Lumumba murdered in Katanga
Algerian peace-talks begin in Evian, Switzerland
Rebellion begins in Angola against the Portuguese
Sierra Leone becomes an independent state within the Commonwealth
South Africa becomes a republic and leaves the Commonwealth
Tanganyika becomes an independent state within the Commonweath
Rhodesia Front party formed

1962 Rwanda and Burundi become independent
Plots against President Nkrumah's life in Ghana
Uganda becomes an independent state within the Commonwealth
Algerian independence agreed to at end of Evian peace-talks
First African government formed in Northern Rhodesia
Frelimo headquarters set up in Dar es Salaam, Tanganyika

1963 End of Katanga secession in Congo
President Olympio killed in Togo coup
General Law Amendment Act passed to give South African government wide powers of arrest
Organisation of African Unity (OAU) formed in Addis Ababa by thirty heads of state
End of the Federation of Rhodesia and Nyasaland
Jomo Kenyatta becomes Prime Minister of Kenya
Zanzibar becomes an independent state within the Commonwealth
French evacuate the naval base at Bizerta, Tunisia
Kenya becomes an independent state within the Commonwealth

1964 Massacre of Tutsi in Rwanda
Revolution in Zanzibar; Sultan overthrown and Karume becomes President
Army mutinies in Kenya, Tanganyika and Uganda; British troops called in to help restore order
Union of Tanganyika and Zanzibar as Tanzania
Rivonia trial in South Africa; Nelson Mandela sentenced to life-imprisonment
Tshombe becomes President of Congo; revolts in Congo provinces and Belgian parachutists land at Stanleyville and elsewhere to rescue Europeans
Malawi and Zambia become independent states within the Commonwealth
Frelimo begins armed struggle against Portuguese in Mozambique

1965   Organisation Commune Africaine et Malagache (OCAM) formed at conference of French-speaking heads of state at Noukachott
Chou En-lai, the Chinese premier, visits Tanzania
One-party state adopted in Tanzania
Rhodesia Front party wins general election in Southern Rhodesia; Ian Smith declares Rhodesia's 'unilateral declaration of independence' (UDI); UN Security Council embargo placed on Rhodesia
Gen. Mobutu takes over complete power in Congo

1966   Commonwealth Conference at Lagos
First military coup in Nigeria led by Igbo officers; a counter-coup follows six months later
President Nkrumah deposed by military and police coup in Ghana
Milton Obote seizes the Kabaka's palace in Kampala and makes Uganda into a centralised state
Botswana becomes an independent state within the Commonwealth
Union Minière du Haut-Katanga taken over by Congo government

1967   Arusha Declaration issued in Tanzania
Two army coups in Sierra Leone
Arab–Israeli 'Six-Day War'; Israelis occupy Sinai
Uprising in eastern and northern Congo ended by foreign mercenaries employed by Gen. Mobutu's central government
East African Community established by Kenya, Tanzania and Uganda
Secession of Eastern Region as independent state of Biafra and start of civil war in Nigeria (to 1970)

1968   Malawi establishes diplomatic relations with South Africa
Start of guerrilla war in Rhodesia
Tanzania, Ivory Coast and two other African states recognise Biafran independence
Equatorial Guinea becomes independent of Spain
Military coup in Mali
Swaziland becomes an independent state within the Commonwealth

1969   King Idris deposed by a military coup in Libya; Col. Gaddafi comes to power
General election in Ghana returns Dr Busia as Prime Minister
Serious political disturbances in western Kenya
Ghana expels thousands of aliens

1970   End of Nigerian civil war
British withdrawal from military bases in Libya
President Obote's 'Common Man's Charter' introduced in Uganda

Chinese offer aid to Tanzania to build railway from Dar es Salaam to the Zambian copperbelt

Aswan High Dam in Egypt comes into operation

1971 Gen. Amin leads military coup which overthrows President Obote of Uganda

Central African Republic recognises South Africa and receives economic aid from it

Congo renamed Zaïre

President Banda of Malawi on state visit to South Africa and Mozambique; Ivory Coast delegation to South Africa

Declaration of Mogadishu issued by eastern and central African states stating their intention to continue the armed struggle to liberate South Africa

African National Council (ANC) formed in Rhodesia by Bishop Muzorewa

1972 'African authenticity' campaign launched by President Mobutu in Zaïre

Army coup in Ghana: Gen. Acheampong overthrows Busia government

Pearce Commission in Rhodesia reports an overwhelming 'no' by African population to settlement proposals

President Amin begins to expel Asians from Uganda

Agreement in Sudan of 'southern problem'; regional autonomy granted to the south

Hutu rising in Burundi suppressed with great loss of life

Serious drought in Sahelian region

Military coup in Madagascar

1973 Zambia–Rhodesia border closed by President Kaunda

Serious strikes by black workers in South Africa

African Games at Lagos

Prime Minister Smith of Rhodesia begins talks with African nationalists in an attempt to find some form of internal settlement

Israel–Egypt war; Egyptian troops retake part of Sinai

Oil crisis brings great increase in prices for African states

Widespread drought in Ethiopia

1974 Emperor Haile Selassie overthrown by a military coup; Dergue established to rule the country

Coup in Lisbon by army officers disillusioned with the African wars brings down the Caetano regime and begins the process of decolonisation in the Portuguese empire in Africa

Guinea-Bissau becomes independent

1975   Lomé Agreement signed between EEC and 37 African states
        Economic Community of West African States (Ecowas) Treaty signed by
            15 states
        Portugal's withdrawal from Africa: independence for Cape Verde
            Islands, São Tomé and Principe, Mozambique (June), and Angola
            (Nov). Civil war in Angola
        Tanzam railway officially opened between Zambia and Tanzania
        Four 'front-line' presidents at Quilemane pledge support for the Zim-
            babwe National Liberation Army
        Gen. Murtala Mohamed, President of Nigeria, assassinated in Lagos
        South African troops invade Angola in support of UNITA forces

1976   Soweto riots in South Africa
        Spain withdraws from Western Sahara; territory partitioned between
            Morocco and Mauritania. Proclamation of Sahara Arab Democratic
            Republic, which through its armed Polisario Front wages a guerrilla
            war against both occupying states
        South Africa declares Transkei independent
        'Palace coup' in Addis Ababa

1977   Djibouti became an independent state; final withdrawal of France from
            African territory
        Invasion of Shaba province, Zaïre, by Katangese rebels
        Somali-supported forces invade Ogaden; serious fighting in the region.
            Cuban aid to Ethiopia in the war
        Central African Empire proclaimed by Bokassa
        Widespread purge in Ethiopia by the Dergue
        Constituent Assembly meets in Nigeria in preparation for a return to
            civilian government

1978   Serious strikes in Tunisia
        Internal agreement in Rhodesia: transitional government formed
        Somali forces defeated by Ethiopia in Ogaden war; Ethiopia steps up its
            attacks on Eritrean nationalist forces
        Reconciliation of Guinea with France
        Uganda invasion of Kagera salient in north-west Tanzania
        'Muldergate' scandal in South Africa
        Gen. Acheampong deposed in Ghana

1979   Tanzania supports Ugandan Liberation Front in invasion of Uganda;
            President Amin overthrown
        Emperor Bokassa overthrown and Central African Republic re-estab-
            lished
        President Macia Nguema of Equatorial Guinea overthrown

Junior officers coup in Ghana led by Flight-Lt Rawlings; three former heads of state executed

Elections in Ghana and Nigeria return both countries to civilian rule

Lancaster House talks in London on a settlement for Zimbabwe; the country reverts to British rule for a transitional period.

1980   Elections in Zimbabwe result in an overwhelming victory for Robert Mugabe's ZANU–PF party. Mugabe becomes Prime Minister of an independent Zimbabwe

Military coup in Liberia by junior army officers.

2 GOVERNORS AND HEADS OF STATE*

ALGERIA

Ruled by France to 1962, when it became an independent republic.

GOVERNORS-GENERAL
1944–8	Yves Chataigneau
1948–51	Marcel Édmond Naegelen
1951–5	Roger Étienne Joseph Leonard
1955–6	Jacques Émile Soustelle

MINISTERS-RESIDENT
1956	Georges Albert Julien Catroux
1956–8	Robert Lacoste

DELEGATES-GENERAL
1958	Raoul Salan
1958–60	Paul Albert Louis Delouvrier
1960–2	Jean Morin
1962	Christian Fouchet

PRESIDENTS
1962–3	Ferhat Abbas
1963–5	Ahmed Ben Bella
1965–79	Houari Boumédienne
1979–	Chadli Benjeddid

ANGOLA

A Portuguese colony to 1975, when it became a republic.

GOVERNORS-GENERAL
1943–7	Vasco Lopes Alves

* In compiling this chapter, the authors are deeply indebted to two published sources – David Henige's indispensable *Colonial Governors from the Fifteenth Century to the Present* (University of Wisconsin Press, 1971) and *The Statesman's Year-Book* (edited by Dr John Paxton).

1947	Fernando Falcão Pacheco Mena
1947–55	José Agapito da Silva Carvalho
1956–9	Horácio de Sá Viana Rebelo
1960–1	Álvaro Rodrigues da Silva Tavares
1961–2	Venâncio Augusto Deslandes
1962–6	Jaime Silvério Marquês
1966–72	Camilo Augusto de Miranda Rebocho Vaz
1972–4	Fernando Augusto Santos E. Castro

HIGH COMMISSIONER

1974–5	Antonio Alba Rosa Coutinho

PRESIDENTS

1975–9	Antonio Agostinho Neto
1979–	José Eduardo dos Santos

BENIN

The French colonial territory of Dahomey to 1960, when it became an independent republic under the same name; the People's Republic of Benin was proclaimed in 1975.

GOVERNORS

1943–5	Charles André Maurice Assier de Pompignan
1945–6	Marc Antoine Christian Laurent de Villedeuil
1946–8	Robert Legendre
1948	Jean Georges Chambon
1948–9	Jacques Alphonse Boissier
1949–51	Claude Valluy
1951–5	Charles Henri Bonfils
1955–8	Casimir Marc Biros

HIGH COMMISSIONER

1959–60	René Tirant

PRESIDENTS

1960–3	Hubert Maga
1963–4	Christophe Soglo
1964–5	Sourou Migan Apithy
1965–7	Christophe Soglo
1967–8	Maurice Kouandcté
1968–9	Émile Derlin Zinsou
1969–70	[Presidency suspended: presidential council of three]
1970–2	Hubert Maga

1972	Justin Ahomadegbé
1972–	Mathieu Kerekou

BOTSWANA

The British High Commission territory of Bechuanaland until 1966, when it became a republic.

HIGH COMMISSIONERS
[also for Basutoland (Lesotho, q.v.) and Swaziland (q.v.)]

1944–51	Evelyn Baring
1951–5	J. le Rougetel
1955–8	Percivale Liesching
1959–63	R. R. Ratcliffe Maud
1963–4	H. S. Stephenson
1964	[post abolished]

COMMISSIONERS

1946–50	A. Sillery
1950–3	E. B. Beetham
1953–5	W. F. MacKenzie
1955–9	M. O. Wray
1965–6	H. S. Norman-Walker

PRESIDENTS

1966–80	Sir Seretse Khama
1980–	Quett K. J. Masire

BURUNDI

A Belgian-mandated territory; an independent kingdom in 1962 and a republic from 1966. (For governors see under Ruanda-Urundi.)

HIGH REPRESENTATIVE

1962	E. Hennequiau

KINGS

1961–6	Mwambutsa IV
1966	Ntare V

PRESIDENTS

1966–76	Michel Micombero
1976–	Jean Baptiste Bagaza

CAMEROON

A trust territory divided between France and the United Kingdom, Cameroon achieved independence in 1960.

HIGH COMMISSIONERS
1944–6	Henri Pierre Nicolas
1946–7	Robert Louis Delavignette
1947–9	René Hoffherr
1949–54	Jean Louis Maurice André Soucadaux
1954–6	Roland Joanes Louis Pré
1956–7	Pierre Auguste Joseph Messmer
1958	Jean Paul Ramadier
1958–60	Xavier Antoine Torré

PRESIDENT
1960	Ahmadou Ahidjo

CAPE VERDE ISLANDS

A Portuguese colony from the fifteenth century until 1975, when a republic was formed.

GOVERNORS
1943–9	João de Figueiredo
1949–53	Carlos Alberto Garcia Alves Roçadas
1953–7	Manuel Marques de Abrantes Amaral
1957–8	António Augusto Peixoto Correia
1958–63	Silvino Silvério Marques
1963–73	Leão Maria de Tavares Rosado do Sacramento Monteiro
1973–4	António Lopes dos Santos
1974–5	Henrique da Silva Horta

PRESIDENT
1975–	Aristides Maria Pereira

CENTRAL AFRICAN REPUBLIC

The French colonial territory of Ubangi-Chari to 1960, when it became a republic. From 1976 to 1979 it was known as the Central African Empire.

LIEUTENANT GOVERNOR
1942–6	Henri Camille Sautot

GOVERNORS
1946–8   Jean Victor Louis Joseph Chalvet
1949–50   Pierre Jean Marie Delteil
1950–1   Ignace Jean Aristide Colombani
1951–4   Aimé Marius Louis Grimald
1954–8   Louis Marius Pascal Sanmarco
1958   Paul Camille Bordier

HIGH COMMISSIONER
1959–60   Paul Camille Bordier

PRESIDENTS
1960–6   David Dacko
1966–76   Jean Bédel Bokassa

EMPEROR
1976–9   Jean Bédel Bokassa

PRESIDENT
1979–   David Dacko

CHAD

A French colonial territory to 1960, when it became a republic.

LIEUTENANT GOVERNORS
1944–6   Jacques Camille Marie Rogué

GOVERNORS
1946–9   Jacques Camille Marie Rogué
1949   Paul Hippolyte Julien Marie le Layec
1950–1   Henri Jean Marie de Mauduit
1951   Charles Émile Hanin
1951–6   Ignace Jean Aristide Colombani
1956–8   Jean René Troadec

HIGH COMMISSIONER
1959–60   Daniel Marius Doustin

PRESIDENTS (AND MILITARY RULERS)
1960–75   François (later N'Garta) Tombalbaye
1975–9   Félix Malloum
1979 (Mar–
   Apr)   Goukouni Oueddei

1979 (Apr–
  Nov)   Lol Mohamed Shawwa
1979 (Nov)– Goukouni Oueddei

COMORO ISLANDS

A French protectorate to 1975, when a republic was proclaimed in three islands while Mayotte remained French.

GOVERNORS
1947–9   Eugène Alain Charles Louis Alaniou
1949–50   Marie Emmanuel Adolphe Roger Remy
1950–7   Pierre Léonard Alphonse Coudert
1957–60   Georges Arnaud
1961   Louis Joseph Édouard Saget

HIGH COMMISSIONERS
1961–3   Louis Joseph Édouard Saget
1963–7   Henri Joseph Marie Bernard
1967–71   Antoine Padouan Columbani
1971–3   Jacques Mouradian

DELEGATES-GENERAL
1973–4   Georges Poulet
1974–5   Henri Beaux

PRESIDENTS
1975   Ahmed Abdallah
1975–6   Said Mohamed Jaffar
1976–8   Ali Soilih
1978   Said Alloumani
1978–9   Ahmed Abdallah and Mohamed Ahmed (co-pres.)
1979   Ahmed Abdallah

CONGO

The French colonial territory of Middle Congo to 1960, when it became a republic.

LIEUTENANT GOVERNORS
1944–6   Ange Marie Charles André Bayardelle
1946   Christian Robert Roger Laigret

1946–7	Numa Henri François Sadoul
1947–50	Jacques Georges Fourneau
1950–2	Paul Hippolyte Julien Marie Le Layec
1952–3	Jean Jacques Chambon
1953–6	Ernest Eugène Rouys
1956–8	Jean Michel Soupault
1958	Paul Charles Dériaud

HIGH COMMISSIONER
| 1959–60 | Gui Noël Georgy |

PRESIDENTS
1960–3	Abbé Fulbert Youlou
1963–8	Alphonse Massemba-Débat
1968–9	Alfred Raoul
1968–77	Marien N'Gouabi
1977–9	Joachim Yhombi-Opango
1979–	Denis Sassou-Nguesso

CONGO (ex-Belgian): see ZAÏRE

DAHOMEY: see BENIN

DJIBOUTI

Formerly French Somaliland; in 1967 it became the French territory of the Afars and Issas, and in 1977 an independent republic.

GOVERNORS
1946–50	Paul Henri Siriex
1950–4	Numa Henri François Sadoul
1954	Roland Joanes Louis Pré
1954–7	Jean Albert René Petitbon
1957–8	Maurice Meker
1958–62	Jacques Marie Julien Campain
1962–6	René Tirant
1966–7	Louis Joseph Édouard Saget

HIGH COMMISSIONERS
1967–9	Louis Joseph Édouard Saget
1969–72	Dominique Ponchardier
1972–7	Georges Thiercy

PRESIDENT
1977–   Hassan Gouled

EGYPT

An independent monarchy from 1922 until 1953, when a republic was established.

KINGS
1936–52   Farouk I
1952–3   Fuad II

PRESIDENTS
1953–4   Mohamed Neguib
1954–70   Gamal Abdul Nasser
1970–81   Mohamed Anwar El Sadat
1981–   Hosni Mubarak

EQUATORIAL GUINEA

Rio Muni and the island of Fernando Po were Spanish territories until 1968, when they were merged to form an independent republic.

GOVERNORS
1943–9   Juan Marian Bonelli Rubío
1949–62   Faustino Ruíz González
1962–3   Francisco Núñez Rodríguez

HIGH COMMISSIONERS
1963–4   Francisco Núñez Rodríguez
1964–6   Pedro Latorre Alcubierre
1966–8   Victor Suances Díaz del Río

PRESIDENTS
1968–79   Francisco Macias Nguema
1979–   Teodoro Nguema

ERITREA

An Italian colony until 1942, when it was conquered by the British. Under British administration until 1952, when it was incorporated into Ethiopia.

CHIEF ADMINISTRATORS
1944–5   C. D. McCarthy
1945–6   John Meredith Benoy
1946–51   Francis Greville Drew
1951–2   Duncan Cameron Cumming

ETHIOPIA

An independent kingdom which was ended in 1975, when a republic was proclaimed.

EMPEROR
1930–74   Haile Selassie (in exile 1936–41)

HEADS OF GOVERNMENT
1974   Aman Mikhail Andom
1974–5   Teferi Benti
1976–   Mengistu Haile Mariam

FRENCH EQUATORIAL AFRICA

The four French colonial territories of Chad, Ubangi-Chari, Middle Congo and Gabon, which were administered as a federal unit to 1958.

GOVERNORS-GENERAL
1944–7   Ange Marie Charles André Bayardelle
1947   Charles Jean Luizet

HIGH COMMISSIONERS
1947–51   Bernard Cornut-Gentille
1951–8   Paul Louis Gabriel Chauvet
1958   Pierre Auguste Joseph Messmer
1958   Yvon Bourges

HIGH COMMISSIONER-GENERAL
1959–60   Yvon Bourges

FRENCH WEST AFRICA

The French colonial territories of West Africa were administered as a federal unit until 1958.

HIGH COMMISSIONERS
1943–6	Pierre Charles Albert Cournarie
1946–8	René Victor Marie Barthes
1948–51	Paul Léon Albin Bechard
1951–6	Bernard Cornut-Gentille
1956–8	Gaston Cusin

HIGH COMMISSIONER-GENERAL
1958–9	Pierre Auguste Joseph Messmer

GABON

A French colonial territory to 1960, when it became a republic.

LIEUTENANT GOVERNORS
1944–6	Numa François Henri Sadoul
1946–7	Roland Joanes Louis Pré
1947–9	Numa François Henri Sadoul
1949–51	Pierre François Pelieu
1951–2	Charles Émile Hanin
1952–8	Yves Jean Digo
1958	Louis Marius Pascal Sanmarco

HIGH COMMISSIONER
1959–60	Jean Risterucci

PRESIDENTS
1960–7	Léon M'Ba
1967–	Albert Bernard (later Omar) Bongo

THE GAMBIA

A British colony to 1965, when it was proclaimed an independent dominion. In 1970 the Gambia became a republic within the Commonwealth.

GOVERNORS
1942–7	H. R. Blood
1947–9	A. B. Wright
1949–58	P. Wyn-Harris
1958–62	E. H. Windley
1962–5	J. W. Paul

GOVERNORS-GENERAL
1965–6   J. W. Paul
1966–70   F. M. Singhateh

PRESIDENT
1970–   Dauda Kairaba Jawara

GHANA

Britain's Gold Coast colony became the dominion of Ghana in 1957 and a republic in 1960.

GOVERNORS
1941–8   A. C. M. Burns
1948–9   G. H. Creasy
1949–57   C. N. Arden-Clarke

ASHANTI: CHIEF COMMISSIONERS
1941–6   E. G. Hawkesworth
1946–51   C. O. Butler
1951–2   W. H. Beaton

ASHANTI: REGIONAL OFFICERS
1952–4   W. H. Beaton
1954–5   A. J. Loveridge
1955–7   A. C. Russell

GOLD COAST COLONY: CHIEF COMMISSIONERS
1945–50   T. R. O. Mangin
1950–3   A. J. Loveridge

NORTHERN TERRITORIES: CHIEF COMMISSIONERS
1942–6   W. H. Ingrams
1948–50   E. N. Jones
1950–3   G. N. Burden

NORTHERN TERRITORIES: REGIONAL OFFICERS
1953–4   A. J. Loveridge
1954–7   S. McDonald-Smith

GOVERNOR-GENERAL
1957–60   W. F. Hare, Earl of Listowel

PRESIDENTS (AND MILITARY RULERS)

1960–6	Kwame Nkrumah
1966–9	Joseph Arthur Ankrah
1969–70	Akwasi A. Afrifa
1970–2	Edward Akufo-Addo
1972–8	Ignatius Kutu Acheampong
1978–9	Frederick W. K. Akuffo
1979	Jerry Rawlings
1979–81	Hilla Limann

GUINEA

A French colonial territory to 1958, when it became a republic.

GOVERNORS

1944–6	Jacques Georges Fourneau
1946–8	Édouard Louis Barthélemy Marie Joseph Terrac
1948–50	Roland Joanes Louis Pré
1950–3	Paul Henri Siriex
1953–5	Jean Paul Parisot
1955–6	Charles Henri Bonfils
1956–7	Jean Paul Ramadier
1958	Jean Mauberna

PRESIDENT

1958–	Ahmad Sekou Touré (1966–72 Kwame Nkrumah as titular co-president)

GUINEA-BISSAU

A Portuguese colony until 1974, when it became a republic.

GOVERNORS

1949–53	Raimundo António Rodrigues Serrão
1953–6	Diogo António José Leite Pereira de Melo e Alvim
1956–8	Álvaro Rodrigues da Silva Tavares
1958–62	António Augusto Peixoto Correia
1962–5	Vasco António Marints Rodrigues
1965–8	Arnaldo Schultz
1968–73	António Sebastião Ribeiro de Spínola
1974	Arnaldo Schultz

PRESIDENT

1974–80	Luiz Cabral
1980–	João Bernardo Vieira

IVORY COAST

A French colonial territory to 1960, when it became a republic.

GOVERNORS

1943–7	André Jean Gaston Latrille
1947–8	Oswald Marcellin Maurice Marius Durand
1948	Georges Louis Joseph Orselli
1948–51	Laurent Élisée Pecheux
1951–2	Pierre François Pelieu
1952–4	Camille Victor Bailly
1954–6	Pierre Joseph Auguste Messmer
1956–7	Pierre Auguste Michel Marie Lami
1957–8	Ernest de Nattes

HIGH COMMISSIONERS

1959	Ernest de Nattes
1959–60	Yves René Henri Guena

PRESIDENT

1960–	Félix Houphouët-Boigny

KENYA

A British colony from 1920 to 1963, when it became an independent dominion; a republic was proclaimed in 1964.

GOVERNORS

1944–52	P. E. Mitchell
1952–7	E. Baring
1957–9	F. Crawford
1959–63	P. M. Renison
1963–4	M. J. MacDonald

PRESIDENTS

1963–78	Jomo Kenyatta
1978–	Daniel T. Arap Moi

LESOTHO

The British High Commission territory of Basutoland until 1966, when it became an independent kingdom.

RESIDENT COMMISSIONERS
1942–6	C. N. Arden-Clarke
1947–51	A. D. F. Thompson
1951–5	E. P. Arrowsmith
1955–61	A. G. T. Chaplin
1961–6	A. F. Giles

KING
1966–	Moshoeshoe II

LIBERIA

An independent republic since 1847.

PRESIDENTS
1944–71	William V. S. Tubman
1971–80	William Richard Tolbert

CHAIRMAN OF PEOPLE'S REDEMPTION COUNCIL
1980–	Samuel K. Doe

LIBYA

An Italian colony from 1912 to 1942, when it came under British administration. In 1951 it was created an independent kingdom by the United Nations. Libya was proclaimed a republic in 1969.

CYRENAICA: CHIEF ADMINISTRATORS
1942–5	D. C. Cumming
1945–6	P. B. E. Acland
1946–8	J. W. N. Haugh
1948–51	E. A. V. de Candole

TRIPOLITANIA: CHIEF ADMINISTRATOR
1943–51	T. R. Blackley

KING
1951–69	Idris I

PRESIDENT
1969–	Mu'ammar Mohamed al-Gaddafi

MADAGASCAR (MALAGASY REPUBLIC)

A French colony to 1960, when it became a republic.

GOVERNOR-GENERAL
1944–6   Paul de Saint-Mart

HIGH COMMISSIONERS
1946–8   Jules Marcel de Coppet
1948–50   Pierre de Chevigné
1950–4   Isaac Robert Bargues
1954–60   Jean Louis Maurice André Soucadaux

PRESIDENTS (AND MILITARY RULERS)
1960–72   Philibert Tsirinana
1972–5   Gabriel Ramanantsoa
1975 (Feb)   Richard Ratsimandrara
1975 (Feb–   Gilles Andriamahazo
  June)
1975 (June)–   Didier Ratsiraka

MALAWI

The British colony of Nyasaland became part of the Central African Federation from 1953 to 1963. It was proclaimed an independent dominion in 1964 and a republic in 1966.

GOVERNORS
1942–7   E. C. S. Richards
1948–56   G. F. T. Colby
1956–61   R. P. Armitage
1961–6   G. S. Jones

PRESIDENT
1966–   Hastings Kamuzu Banda

MALI

The French colonial territory of Soudan joined Senegal in the Mali Federation in 1960 (June–Aug) and then became the republic of Mali.

GOVERNORS
1942–6   Auguste Maurice Léon Calvel

1946–52	Edmond Jean Louveau
1952	Camille Victor Bailly
1952–3	Salvador Jean Etcheber
1953	Albert Jean Mouragues
1953–6	Lucien Eugène Geay
1956–8	Henri Marie Joseph Gipoulon

HIGH COMMISSIONER
1959–60	Jean Charles Sicurani

PRESIDENTS
1960–8	Mobido Keita
1968–	Moussa Traoré

MAURITANIA

A French colonial territory to 1960, when it became a republic.

GOVERNORS
1944–6	Christian Robert Roger Laigret
1947–8	Lucien Eugène Geay
1948–9	Henri Jean Marie de Mauduit
1949–50	Édouard Louis Barthélemy Marie Joseph Terrac
1950–1	Jacques Camille Marie Rogué
1951–4	Pierre Auguste Joseph Messmer
1954–5	Albert Jean Mouragues
1955–6	Jean Paul Parisot
1956–8	Albert Jean Mouragues

HIGH COMMISSIONER
1959–60	Pierre Amédée Joseph Émile Jean Anthonioz

PRESIDENTS
1960–78	Mokhtar Ould Daddah
1978–9	Mustapha Ould Mohamed Salek
1979–80	Mohamed Ould Ahmed Louly
1980–	Mohamed Khouna Ould Kaydalla

MAURITIUS

The island was ruled by Britain from 1810 to 1968, when an independent dominion was established.

GOVERNORS
1942–9	H. C. D. C. Mackenzie-Kennedy
1949–53	H. R. R. Blood
1953–9	R. Scott
1959–62	C. M. Deverell
1962–8	J. S. Rennie

GOVERNORS-GENERAL
1968	J. S. Rennie
1968–72	A. L. Williams
1972–8	Sir Rainan Osman
1978–	Sir D. Burrenchobay

MOROCCO

From 1912 to 1956 the sultanate of Morocco was divided into French and Spanish protectorates and an internationally administered area around Tangier.

RESIDENTS-GENERAL
1943–6	Gabriel Puaux
1946–7	Eirik Labonne
1947–51	Alphonse Pierre Juin
1951–4	Augustin Léon Guillaume
1954–5	François Lacoste
1955	Gilbert Yves Édmond Grandval
1955	Pierre Boyer de la Tourdu Moulin
1955–6	André Louis Dubois

SULTAN
1927–53	Mohammed V

KINGS
1927–61	Mohammed V (Sultan 1927–56; deposed by French 1953–5)
1961–	Hassan II

MOZAMBIQUE

A Portuguese colony to 1975, when it became a republic.

GOVERNORS-GENERAL
1940–7	José Tritão de Bettencourt
1947–58	Gabriel Maurício Teixeira

1958–61	Pedro Correia de Barros
1961–4	Manuel Maria Sarmento Rodrigues
1964–8	José Augusto da Costa
1968–70	Baltasar Rebêlo de Sousa Almeida
1970–1	Eduardo de Arantes de Oliveira
1971–4	Manuel Pimental dos Santos

HIGH COMMISSIONER
1974–5	Vítor Crespo

PRESIDENT
1975–	Samora M. Machel

NAMIBIA

Former German colony administered by South Africa as a mandated territory. South Africa's continuing control of the country is contested by the United Nations.

ADMINISTRATORS
1943–51	P. I. Hougenhout
1951–3	A. J. R. van Rhijn
1953–63	D. T. du P. Viljoen
1963–8	W. C. du Plessis
1968–71	J. G. H. van der Wath
1971–5	B. J. van der Walt

ADMINISTRATORS-GENERAL
1977–9	M. T. Steyn
1979–	G. Viljoen

NIGER

A French colonial territory to 1960, when it became a republic.

GOVERNORS
1942–54	Jean François Toby
1955–6	Jean Paul Ramadier
1956–8	Paul Camille Bordier
1958	Louis Félix Rollet
1958	Don Jean Colombani

HIGH COMMISSIONER
1959–60   Don Jean Colombani

PRESIDENTS
1960–74   Hamani Diori
1974–   Seyni Kountché

NIGERIA

A British colony which became an independent dominion in 1960 and a republic in 1963.

GOVERNORS
1943–8   A. F. Richards
1948–54   J. S. Macpherson

GOVERNORS-GENERAL
1954–5   J. S. Macpherson
1955–60   J. Robertson
1960–3   B. M. Azikiwe

NORTHERN REGION: CHIEF COMMISSIONERS
1943–7   J. R. Patterson
1947–51   E. W. Thompstone

NORTHERN REGION: LIEUTENANT GOVERNORS
1951–2   E. W. Thompstone
1952–4   B. E. Sharwood-Smith

NORTHERN REGION: GOVERNORS
1954–7   B. E. Sharwood-Smith
1957–62   G. W. Bell

EASTERN REGION: CHIEF COMMISSIONERS
1943–8   F. B. Carr
1948–51   J. G. Pyke-Nott

EASTERN REGION: LIEUTENANT GOVERNORS
1951–2   J. G. Pyke-Nott
1952–4   C. J. Pleass

EASTERN REGION: GOVERNORS
1954–6   C. J. Pleass
1956–60   R. de S. Stapledon

WESTERN REGION: CHIEF COMMISSIONERS
1939–46   G. C. Whiteley
1946–51   T. C. Hoskyns-Abrahall

WESTERN REGION: LIEUTENANT GOVERNORS
1951   T. C. Hoskyns-Abrahall
1951–4   H. F. Marshall

WESTERN REGION: GOVERNOR
1954–60   J. D. Rankine

PRESIDENTS (AND MILITARY RULERS)
1963–6   Benjamin Mhamdi Azikiwe
1966 (Jan) Nwafoi Orzu
1966 (Jan– Johnson Aguiyi-Ironsi
  Aug)
1966–75   Yakubu Gowon
1975–6   Murtala Ramal Mohamed
1976–9   Olusegun Obasanjo
1979–   Alhaji Shehu Usman A. Shagari

RHODESIA: see ZIMBABWE

RHODESIA AND NYASALAND

The Federation of Northern and Southern Rhodesia and Nyasaland came into being in 1953 and lasted until 1963.

GOVERNORS-GENERAL
1953–7   J. J. Llewellin, Baron Llewellin
1957–63   S. Ramsey, Earl of Dalhousie

RUANDA-URUNDI

A Belgian mandated territory which in 1962 became the independent republic of Rwanda (q.v.) and the kingdom of Burundi (q.v.).

GOVERNORS
1932–46   Eugène Jacques Pierre Louis Jungers
1946–52   Léon Antonin Marie Pétillon
1952–5   Alfred Maria Josephus Ghislencus Claeys-Bouuaert
1955–62   Jean Paul Harroy

HIGH REPRESENTATIVE
1962　　　　Édouard Hennequiau

RWANDA

A Belgian territory which became an independent republic in 1962.

PRESIDENTS
1962–73　　　Grégoire Kayibanda
1973–　　　　Juvénal Habyarimana

SAINT HELENA, ASCENSION ISLAND AND TRISTAN DA CUNHA

A British dependency in the South Atlantic.

GOVERNORS
1941–7　　　W. B. Gray
1947–54　　　G. A. Joy
1954–8　　　J. D. Harford
1958–62　　　R. E. Alford
1962–8　　　J. O. Field
1968–74　　　D. A. P. Murphy
1974–8　　　T. Oates
1978–　　　　G. C. Guy

SÃO TOMÉ AND PRINCIPE

A Portuguese colony from 1483, the islands formed a republic in 1975.

GOVERNORS
1941–5　　　Amadeu Gomes de Figueiredo
1945–53　　　Carlos de Sousa Gorgulho
1953–7　　　Francisco António Pires Barata
1957–63　　　Manuel Marques de Abrantes Amaral
1963–71　　　António Jorge da Silva Sebastião
1972–4　　　João Cecilio Goncalves
1974–5　　　António E. C. Peres Veloso

PRESIDENT
1975–　　　　Manuel Pinto da Costa

SENEGAL

A French colonial territory to 1960, when Senegal became independent within the Federation of Mali. The Federation split after a few months and Senegal was proclaimed a separate republic.

GOVERNORS

1945–6	Pierre Louis Maestracci
1946–7	Oswald Marcellin Maurice Marius Durand
1947–50	Laurent Marcel Wiltord
1950–2	Camille Victor Bailly
1952–3	Lucien Eugène Geay
1953–4	Daniel Henri Marie Goujon
1954–5	Maxime Marie Antoine Jourdain
1955–7	Don Jean Colombani
1957–8	Pierre Auguste Michel Marie Lami

HIGH COMMISSIONER

1959–60	Pierre Auguste Michel Marie Lami

PRESIDENT

1960–	Léopold Sédar Senghor

SEYCHELLES

A British colony which became an independent republic in 1976.

GOVERNORS

1942–7	W. M. Logan
1947–51	P. S. Selwyn-Clarke
1951–3	F. Crawford
1953–8	W. Addis
1958–61	J. K. Thorp
1961–7	J. E. Asquith, Earl of Oxford and Asquith
1967–9	H. S. Norman-Walker
1969–74	B. Greatbatch
1974–6	C. H. Allan

PRESIDENTS

1976–7	James Richard Mancham
1977–	France Albert René

SIERRA LEONE

A British colony which became an independent dominion in 1961 and a republic in 1971.

GOVERNORS
1941–8	H. C. Stevenson
1948–53	G. B. Stooke
1953–6	R. D. Hall
1956–61	M. H. Dorman

GOVERNORS-GENERAL
1961–2	M. H. Dorman
1962–8	H. J. L. Boston
1968–71	B. Tejan-Sie

PRESIDENT
1971–	Siaka Probyn Stevens

SOMALIA

The republic was created in 1960, incorporating British Somaliland, a former colony, and Italian Somaliland, which was a United Nations trust territory from 1945.

BRITISH SOMALILAND: GOVERNORS
1943–8	G. T. Fisher
1948–54	G. Reece
1954–9	T. O. Pike
1959–60	D. B. Hall

ITALIAN SOMALILAND: GOVERNORS

(under United Kingdom)
1943–8	D. H. Wickham
1948	E. A. V. de Candole
1948–50	G. M. Gamble

(under Italy)
1950–3	G. Fornari
1953–5	E. Martino
1955–8	E. Anzilotti
1958–60	M. di Stefani

PRESIDENTS
1960–7	Adan Abdullah Osman
1967–9	Abdelrashid Ali Shermarke
1969–	Mohamed Siad Barre

SOUTH AFRICA

The Union of South Africa was created in 1910. South Africa became a republic in 1961 and left the Commonwealth.

GOVERNORS-GENERAL
1943–6	N. J. de Wet
1946–51	G. B. van Zyl
1951–9	E. Jansen
1959–61	C. R. Swart

STATE PRESIDENTS
1961–7	C. R. Swart
1967	T. E. Dönges (never assumed office, owing to illness; J. F. T. Naude was acting president)
1968–75	J. J. Fouché
1975–8	N. Diederichs
1978–9	B. J. Vorster
1979–	M. Viljoen

Under the policy of apartheid three homelands, or 'bantustans', have been declared republics by the South African government: Transkei in 1976, Bophuthatswana in 1977 and Venda in 1979. None of these 'independent' states has received any international recognition.

TRANSKEI: PRESIDENT
1976–9	Chief Botha Sigeau
1979–	Chief Kaiser Matanzima

BOPHUTHATSWANA: PRESIDENT
1977–	Chief Lucas L. M. Mangope

VENDA: PRESIDENT
1979–	Chief Mphephu

SOUTH WEST AFRICA: see NAMIBIA

SPANISH WEST AFRICA

The Spanish territories of West Africa were administered as a single unit until 1958, when they were divided into two provinces. Spain handed over Ifni to Morocco in 1969. In 1976 Spain withdrew from Spanish Sahara and the territory was divided between Morocco and Mauritania.

GOVERNORS

1939–49	J. B. Lopez
1949–52	F. R. Burguet
1952–4	V. T. Gil
1954–7	R. P. de Santallana
1957–8	E. G. Z. Quirce

SPANISH SAHARA: GOVERNORS

1958	José Hector Vázquez
1958–61	Mariano Alonso Alonso
1961–4	Pedro Latorre Alcubierre
1964–5	Joaquín Agulla Jiménez Coronado
1965–7	Angel Enríquez Larrondo
1967–71	José María Pérez de Lema Tejero
1971–4	Don Fernando de Santiago y Diaz de Mendevil
1974–6	Federico Gomez de Salazar y Nieto

IFNI: GOVERNORS

1958–9	M. G. Z. Quirce
1959–61	P. L. Alcubierre
1961–3	J. A. J. Coronado
1963–5	A. A. Campos
1965–7	M. T. Larrasquito
1967–9	J. M. V. Rodríguez

SUDAN

The territory which formed the Anglo-Egyptian condominium from 1899 became an independent republic in 1956.

GOVERNORS-GENERAL

1940–7	H. J. Huddleston
1947–54	R. G. Rowe
1954–5	A. K. Helm

HEADS OF GOVERNMENT, PRIME MINISTERS

1956–8	[Presidential Council]
1958–64	Ferik Ibrahim Abboud
1964–5	[Supreme Council of State]
1965–9	Ismail al-Azhari
1969–	Jaafar Mohamed al-Nemery

SWAZILAND

A British protectorate from 1906, Swaziland became an independent kingdom within the Commonwealth in 1968.

RESIDENT COMMISSIONERS

1946–50	E. B. Beetham
1950–6	D. L. Morgan
1956–63	B. A. Marwick
1963–8	F. A. Loyd

KING
1921–	Sobhuza II

TANGANYIKA/TANZANIA

The United Republic of Tanzania was formed in 1964 from the Republic of Tanganyika, a British trust territory until 1961, and Zanzibar, which had become an independent sultanate in 1963 and a republic in 1964.

GOVERNORS OF TANGANYIKA

1942–5	W. E. Jackson
1945–9	W. D. Battershill
1949–58	E. F. Twining
1958–61	R. G. Turnbull

PRESIDENT
1961–	Julius K. Nyerere

TOGO

A French trust territory which became an independent republic in 1960.

HIGH COMMISSIONERS
1944–8	Jean Noutary
1948–51	Jean Henri Arsène Cédile

1951–2   Yves Jean Digo
1952–4   Laurent Elisée Péchoux
1955–7   Jean Louis Philippe Bérard
1957–60   Georges Léon Spénale

PRESIDENTS
1960–3   Sylvanus Olympio
1963–7   Nicolas Grunitzky
1967   Kléber Dadjo
1967–   Étienne (later Gnassingbe) Eyadéma

TUNISIA

Under French rule from 1881 to 1956, when Tunisia became an independent monarchy. A republic was proclaimed in 1957.

BEYS
1943–56   Mohamed al-Amin
1956–7   Sidi Lamine

RESIDENTS-GENERAL
1946–50   Jean Mons
1950–2   Louis Marcelin Marie Perillier
1952–3   Jean de Hauteclocque
1953–4   Pierre Voizard
1954–5   Pierre Georges Jacques Marie Boyer de la Tour du Moulin

HIGH COMMISSIONER
1955–6   Roger Seydoux Fornier de Clausonne

PRESIDENT
1957–   Habib Ben Ali Bourguiba

UGANDA

A British Colony which became an independent dominion in 1962 and a republic in 1967.

GOVERNORS
1944–52   J. H. Hall
1952–7   A. B. Cohen
1957–61   F. Crawford
1961–2   W. F. Coutts

GOVERNOR-GENERAL
1962–3   W. F. Coutts

PRESIDENTS
1962–6   Mutesa II, Kabaka of Buganda
1966–71   A. Milton Obote
1971–9   Idi Amin
1979 (Apr–   Yusaf Lule
  June)
1979–80   Godfrey Binaisa
1980–   A. Milton Obote

UPPER VOLTA

A French colonial territory, separated from the Ivory Coast in 1947, and proclaimed an independent republic in 1960.

GOVERNORS
1947–8   Gaston Mourgies
1948–52   Albert Jean Mouragues
1952–3   Roland Joanes Louis Pré
1953–6   Salvador Jean Étcheber
1956–8   Yvon Bourges

HIGH COMMISSIONER
1959–60   Paul Jean Marie Masson

PRESIDENTS
1960–6   Maurice Yameogo
1966–   Sangoulé Lamizana

ZAÏRE

The Belgian Congo, which achieved independence as the Republic of Congo in 1960. The name Zaïre was adopted in 1971.

GOVERNORS
1934–46   Pierre Marie Joseph Ryckmans
1946–52   Eugène Jacques Pierre Louis Jungers
1952–8   Léon Antonin Marie Pétillon
1958–60   Henri Arthur Adolf Antoon Marie Christophe Cornelis

PRESIDENTS
1960–5   Joseph Ileo Kasavubu
1965–   (Joseph Désiré) Mobutu Sese Seko

ZAMBIA

The British colony of Northern Rhodesia, which became an independent republic in 1964.

GOVERNORS
1941–7   E. J. Waddington
1948–54   G. M. Rennie
1954–8   A. E. T. Benson
1958–64   E. D. Hone

PRESIDENT
1964–   Kenneth David Kaunda

ZANZIBAR

A British territory which became an independent sultanate in 1963 and a republic in 1964. In the same year Zanzibar joined Tanganyika to form a united republic, now Tanzania.

SULTANS
1911–60   Seyyid Sir Khalifa bin Harub
1960–3   Seyyid Abdullah
1963–4   Seyyid Jamshid

RESIDENTS
1941–46   H. G. Pilling
1946–51   V. G. Glenday
1952–4   J. D. Rankine
1954–60   H. S. Potter
1960–3   G. R. Mooring

PRESIDENT
1964–5   Sheikh Abeid Karume

ZIMBABWE (formerly RHODESIA)

The British territory of Southern Rhodesia became self-governing in 1923. In 1965 the white minority government unilaterally declared the country an independent state as Rhodesia. A republic was proclaimed in 1970 but it failed to gain international recognition. By 1978 agreement had been reached between the regime and African nationalists within the country to form a more representative government for the state of Zimbabwe–Rhodesia. A provisional government was established, but continuing guerrilla warfare forced that government to return the territory temporarily to British supervision. Zimbabwe became an independent republic in 1980.

GOVERNORS

1944–6	W. C. Tait
1947–53	J. N. Kennedy
1954–9	P. B. R. W. William-Powlett
1959–69	H. V. Gibbs

PRESIDENTS

1970–5	C. Dupont
1975–8	J. J. Wrathall
1979	J. Gumede

GOVERNOR

1980	Christopher Soames, Lord Soames

PRESIDENT

1980–	Canaan Banana

3 MAJOR MINISTERIAL APPOINTMENTS

Pres – President; PM – Prime Minister; FA – Foreign Affairs; Ext – External Affairs; Fin – Finance.

ALGERIA

1 July 62	Independence granted; first effective government formed after elections of Sep 63 – before that, wrangling factions shoved each other in and out
18 Sep 63	*Pres/PM* Ahmed Ben Bella *FA* Abdul Aziz Bouteflika *National Economy* (incorporating Finance, Commerce and industry) Bachir Boumaza
28 Sep 63	*FA* Mohamed Khemisti *Fin* Ahmed Francis
19 June 65	Coup under Col. Boumédienne; Revolutionary Council assumes power
10 July 65	Boumédienne forms a cabinet *PM* Col. Houari Boumédienne *FA* Abdul Aziz Bouteflika *Fin* Ahmed Kaïd
10 Dec 67	*Fin* (acting; later confirmed) Ahmed Medhegri
28 July 70	*Fin* Ismaïl Mahroug
16 Feb 76	*Fin* Abdelmalek Temam
21–27 Apr 77	Cabinet reshuffle *Fin* Mohamed Seddik Benyahia

40

9 Feb 79   *President of the Republic, Council of Revolution, Council of Ministers*   Col. Benjeddid Chadli

8 Mar 79   *PM*   Mohamed Ben Ahmed Abdelghani
            FA   Mohamed Seddik Benyahia
            Fin   Mohamed Hadj Yalla

ANGOLA

11 Nov 75   Independence

14 Nov 75   Neto's government sworn in:

            PM   Lopo do Nascimento
            FA   José Eduardo dos Santos
            Fin   none; Carlos Rocha is Minister for Planning and Economic Co-ordination

23 Nov 75   Roberto government:

            PM   Johnny Eduardo/José N'dale (coalition of FNLA/UNITA, joint premiership)
            FA   Hendrik Vaal Neto
            Fin   Craca Tavares

26 Nov 76   *PM*   Lopo do Nascimento
            FA   Paulo Teixeira Jorge
            Fin   Saidi Vieira Dias Mingas

27 May 77   Mingas killed in an attempted coup

31 Aug 77   *Fin*   Ismael Gaspar Martins

Dec 78   Post of PM abolished

17 Jan 79   Death of Neto
            Pres   José Eduardo dos Santos

12 July 80 *FA*   Paulo Teixeira Jorge
            Fin   Ismael Gaspar Martins

BENIN (formerly DAHOMEY)

4 Dec 58   Independence as Dahomey, an autonomous republic within the French Community

            PM   Sourou Migan Apithy

22 May 59	*PM* Hubert Maga *FA* Émile Derlin Zinsou
1 Aug 60	Full independence
2 Nov 60	*Fin* Sourou Migan Apithy
12 Dec 60	*FA* Oké Assaba
Feb 62	*FA* Émile Zinsou
July 62	Reference to Borna Bertin as Fin Minister
28 Oct 63	Army coup
29 Oct 63	*Pres/PM* Col. Christophe Soglo *FA* Hubert Maga *Fin* Sourou Migan Apithy
25 Jan 64	*PM* Justin Ahomadegbé *FA* Gabriel Lozès *Fin* François Aplogan
29 Nov 65	Ahomadegbé resigns as PM
1 Dec 65	*PM/FA* Tahirou Congacou *Fin* Antoine Boya
23 Dec 65	*Pres/PM* Christophe Soglo *FA* Émile Derlin Zinsou *Fin* Nicéphore Soglo
Dec 66	*Fin* Bertin Borna
17 Dec 67	Army coup
18 Dec 67	*Pres/PM* Maj. Maurice Kouandeté *FA* Émile Derlin Zinsou *Fin* Pascal Tchabi Kao
17 July 68	Zinsou elected President, and asked to form a government, which he does on 31 July 68: *Pres/PM* Émile Derlin Zinsou *FA* Daouda Badarou *Fin* Stanislas Kpognon
10 Dec 69	Army coup
12 Dec 69	Directorate installed under Lt-Col. Émile de Souza; the former Cabinet resigns on 16 Dec 69 *FA* Lt-Col. Benoît Sinzogan *Fin* Lt-Col. Maurice Kouandeté

Apr 70	Introduction of presidency by rotation; the President heads the Cabinet during his two-year term

1 May 70   *Pres/PM*   Hubert Maga
            FA   Daouda Badarou
            Fin   Pascal Tchabi Kao

4 Aug 71   *FA*   Michel Ahouanmenou

7 May 72   *Pres/PM*   Justin Ahomadegbé

26 Oct 72   Army coup

27 Oct 72   *Pres/PM*   Maj. Mathieu Kerekou
            FA   Maj. Michel Aladaye
            Fin   Thomas Lahami

30 Mar 73   *Fin*   Janvier Assogba

21 Oct 74   *Fin*   Quartermaster Isidore Amoussou

BOTSWANA (formerly BECHUANALAND)

3 Mar 65   *PM*   Seretse Khama (forms a cabinet 4 Mar 65; contains no FA minister)

30 Sep 66   First cabinet on Independence:

            Pres   Sir Seretse Khama
            Ext   M. P. K. Nwako
            Fin   B. C. Thema

22 Oct 69   Sir Seretse Khama appointed PM once more; chooses cabinet on 23 Oct 69

            Fin   J. G. Haskins

30 Oct 74   *Fin*   Quett K. J. Masire
            Ext   A. M. Mogwe

18 July 80   *Pres*   Quett K. J. Masire
            Fin   Peter S. Mmusi

BURUNDI

1 July 62   Independence

            PM   André Muhirwa

June 63   *PM*   Pierre Ngendandumwe

Apr 64	*PM*	Albin Nyamoya
11 Jan 65	*PM*	Pierre Ngendandumwe (assassinated 15 Jan 65)
23 Jan 65	*PM*	Joseph Bamina
Oct 65	*PM*	Léopold Biha
11 July 66	*PM*	Michel Micombero (he appointed his cabinet on 13 July 66)
	FA	Pie Masumbuku
Sep 66		Masumbuku resigns; replaced by Prime Nyongabo
29 Nov 66		PM Micombero deposes the head of state and becomes Pres as well as PM. He dissolves the government and forms a new one on 6 Dec 66:
	FA	Prime Nyongabo
	Fin	Donatien Bihute
14 Mar 67	*PM*	takes FA portfolio
Aug 68	*FA*	Lazare Ntawurishira
	Fin	André Kabura (imprisoned 8 Oct 69)
29 Apr 72		Pres Micombero dissolves the government and takes full powers till 14 July 72
15 July 72	*PM*	Albin Nyamoya
	FA	Artemon Simbananiye
	Fin	Joseph Hicuburundi
5 June 73		Nyamoya sacked
11 July 74		Constitution comes into force
13 Mar 74	*Fin*	Maj. Samuel Nduwingoma
11 Nov 74	*FA*	Gilles Bimazubute
	Fin	Gabriel Mpozagara
27 Nov 75	*FA*	Melchior Bakwira
1 Nov 76		Pres Micombero overthrown
9 Nov 76	*Pres*	Lt-Col. Jean Baptiste Bagaza
11 Nov 76	*PM*	(office re-created) Lt-Col. Edouard Nzambimana
13 Nov 76	*FA*	Albert Muganga
	Fin	Dominique Shiramanga

13 Oct 78	*PM*	(office abolished)
	FA	E. Nzambimana
	Fin	Astère Girumkwigomba

CAMEROON

1 Jan 60	Independence	
	Pres/PM	Ahmadou Ahidjo
	FA	Charles Okala
Oct 61	*FA*	Jean Betayene
1964	*FA*	Benoît Balla
May 65	*FA*	Simon Nko'o Efoundgou
July 66	*Fin*	Simon Nko'o Efoundgou
Jan 68	*FA*	Simon Nko'o Efoundgou
13 June 70	*FA*	Raymond Ntheppe
25 Jan 71	*FA*	Jean Keutcha
June 72	*FA*	Vincent Efon
	Fin	Charles Ouana Awana
2 June 75	Post of PM recreated, but no date for when it previously lapsed, as Ahidjo was originally PM	
30 June 75	*PM*	Paul Biya
	FA	Jean Keutcha
	Fin	Marcel Yondo
8 Nov 79	*Fin*	Gilbert Ntang
19 July 80	*FA*	Paul Doutsop

CAPE VERDE ISLANDS

5 July 75	Independence	
	Pres	Aristides Maria Pereira
	PM	Pedro Pires
	FA	Abilio Duarte
	Fin	Amaro da Luz

CENTRAL AFRICAN REPUBLIC (formerly UBANGI-CHARI)

Apr 59	PM Barthelemy Boganda killed in an air crash; new PM appointed, David Dacko
12 Aug 60	Independence
	PM David Dacko
	FA Maurice Dejean
17 Nov 60	PM Dacko is also elected Pres
1 Jan 66	Pres Dacko imprisoned by Col. Jean Bédel Bokassa
3 Jan 66	*Pres/PM* Col. Jean Bédel Bokassa
	FA Antoine Guimali
	Fin Alexandro Banza
12 Jan 67	*FA* Jean Arthur Bandio
13 Feb 68	*Fin* Antoine Guimali
19 Aug 70	*FA* Nestor Kombot Naguemon
5 Feb 71	*FA* Clément N'Gai Voueto
4 Aug 71	*FA* Joseph Potelot
29 Dec 71	*Fin* Derant Enoch-Lakoué in place of François Gon, but no date for the appointment of Gon
16 Oct 73	*FA* Louis Alazoula
	Fin Alphonse Koyamba
1 Jan 75	*PM* (newly created post) Elisabeth Domitien
15 June 74	*FA* Joseph Potelot
23 June 75	*FA* Antonio Franck
	Fin Marie Christiane Ghoukou
1976	PM Domitien sacked and replaced by Pres Bokassa
5 Sep 76	*PM* Ange Patassé
4 Dec 76	Empire proclaimed, with Bokassa as Emperor
14 Dec 76	*FA* Jean Paul Mokodopo
	Fin Alphonse Koyamba
Oct 77	*FA* Michel Gbezera-Bria
	Fin Hugues Dobozeildi
17 July 78	*PM* Henri Madou
	Fin François Estrade

24 Sep 79	Restoration of Central African Republic

Pres David Dacko
PM Bernard Christian Ayandho
FA Sylvestre Bangui
Fin François Gueret

CHAD

28 Nov 58	Autonomous republic within the French Community

PM Gabriel Lisette (defeated 10 Feb 59)

10 Feb 59	*PM* Goutchomo Sahoulba (resigns 13 Mar 59)
13 Mar 59	*PM* Ahmed Koulamallah (resigns 24 Mar 59)
24 Mar 59	*PM* François Tombalbaye *Fin* Ahmed Kotoko
11 Aug 60	Independence
Dec 60	*Pres/PM* François Tombalbaye *Fin* Djibrine Kherallah
22 Aug 61	*FA* Djibrine Kherallah *Fin* Michel Djidingar
6 Mar 63	*FA* Maurice Ngantar
24 Nov 64	*FA* Jacques Baroum
20 Apr 66	*Fin* Abakar Sanga Traore
15 Oct 68	*Fin* Abdoulaye Lamana
23 May 71	*FA* Baba Hassane *Fin* Djibrine Kherallah Qui (mention of another FA minister, Élie Romba, 26 Dec 71–9 Mar 73)
1 Oct 73	*FA* Djiriabaye Doralta
30 Aug 73	Pres Tombalbaye changes his forename to N'Garta, Christian names having been abolished by decree, 27 Aug 73
13 Apr 75	Military coup; Tombalbaye assassinated
12 May 75	Provisional government:

PM Brig.-Gen. Félix Malloum
FA Sq.-Ldr Wadal Abdelkader Kamoungue
Fin Brig.-Gen. Negue Djogo

29 Aug 78	*PM* Hissène Habré (resigns Mar 1979) *FA* Kotigua Guerina *Fin* Elie Romba
23 Mar 79	Formation of Provisional State Council: *Chairman* (i.e. *de facto* head of state) Goukouni Oueddei *FA* Barma Ramadan Omer *Fin* Mahamat Saleh Ahmat
29 Apr 79	Provisional government formed *Pres* Lol Mohamed Shawwa *FA* Koumbamba Dering
10 Nov 79	*Pres* Goukouni Oueddei *FA* Acyl Ahmat *Fin* Mahamat Saleh Ahmat

COMORO ISLANDS

26 Dec 72	Government elected to work for independence *PM* Ahmed Abdallah
6 July 75	Unilateral declaration of independence from France; the Mayotte islanders refuse to support it. Comoros apart from Mayotte instal a government on 24 July 75 *Pres/PM* Ahmed Abdallah *FA* Ali Mroudjae
3 Aug 75	Coup by Front National Uni
4 Aug 75	Revolutionary Council headed by Prince Said Mohamed Jaffar
6 Jan 76	*PM* Abdellahi Mohamed *FA* Mouzaoir Abdallah *Fin* Tadjidine Massoundi
12 May 78	Coup
15 May 78	*PM* Abdellahi Mohamed *Minister of State* Abbas Djoussouf
23 May 78	*Co-Pres* Ahmed Abdallah and Mohamed Ahmed
24 May 78	New name: Federal and Islamic Republic of the Comoros *PM* Abdellahi Mohamed *FA* Ali Mroudjae *Fin* Said Kafe

22 Dec 79	*Pres*	Ahmed Abdallah
	PM	Salim Ben Ali
	FA	Ali Mroudjae

CONGO (formerly MIDDLE CONGO)

28 Nov 58	Independence as an autonomous republic within the French Community
	PM Abbé Fulbert Youlou
14 Aug 60	Full independence
	FA Stéphane Tchichelle
15 Aug 63	Youlou, Pres/PM, overthrown
16 Aug 63	*Pres/PM* Alphonse Massemba-Débat
	FA Charles Ganao
	Fin Edouard Babackas
24 Dec 63	*PM* Pascal Lissouba
	FA Charles Ganao
	Fin Edouard Babackas
26 Apr 66	PM Lissouba resigns
6 May 66	*PM* Ambroise Noumazalay
12 Jan 68	*FA* Nicolas Mondjo
1 Aug 68	Pres Massemba-Débat announces dissolution of National Assembly; he will rule himself by decree
3 Aug 68	Pres deposed by the army
4 Aug 68	Pres recalled. Cabinet resigns
5 Aug 68	New cabinet:
	Pres/PM Alphonse Massemba-Débat
	FA Nicolas Mondjo
	Fin Edouard Babackas
22 Aug 68	*Pres/PM* Capt. Alfred Raoul
6 Sep 68	*Fin* Pierre-Félicien Koua
21 June 69	*FA* Charles Assemekeng
3 Jan 70	Cabinet resigns

4 Jan 70   New cabinet:

                    Pres/PM   Maj. Marien N'Gouabi
                    FA   Auxence Ikonga
                    Fin   Edouard Madingou

13 June 71   Keesing's gives a new Fin Minister, Edouard Ange Poungui, and says he replaced Boniface Matingou. Probably a confusion of names

16 Dec 71   *FA*   Henri Lopes

8 Jan 73   *FA*   David Charles Ganao
                    Fin   Saturnin Okabe

9 Nov 74   *PM* (post separated from presidency)   Henri Lopes

12 Dec 75   Lopes resigns

18 Dec 75   *PM*   Louis Sylvain Goma
                    FA   Théophile Obenga
                    Fin   Alphonse Poaty

18 Mar 77   Pres N'Gouabi assassinated

3 Apr 77   *Pres*   Col. Joachim Yhombi-Opango

5 Apr 77   New council of ministers appointed by new Pres:

                    PM and *FA* as before
                    Fin   Henri Lopes

4 Apr 79   *Pres*   Denis Sassou Nguessou
                    V Pres   Jean-Pierre Thystère Tchicaya
                    PM   Louis Sylvain Goma
                    FA   Pierre Nze
                    Fin   Henri Lopes

DJIBOUTI (formerly FRENCH SOMALILAND, then TERRITORY OF THE AFARS AND ISSAS)

26 June 77   Independence

                    Pres/PM   Hassan Gouled Aptidon

12 July 77   *PM*   Ahmed Dini Ahmed

15 July 77   *Fin*   Ibrahim Harbi Farah (dies 22 Nov 77; replacement unknown)
                    FA   Abdallah Mohamed Kamil

17 Dec 77	PM Ahmed resigns; Pres Aptidon takes on post of PM

2 Oct 78	*PM*	Barkat Gourad Hamadou
	FA	Moumin Bahdon Farah
	Fin	Ibrahim Soultan

EGYPT

9 Oct 44	*PM*	Ahmed Maher
	FA	Mahmoud Fahmy al-Noukrachy
	Fin	Makram Ebeid

24 Feb 45	PM assassinated

25 Feb 45	*PM/FA* Mahmoud Fahmy al-Noukrachy

7 Mar 45	*FA* Abdul Hamid Badawy

15 Feb 46	PM resigns; Ebeid had resigned as Fin Minister 13 Feb 46

17 Feb 46	*PM/Fin* Ismail Sidky
	FA Ahmed Lufty es-Sayed

8 Dec 46	PM Sidky resigns

9 Dec 46	*PM/FA* Mahmoud Fahmy al-Noukrachy
	Fin Ibrahim Abdul Hadi

17 Feb 47	*Fin* Abdul Magid

20 Nov 47	*PM/Fin* Mahmoud Fahmy al-Noukrachy
	FA Khashaba Pasha

28 Dec 48	Noukrachy assassinated
	PM/Fin Ibrahim Abdul Hadi
	FA Ibrahim Dessuky Abaza

27 Feb 49	*FA* Ahmed Mohamed Khashaba

25 July 49	PM Hadi resigns

26 July 49	*PM/FA* Hussein Sirry (leads a caretaker government pending elections in Oct)

3 Nov 49	PM Sirry resigns and forms a new cabinet on the same day:
	PM/FA Hussein Sirry
	Fin Mohamed Zaki Abdul Motaal

3 Jan 50	Fresh elections

12 Jan 50   *PM*   Mustapha Nahas
               FA   Mohamed Saleh al-Din
               Fin   Mohamed Zaki Abdul Motaal

11 Nov 50   *Fin*   Fuad Sirag el-Din

26 Jan 52   PM Nahas dismissed

27 Jan 52   *PM/FA*   Aly Maher
               Fin   Mohamed Zaki Abdul Motaal

 1 Mar 52   Maher resigns

 2 Mar 52   *PM*   Ahmed Naguib Hilaly
               FA   Abdul Khalek Hassouna
               Fin   Mohamed Zaki Abdul Motaal

30 June 52   Hilaly resigns

 2 July 52   *PM/FA*   Hussein Sirry
               Fin   Naguib Ibrahim

20 July 52   *PM*   Sirry resigns

22 July 52   *PM*   Ahmed Naguib Hilaly

23 July 52   Coup under Maj.-Gen. Mohamed Neguib; Hilaly resigns

24 July 52   *PM/FA*   Aly Maher
               Fin   Abdul Gelil al-Emary

 7 Sep 52   *PM*   Mohamed Neguib
               FA   Ahmed Farrag Tayeh

 9 Dec 52   *FA*   Mohamed Fawzi

25 Feb 54   Neguib resigns

               PM   Lt-Col. Gamal Abdul Nasser
               FA   Mohamed Fawzi
               Fin   Aly al-Gereitly

 8 Mar 54   *PM*   Mohamed Neguib (Nasser having withdrawn and the
               government having made it up with Neguib)

17 Apr 54   *PM*   Gamal Abdul Nasser
               Fin   Abdul Hamid al-Sherif

 1 Sep 54   *Fin*   Abdul Moneim al-Khaissouny

17 Aug 61   Fin is now the responsibility of three ministers:

               Abdul Moneim al-Khaissouny
               Hassan Abbas Zaky
               Col. Akram Deiry

19 Oct 61	*Fin*	Abdul Latif al-Boghdadi
29 Sep 62	(Nasser now Pres)	
	PM	Wing-Commander Ali Sabry
	Fin	Abdul Moneim al-Khaissouny
25 Mar 64	*FA*	Mohamed Riad
	Fin	Nazih Deif
2 Oct 65	*PM*	Zakaria Mohieddin
	FA	Mohamed Fawzi
	Fin	Abdul Moneim al-Khaissouny
10 Sep 66	*PM*	Mohamed Sidki Soliman
	Minister of the Economy	Hassan Abbas Zaky
	Minister for the Treasury	Nazih Deif
20 Mar 67	*Pres/PM*	Gamal Abdul Nasser
	Presidential adviser on FA	Mohamed Fawzi
	FA	Mohamed Riad
	Fin	Abdul Aziz Mohamed Hegazy
19 June 67	*Fin*	Nazih Ahmed Deif
28 Sep 70	Pres Nasser dies	
21 Oct 70	*PM*	Mohamed Fawzi
16 Nov 70	Fawzi's cabinet resigns	
18 Nov 70	New cabinet:	
	PM	Mohamed Fawzi
	FA	Mohamed Riad
	Fin	Abdul Aziz Mohamed Hegazy
16 Jan 72	*PM*	Aziz Sidky
17 Jan 72	*FA*	Mohamed Murad Ghaleb
8 Sep 72	*FA*	Mohamed Hassan al-Zayat
27 Mar 73	*Pres/PM*	Mohamed Anwar El Sadat
	Vice-Premier for Finance (new title) Abdul Aziz Mohamed Hegazy	
31 Oct 73	*FA*	Ismail Fahmy
26 Apr 74	Hegazy promoted to First Vice-Premier, Economy and Commerce, which gives him a supervisory position over new Fin Minister, Abdul Fattah Ibrahim	
25 Sep 74	*PM*	Abdul Aziz Mohamed Hegazy

13 Apr 75	Government resigns
14 Apr 75	*PM* Mamdouh Mohamed Salem
15 Apr 75	*FA* Ismail Fahmy *Fin* Ahmed Abu Ismail
28 Oct 76–	Elections; government resigns and forms again, 9 Nov 76
4 Nov 76	*Deputy PM for Financial and Economic Affairs* Abdul Moneim al-Khaissouny *FA* Ismail Fahmy *Fin* Mahmoud Sakaheddin Hamid
17 Nov 77	Fahmy resigns; temporarily replaced by Mohamed Riad. He resigns at once and is in turn replaced by Boutros-Ghali
24 Dec 77	*FA* Mohamed Ibrahim Kamel
1 May 78	*FA* Boutros Boutros-Ghali
2 Oct 78	*PM* (of the 'Peace Cabinet') Mustapha Khalil
17 Feb 79	*PM/FA* Mustapha Khalil
19 June 79	*Fin* Ali Lutfi Mohamed Lutfi

EQUATORIAL GUINEA

12 Oct 68	Independence
	Pres/PM Francisco Macias Nguema *FA* Atanasio Ndongo
5 Mar 69	*Pres/PM/FA* Francisco Macias Nguema
4 Aug 73	New constitution, forming a unitary state out of two formerly autonomous provinces, Fernando Po and Rio Muni. Pres Macias Nguema is made Life Pres
Dec 78	*V Pres/FA* Nguema Esono Nchama
3 Aug 79	Pres Macias Nguema overthrown
25 Aug 79	*Pres of Supreme Military Council* Teodoro Nguema *V Pres/FA* Florencio Maye *Fin* Salvador Ela

ETHIOPIA

FA (from 1943)   Akilou Habtewold
Fin (no date)   Makonnen Habtewold

| 3 Apr 58 | *FA* | Yilma Deressa |
| | *Fin* | M. Woldemaskal |

17 Apr 61   List published of the cabinet then in office:

	PM	Akilou Habtewold
	FA	Mikael Imru
	Fin	Yilma Deressa

23 Mar 66   Decree giving the PM power to appoint the cabinet (previously the Emperor did it)

11 Apr 66	*FA*	Ketema Yifru
18 Feb 69	*Fin*	Mammo Tadesse
19 Aug 71	*FA*	Minassie Haile

27 Feb 74   Government resigns

| 28 Feb 74 | *PM* | Lij Endalkatchew Makonnen |

| 3 Mar 74 | *PM/FA* | Lij Endalkatchew Makonnen |
| | *Fin* | none |

| 21 Mar 74 | *Fin* | Negash Desta |
| 29 May 74 | *FA* | Dejazmatch Zewde Gabre Selassie |

12 Sep 74   Provisional military government headed by Gen. Aman Mikhail Andom takes power and deposes Emperor

15 Nov 74   Gen. Andom resigns

17 Nov 74   *Head of Executive Committee of the Military Council*   Maj. Mengiste Haile Mariam

23 Nov 74   Gen. Andom executed

28 Nov 74   *Chairman of Provisional Military Administration Council* Brig.-Gen. Teferi Benti

| 6 Dec 74 | *FA* | Kifle Wodajo |

3 Feb 77   Teferi Benti assassinated

11 Feb 77   Provisional Military Council to be known as the Dergue and appoint a council of ministers. Lt-Col. Mengistu Haile Mariam head of the Dergue and all its committees

| 11 Mar 77 | *FA* | Feleke Gedle-Ghiorgis (Wodajo had defected) |

GABON

Independence as an autonomous republic within the French Community

28 Nov 60	Independence	
	Pres/PM	Léon M'Ba
1963	*FA*	Jean François Ondo
1964	*FA*	Pierre Avaro
20 Mar 65	*FA*	Jean Engone
	Fin	Léonard Badinga
20 Apr 67	*FA*	Jean Rémy Ayouné
	Fin	Pierre Mebaley
28 Nov 67	*Pres/PM*	Albert Bernard Bongo
July 68	*Fin*	Augustin Boumah
8 Feb 71	*FA*	Georges Rawiri
Feb 72	*Fin*	Paul Moukambi
4 Oct 73	*Pres/FA*	Albert Bernard Bongo
16 Apr 75	*V Pres/PM*	Léon Mébiane
15 Mar 76	*FA*	Paul Okumba D'Okwatsegue
	Fin	Jérome Okinda
17 Oct 76	*FA*	Martin Bongo

THE GAMBIA

17 Feb 65	Independence. Pierre N'Jie had been appointed Chief Minister in Mar 61. PM at Independence, Dauda Kairaba Jawara
Sep 72	Reference to

FA Andrew Camara
Fin S. M. Dibba

9 Apr 77	Reference to

Pres/PM Sir Dauda Kairaba Jawara
FA Lamine Jabang
Fin Lamine Bora M'Boge

| 13 June 77 | *Fin* | Assane Moussa Camara (formerly Andrew Camara) |

| 19 Aug 78 | *V Pres* | Assane Moussa Camara |
| | *Fin* | Alhaji Mohamadu Cadi Cham |

GHANA (formerly GOLD COAST)

| 5 Mar 52 | *PM* | Kwame Nkrumah |

| 10 Mar 52 | Nkrumah institutes cabinet government, but there are no FA or Fin Ministers |

| 17 June 54 | *Fin* | Agbeli Gbedemah |

| 5 Mar 57 | Independence |

| 18 Jan 59 | *FA* | Kojo Botsio |

| 9 Apr 59 | *FA* | Ako Adjei |

| 1 July 60 | Republican constitution (cabinet as before) |

| May 61 | Reshuffle between 2 May and 20 May |
| | *Fin* | F. K. D. Goka |

| 29 Aug 62 | Adjei dismissed |

| 3 Sep 62 | PM Nkrumah takes on the FA portfolio; Adjei is arrested |

| 17 Mar 63 | *FA* | Kojo Botsio |

| 19 Feb 64 | Goka resigns; PM Nkrumah takes on Fin portfolio |

| 12 June 65 | *FA* | Alex Quaison-Sackey |
| | *Fin* | Kwesi Amoako-Atta |

| 24 Feb 66 | Nkrumah deposed; National Liberation Council formed under Maj.-Gen. Joseph A. Ankrah |

| 1 July 67 | Executive Council of the National Liberation Council formed: |

Chairman Lt-Gen. Joseph A. Ankrah
FA J. W. K. Harlley
Fin Brig. Akwasi A. Afrifa

| 7 Sep 69 | Civilian cabinet: |

PM Kofi Abrefa Busia
FA Victor Owusu
Fin J. H. Mensah

| 28 Jan 71 | *FA* | William Ofori-Atta |

13 Jan 72   Coup

15 Jan 72   Office of PM abolished by proclamation, Parliament dissolved, constitution suspended

29 Jan 72   Formation of Commissioners' Council:

Head of Council and Finance Commissioner   Lt-Col. Ignatius Kutu Acheampong
Commissioner for FA   Maj.-Gen. Nathan A. Aferi

1 Jan 74   *FA*   Maj. Kwame Baah

9 Oct 75   Reorganisation: National Redemption Council replaced by Supreme Military Council

FA Commissioner   Roger J. A. Felli

15 June 77   *Fin Commissioner*   A. K. Appiah

1 Jan 79   *Pres of Supreme Military Council and head of state*   Fred W. K. Akuffo

4 June 79   Coup. Armed Forces Revolutionary Council:

Chairman   Flight-Lt Jerry Rawlings
Fin   Joseph L. S. Abbey
FA   Gloria A. Nikoi

24 Sep 79   Civilian government:

Pres   Hilla Limann
FA   Isaac K. Chinebuah
Fin   Amon Nikoi

13 Nov 80   *Fin*   George Bennet

GUINEA

2 Oct 58   Independence

Pres/PM/FA   Ahmad Sekou Touré
Fin   Drame Alioune

Jan 68   *FA*   Louis Lansana Beavogui
Fin   Diallo Saifoulaye

16 May 69   *FA*   Diallo Saifoulaye
Fin   Ismaël Touré

26 Apr 72   *PM/FA*   Louis Lansana Beavogui

11 Dec 76–   Reshuffle

Feb 77   *FA*   Fily Sissoko
           Fin   Fodé Mamadou Touré
           Minister of the Domain of Economy and Finance (over F. M. Touré) Ismaël Touré

GUINEA-BISSAU

10 Sep 74   Independence

18 Mar 77   Reference to

           PM (from 1973)   Maj. Francisco Mendes
           FA   Victor Maria Saudé
           Fin   Carlos Correia

1978   *PM*   João Bernardo Vieira

IVORY COAST

4 Dec 58   Independence as an autonomous republic within the French Community

1 May 59   *PM/FA*   Félix Houphouët-Boigny

11 Aug 60   Full independence

4 Jan 61   *Fin*   Raphaël Saller

5 Jan 70   *FA*   Arsène Assouane Usher
           Fin   Henri Konan Bédié

1977   *FA*   Siméon Ake
           Fin   Abdoulaye Koné

KENYA

1 June 63   Ministry in preparation for independence:

           PM/FA   Jomo Kenyatta
           Fin   James Gichuru

12 Dec 63   Independence

10 Dec 64   First republican cabinet:

           Pres/PM   Jomo Kenyatta
           FA   Joseph Murumbi
           Fin   James Gichuru

3 May 66   Murumbi appointed a V Pres; FA portfolio to be dealt with by a committee under Pres Kenyatta

5 Jan 67   *FA*   James Myamweya (mention of his having replaced Mbiyu Koinange, who is said to have served from 3 May 66, so maybe he headed FA committee)

24 July 69   *Fin*   Robert Ouko (said to have replaced Joseph Odero Jowi, but no date given for the beginning of Jowi's term)

22 Dec 69   *FA*   Njoroge Mungai
                Fin   Mwai Kibaki

3 Oct 74   *FA*   Munyua Waiyaki

10 Oct 78   *Pres*   Daniel T. Arap Moi
                FA   Mwai Kibaki

LESOTHO

11 May 65   *PM/FA*   Chief Sekonyana Maseribane
                Fin   Benedict Leseteli

7 July 65   *PM* and *FA* Chief Leabua Jonathan

3 Oct 66   Independence

Jan 70   Constitution suspended

27 Apr 73   Interim Assembly meets (still mention of ministers – Peete mentioned as FA Minister).

5 July 74   *FA*   J. R. Kostsokoane

12 Nov 75   *FA*   C. D. Molapo
                Fin   E. R. Sekhonyana

1977   *PM*   Chief Leabua Jonathan
                FA   Charles Molapo
                Fin   E. R. Sekhonyana

LIBERIA

No mention of any cabinet or ministers during the whole of Pres Tubman's reign (1944–71)

3 Jan 72   *Pres/PM*   Richard Tolbert
                FA   Rocheford Weeks
                Fin   Cyril Bright

2 July 74		Rocheford Weeks suspended
16 July 74	*FA*	Cecil Dennis
28 Apr 75	*Fin*	Edwin Williams
12 Jan 76	*Fin*	James T. Phillips
1 Aug 79	*Fin*	Ellen Johnson-Sirleaf
13 Apr 1980		Military coup

Chairman of People's Redemption Council   Master-Sgt Samuel
   K. Doe
FA   Gabriel Baccus Matthews
Fin   Perry Zulu

LIBYA

30 Mar 51		Provisional pre-independence government formed

PM   Mahmoud Bey Muntasser
FA   Ali Bey Jerbi
Fin   Said Mansour Gadara

24 Dec 51		Independence
25 Dec 51	*PM/FA*	Mahmoud Bey Muntasser
	Fin	Said Mansour Gadara
15 Feb 54		Muntasser resigns
19 Feb 54	*PM/FA*	Mohamed Saqizly
	Fin (till 60)	Ali Ounaizi
8 Apr 54		Government resigns
12 Apr 54	*PM*	Mustapha Halim
	FA	Abduffalan Albufeiri
25 May 57		Government resigns
26 May 57	*PM*	Abdul Majid Kobar
	FA	Wahbi Bouri
17 Jan 60		General election
6 Feb 60	*PM/FA*	Abdul Majid Kobar
	Fin (*Minister of the Economy*)	Mohamed bin-Othman al-Said
17 Oct 60	*PM*	Mohamed bin-Othman al-Said
	FA	Abdul Qadir Allam
	Fin	Salim al-Qadi

4 May 61	*FA*	Sulaiman Jerbi
	Fin	Ahmed al-Hasairi
29 Jan 62	*FA*	Wanis Gaddafi
15 Oct 62	*Fin*	Mohamed Sulaiman Bu Rabaida
20 Mar 63	*PM/FA*	Mohieddine Fekini
	Fin	Said Mansour Gadara
22 Jan 64	*PM*	Mahmoud Muntasser
	FA	Husain Maziq
	Fin	Salim Lutfi Qadi
21 Mar 65	*PM*	Husain Maziq
	FA	Wahbi Bouri
2 Oct 65	*FA*	Ahmed Bishti
1 Sep 69	Coup	
8 Sep 69	*PM/Fin*	Mahmoud Sulaiman al-Maghrabi
	FA	Salah Bousseir
16 Jan 70	*Pres/PM*	Col. Mu'ammar Mohamed al-Gaddafi
	Fin	Mohamed al-Rabeye
16 Sep 70	*FA*	Maj. Mohamed Najm
	Fin	Capt. Omar al-Meheishi
17 Oct 70	Meheishi resigns	
8 Dec 70	Najm resigns	
13 Aug 71	*Fin*	Maj. Abdul Salam Jallud
10 July 72	*PM*	Abdul Salam Jallud
16 July 72	*FA*	Mansour Rashid Kikhya
	Fin	Mohamed Zarrouk Ragab
Apr 73	Kikhya resigns	
14 Nov 74	*FA*	Maj. Abdul Moneim al-Huni
	Fin	Mohamed Zarrouk Ragab
Nov 75	Huni flees to Egypt	
23 Oct 76	*FA*	Ali Abdessalam al-Turayki
Mar 77	Cabinet renamed 'General People's Committee'	

MADAGASCAR (MALAGASY REPUBLIC)

26 June 60	Independence
	PM (from 1 May 59) Philibert Tsirinana
	FA M. Sylla
22 July 67	*FA* Jacques Rabemananjara
18 May 72	*Pres/PM* Maj.-Gen. Gabriel Ramanantsoa
27 May 72	*FA* Lt-Cdr Didier Ratsikara
	Fin Albert Marie Ramoroson
26 Jan 75	Government dismissed and dissolved
5 Feb 75	Head of state hands over his powers to Col. Richard Ratsimandrava, who forms a government:
	FA Pastor Albert Zakariasy
	Fin Maj. Désiré Rakotoarijaona
11 Feb 75	Ratsimandrava assassinated. New military directorate under Gen. Gilles Andriamahazo; no change in cabinet
15 June 75	*Head of state and government* Didier Ratsiraka
16 June 75	*FA* Rémi Tiandrazana
	Fin Rakotovao Razakaboana
11 Jan 76	*PM* Lt-Col. Joël Rakotomalala
	FA Jean Bemananjara
30 July 76	PM Rakotomalala killed in a helicopter crash
12 Aug 76	*PM* Justin Rakotoniaina
	FA Bruno Rakotomavo
4 Aug 77	*PM* Lt-Col. Désiré Rakotoarijaona
	FA Christian Rémi Richard

MALAWI (formerly NYASALAND)

1 Feb 63	Internal self-government, following break-up of Federation of Rhodesia and Nyasaland
	PM/FA Hastings Banda
	Financial Secretary (permanent official) H. E. Phillips

5 July 64	Full independence	
	FA	none listed
	Fin	J. Z. U. Tembo
7 Sep 64	*FA*	mention of W. K. Chiume, who was dismissed on this date, his portfolio being taken over by Banda on 10 Sep 64
1 Jan 69	*Fin*	Aleke Banda
Apr 72	*Fin*	D. T. Matenje
8 July 77	*Fin*	Edward Bwanalie
11 Nov 77	*Fin*	D. T. Matenje
29 Feb 80	*Fin*	Lewis Chimango
7 Jan 81	*Fin*	Chaziya Phiri

MALI (formerly SOUDAN)

20 June 60	Independence; the Mali Federation, consisting of Senegal and Soudan, comes into being	
	PM	Modibo Keita
20 Aug 60	Senegal withdraws from the Federation	
22 Sep 60	The Soudan creates itself the Republic of Mali	
20 Jan 61	*Pres/PM/FA*	Modibo Keita
mid 61	*FA*	Barema Bocoum
1965	*Pres/PM/FA*	Modibo Keita
19 Nov 68	National Liberation Committee set up:	
	Chairman	Lt Moussa Traoré
	(Reference to Louis Nègre as former Fin Minister)	
23 Nov 68	Provisional government	
	PM	Capt. Yoro Diakité
	FA	Jean Marie Koné
	Fin	Louis Nègre
15 Sep 69	*FA*	Sori Coulibaly
19 Sep 69	*PM/head of state*	Moussa Traoré
10 Sep 70	*FA*	Capt. Charles Semba Sissoko
	Fin	Lt Baba Diarra

2 June 74	New constitution approved by referendum
25 Sep 75	*Fin* Founeké Keita
8 Mar 78	Sissoko arrested
	FA Lt-Col. Youssouf Traoré
1978	*FA* Alioune Blondin Beye
	Fin Madi Diallo

MAURITANIA

28 Nov 60	Independence
	Pres/PM/FA Mokhtar Ould Daddah
20 Sep 61	Resignation of Fin Minister Maurice Compagnet, but no date given for the beginning of his term
27 July 65	*FA* Sidi Ould Sheikh Abdellahi
21 Feb 66	*FA* Malam Ould Braham
Oct 66	*FA* Birame Mamadou Wane (arrested July 1968)
1 Feb 68	*Fin* Sidi Mohamed Dagane
9 Apr 70	*FA* Sheikh Abdellahi replaces Hamdi Ould Mouknass, but no date is given for the beginning of Mouknass's term
18 Aug 71	*Fin* Soumare Diara Mouna
23 Aug 75	Reorganisation into 'super-ministries': *Minister of State for the National Economy* (in charge of three departments) Sidi Ould Sheikh Abdellahi
	Fin (one of the three) Mouly Ould Mohamed
	FA Hamdi Ould Mouknass
31 Jan 77	Mouly Ould Mohamed sacked and his ministry joined to that of Trade. No name given for the Trade Minister, who becomes Minister of Trade and Finance
7 May 77	*Fin* Ba Ibrahima (said to have replaced Ethmane Sidi Ahmed Yessa, but no date given for the beginning of Yessa's term)
4 Aug 77	The super-ministries are abolished
	FA/Fin unchanged
31 May 78	*Fin* Ahmed Ould Daddah

10 July 78	Military coup overthrows Pres Daddah. Military Committee for National Recovery (later Salvation) set up	
	Pres	Mustapha Ould Mohamed Salek
	FA	Ahmedou Ould Abdalla
	Fin	Sidi Mohamed Ould Bigeira
21 Mar 79	*Fin*	Mouly Ould Mohamed
6 Apr 79	*PM*	Ahmed Ould Boussief (dies 25 May 79)
28 May 79	*PM*	Mohamed Khouna Ould Kaydalla
3 June 79	*Pres*	Mohamed Ould Ahmed Louly
	Fin	Ahmed Ould Zein
	FA	Ahmedou Ould Abdalla
4 Jan 80	*Pres/PM*	Mohamed Khouna Ould Kaydalla
	FA	Mohamed El Mokhtar Ould Zamel
15 Dec 80	*PM*	Sidi Ahmed Ould Bneijara

MAURITIUS

12 Mar 68	Independence	
	PM	Sir Seewoosagur Ramgoolam
	FA	Gaetan Duval
2 Mar 73	*PM/FA*	Sir Seewoosagur Ramgoolam
1 June 76	*Fin*	Sir Veerasamy Ringadoo
	FA	Sir Harold Walter

MOROCCO

7 Dec 55	Appointment of first cabinet	
	PM	Si M'Barek Ben Mustapha el-Bekkai
	Fin	Abdelkader Bendjelloun
	FA	none
2 Mar 56	Independence. Morocco incorporates the former international zone of Tangier	
26 Apr 56	*FA*	Ahmed Balafrej
27 Oct 56	*Minister of Economic Affairs*	Abderrahim Bouabid (no Fin minister listed)
16 Apr 58	Government resigns	

12 May 58	*PM/FA* Ahmed Balafrej *Minister of Economic Affairs* unchanged
22 Nov 58	PM Balafrej resigns
24 Dec 58	*PM/FA* Moulay Abdallah Ibrahim
20 May 60	Government dismissed; King Mohamed forms a cabinet as PM
	FA Driss M'Hammedi *Fin* M'Hammed Douiri
2 June 61	*PM/FA* King Hassan II
22 Dec 61	*FA* Ahmed Balafrej
4 Jan 63	*Fin* Driss Slaoui
13 Nov 63	*PM* Hadj Ahmed Bahnini *FA* Ahmed Reda Guedira
15–21 Aug 64	Reshuffle
	FA Ahmed Taïbi Benhima *Fin* Mohamed Cherkaoui
8 June 65	State of emergency; parliamentary government ended
	PM King Hassan II *Fin* Mamoun Tahiri
23 Feb 66	*FA* Mohamed Cherkaoui
11 Mar 67	*FA* Ahmed Laraki
6 July 67	End of state of emergency
	PM Mohamed Benhima
6 Oct 69	*PM* Ahmed Laraki *FA* Abdelhadi Boutaleb
25 Mar 70	*Fin* Abdelkrim Lazarak
12 Oct 70	*FA* Youssef Ben Abbes
23 Apr 71	*FA* Karim Lamrani
4 Aug 71	Cabinet resigns
6 Aug 71	*PM* Karim Lamrani *FA* Abdellatif Filali *Fin* Mohamed Medeghri
12 Apr 72	*Fin* Mustapha Faris

24 May 72	*FA*	Ahmed Taïbi Benhima
19 Nov 72	*PM*	Ahmed Osman
	Fin	Bensallem Guessous
25 Apr 74	*FA*	Ahmed Laraki
	Fin	Abdelkader Benslimane
5 Oct 77	Cabinet dismissed	
10 Oct 77	*FA*	Mohamed Boucetta
	Fin	Abdellatif Ghissassi
22 March 79	*PM*	Maati Bouabid
27 Mar 79	*Fin*	Abdel Kamal Reqhaye

MOZAMBIQUE

20 Sep 74	Transitional government	
	PM	Joaquim Alberto Chissano
	Fin	Mário Fernandes da Graça Machungo
25 June 75	Independence	
1 July 75	*Pres*	Samora M. Machel
	FA	Joaquim Alberto Chissano
	Fin	Salamão Munguambé
22 Jan 79	*Fin*	Rui Baltasar dos Santos Alves

NIGER

2 Aug 60	Independence	
	Pres/PM	Hamani Diori
1970	*FA*	El-Hadj B. Courmo
15 Apr 74	Coup	
17 Apr 74	*Head of the Supreme Military Council and head of state* Lt-Col. Seyni Kountché	
	FA	Capt. Moumouni Amadou Djermakoye
	Fin	Quartermaster Tondi Moussa
1977	*Fin*	Moussa Tondi
	FA	Moumouni Amadou Djermakoye
10 Sep 1979	*FA*	Daouda Diallo

NIGERIA

20 Dec 59	Pre-independence government set up
	PM Sir Abubakar Tafawa Balewa *Fin* Chief Festus Okotie-Eboh *FA* none
30 Sep 60	Independence
	PM/FA Sir Abubakar Tafawa Balewa
17 July 65	*FA* Jaja Wachuku
1963	Nigeria becomes a republic
1 Jan 65	*PM/FA* Sir Abubakar Tafawa Balewa
1 Dec 65	*FA* Alhaji Nuhu Bamali
15 Jan 66	Coup; PM and Fin Minister both killed
16 Jan 66	Maj.-Gen. Johnson Aguiyi-Ironsi sets up a military government with a Federal Executive Council. Office of PM suspended
29 July 66	Coup; Aguiyi-Ironsi killed
1 Aug 66	*Head of military government* Lt-Col. Yakubu Gowon
24 Jan 75	New Federal Executive Council headed by Gowon
	FA Okoi Arikpo *Fin* Alhaji Shehu Shagari
29 July 75	Gowon overthrown
	Head of state and government Brig. Murtala Ramal Mohamed
6 Aug 75	*FA* Lt-Col. Joseph Namvan Garba *Fin* A. E. Ekukinam
13 Feb 76	Gen. Mohamed assassinated
	Head of state and government Lt-Gen. Olusegun Obasanjo *FA/Fin* unchanged
15 Mar 77	*Fin* Maj.-Gen. James Oluleye
1 Oct 79	Civilian government returned
	Pres Alhaji Shehu Usman A. Shagari *FA* Ishaya Andu *Fin* Sunday Matthew Essang
15 Jan 81	*Fin* Victor Masi

RHODESIA AND NYASALAND

7 Sep 53	The PM of Southern Rhodesia, Sir Godfrey Huggins (from 1954 Lord Malvern), resigns to become PM, FA and Fin Minister of an interim federal government
15 Dec 53	*Fin* Donald McIntyre
31 Oct 56	Lord Malvern retires
1 Nov 56	*PM/FA* Sir Roland (Roy) Welensky
3 Sep 62	*Fin* J. M. Caldicott
31 Dec 63	Federation dissolved

RHODESIA (SOUTHERN RHODESIA)

2 Feb 44	*PM* Sir Godfrey Huggins *Fin* Max Danziger *FA* none
23 Sep 46	*Fin* Edgar C. F. Whitehead
15 July 48	Government defeated
21 July 48	Parliament dissolved
12 Nov 48	*PM/FA* Sir Godfrey Huggins *Fin* Edgar C. F. Whitehead
7 Sep 53	*PM* Reginald Stephen Garfield Todd *Fin* Donald McIntyre
17 Dec 53	*PM/Fin* Reginald Stephen Garfield Todd
28 Jan 54	*Fin* Cyril Hatty
11 Jan 58	Hatty resigns (with all other members of the Todd cabinet).
14 Jan 58	New Todd cabinet *Fin* A. E. Abrahamson
17 Feb 58	*PM* Sir Edgar C. F. Whitehead *Treasury* Cyril Hatty (Whitehead didn't have a seat in the house; a member resigned so that he could win his seat in a by-election, but Whitehead lost. Parliament was dissolved 18 Apr 58 pending a general election for 5 June 58, after which all was well)
23 Sep 62	*Fin* Geoffrey Ellman-Brown
17 Dec 62	*PM* Winston Field *Fin* Ian Douglas Smith

14 Apr 64	*PM/FA* Ian Douglas Smith *Fin* J. J. Wrathall
20 Aug 64	*FA* Clifford Dupont
11 Nov 65	Unilateral Declaration of Independence; Dupont becomes Officer Administering the Government and leaves FA Ministry vacant
31 Dec 65	*FA* Lord Graham (Duke of Montrose)
11 Sep 68	*FA* John Howman
2 Aug 74	*FA* Pieter K. van der Byl
13 Jan 76	*Fin* David Smith
21 Mar 78	New Executive Council sworn in
11–12 Apr 78	Ministerial Council chosen; the Government being a coalition, portfolios are held jointly. Smith remains PM, but chairmanship of the Ministerial Council is held in rotation by its members *Fin* David Smith and Ernest Bulle *FA* Pieter K. van der Byl and Elliott Gabellah

RWANDA

1 July 62	Independence *Pres/PM* Grégoire Kayibanda
5 July 73	Coup led by Maj.-Gen. Juvénal Habyarimana
8 Dec 77	*Pres/PM* Juvénal Habyarimana *FA* Lt-Col. Aloys Nsekalije *Fin* Denis Ntirugirimbabazi (The above ministers are listed as having retained posts which they held before the 8 Dec 77 government reorganisation, but there is no date for their original appointments.)
11 Jan 79	*FA* François Ngarukiyintwali

SÃO TOMÉ AND PRINCIPE

12 July 75	Independence *Pres* Manuel Pinta da Costa *PM/FA* Miguel Trouvoada

11 Dec 75	*FA*	Leonel Mário D'Alva
1 Oct 78	*FA*	Mário do Nascimento da Graça Amorim
Apr 79	Post of PM abolished	

SENEGAL

25 Nov 58	Independence as autonomous republic within the French Community	
20 June 60	Independent as part of Mali Federation	
20 Aug 60	Independent republic, having withdrawn from the Mali Federation	
	PM	Mamadou Dia
	FA	Doudou Thiam
12 Nov 62	*FA*	André Guillabert
	Fin	Valdiodio Ndiaye (replaces A. Peytavin, but no date is given for the beginning of Peytavin's term)
17 Dec 62	*Pres/PM* Léopold Sédar Senghor	
19 Dec 62	*FA*	Doudou Thiam
	Fin	André Peytavin
6 Mar 68	*FA*	Alioune Badara Mbengue
22 Feb 70	Referendum on separating the posts of Pres and PM	
26 Feb 70	*PM*	Abdou Diouf
28 Feb 70	*FA*	Amadou Karim Gaye
	Fin	Jean Collin
10 Apr 71	*Fin*	Babacar Bâ
19 June 72	*FA*	Coumba Ndaffène Diouf
5 Apr 73	*Pres/PM* Léopold Sédar Senghor	
	FA	Assane Seck
21 Nov 75	Reference to the cabinet as	
	PM	Abdou Diouf
	FA	Assane Seck
	Fin	Babacar Bâ
13 Mar 78	Government resigns	

15 Mar 78	*PM*	Abdou Diouf
	FA	Babacar Bâ
	Fin	Assane Seck

1980 Senghor resigns

Pres Abdou Diouf
FA Mustapha Niasse

SEYCHELLES

1970 *PM* James Richard Mancham

29 June 76 Independence

Pres/FA James Richard Mancham
PM France Albert René
Fin C. Chetty

5 June 77 Coup

Pres/Fin France Albert René
FA Guy Sinon

28 June 79 *FA* Jacques Hodoul

SIERRA LEONE

14 Aug 58 First cabinet and full ministerial system:

PM M. A. S. (from 1961 Sir Milton) Margai
Fin M. S. Mustapha
FA none

27 Apr 61 Independence

FA J. Karefa-Smart

28 May 62 *Fin* Albert Michael Margai

28 Apr 64 Death of Sir Milton Margai

29 Apr 64 *PM* Albert Michael Margai
FA C B. Rogers-Wright
Fin R. G. O. King

23 Nov 65 *FA* Maigore Kallon

1967	Sierra Leone becomes a republic
23 Mar 67	Army Coup. National Reformation Council set up:
	Chairman/Fin Lt-Col. Andrew Juxon-Smith *FA* William Leigh
18 Apr 68	Counter-coup. National Reformation Council dissolved; National Interim Council set up
26 Apr 68	Cabinet formed by PM Siaka Probyn Stevens (membership unstated)
11 Sep 70	*Fin* Sembu Forna (replaces Mohammed Forna, but no date given for the beginning of Forna's term)
21 Apr 71	*PM* J. J. Koroma *FA* Solomon A. J. Pratt
23 Mar 75	Desmond Fashole Luke resigns as FA Minister but no date given for the beginning of his term
1 Apr 75	*FA* Francis Minah
Mid-July 75	*PM* Christian A. Kamara-Taylor (said to be ex-Fin Minister) *Fin* Sorie I. Koroma
9 May 77	*FA* Abdulai Conteh *Fin* A. B. Kamara
1980	*Fin* Francis Minah

SOMALIA

1 July 60	Independence as union of the former British Somaliland Protectorate and the Italian trusteeship territory of Somalia. The British protectorate had already become independent on 26 June 1960. First PM and cabinet appointed
12 July 60	*PM* Abdelrashid Ali Shermarke *FA* Abdallah Issa *Fin* Abdul Cadir Mohamed Aden
14 June 64	*PM* Abdirizak Hadji Hussein *FA* Ahmed Yussuf Dualeh *Fin* Awil Hadji Abdellahi
6 July 67	*PM/FA* Mohamed Ibrahim Egal *Fin* Hadji Farrah
22 May 69	*Fin* Sufi Omar Mohamed

15 Oct 69	Pres Shermarke assassinated
21 Oct 69	Army coup
1 Nov 69	*Chairman of the Revolutionary Council* Gen. Mohamed Siad Barre
	FA Omar Arteh Ghalib
	Fin Abdi Avaleh
31 Mar 70	*Fin* Ibrahim Meigag Samater
8 Apr 76	Ghalib sacked. No successor appointed
3 July 76	*Fin* Abdurahman Nur Hersi
27 July 77	*FA* Abdurahman Jamma Barreh
7 Feb 1980	*Fin* Abdellahi Ahmed Adow

SOUTH AFRICA

1945	*PM/FA* Jan Christian Smuts
	Fin J. H. Hofmeyr
1948	*Fin* F. C. Sturrock
3 June 48	*PM/FA* D. F. Malan
	Fin N. C. Havenga
30 Nov 54	Malan retires
2 Dec 54	*PM/FA* Johannes Gerhardus Strijdom
	Fin Eric Louw
4 Jan 55	*FA/Fin* Eric Louw
31 July 56	*Fin* J. F. Nande
24 Aug 58	*PM* Hendrik Frensch Verwoerd
20 Oct 58	*Fin* T. E. Dönges
	(Verwoerd had been elected head of the Nationalist Party on the death of Strijdom (24 Aug 58), so he automatically became PM. An acting PM – C. R. Swart – had been sworn in on 21 Aug 58 when Strijdom became too ill to go on. Parliament had adjourned from 25 Aug to 3 Sep; Verwoerd took over on 3 Sep and reorganised his cabinet (as above) on 20 Oct 58)
21 Nov 63	Louw retires
9 Jan 64	*FA* Hilgard Muller

6 Sep 66	Verwoerd assassinated
	Acting PM T. E. Dönges
18 Sep 66	*PM* Balthazar Johannes Vorster
23 Jan 67	*Fin* Nicolaas D. Diederichs
31 Jan 75	*Fin* Owen P. Horwood
1 Apr 77	*FA* Roelof F. ('Pik') Botha
20 Sep 78	Vorster resigns
	Pres Nicolaas D. Diederichs
28 Sep 78	*PM* Pieter Willem Botha
4 June 79	*Pres* Marais Viljoen

SUDAN

9 Jan 54	Ministry set up to manage the transition to self-government:
	PM Ismail al-Azhari
	Fin Hamad Tewfik
	FA none
10 Nov 55	Azhari cabinet resigns, but the opposition unable to form a government and Azhari voted back on 16 Nov 55
1 Jan 56	Independence
2 Feb 56	*FA* Mubarek Zarrouk
	Fin Ibrahim Ahmed
4 July 56	Cabinet resigns
5 July 56	*PM* Abdallah Khalil
	FA Mohamed Ahmed Mahgoub
	Fin Ibrahim Ahmed
17 Nov 58	Coup
18 Nov 58	*Pres/PM* Ferik Ibrahim Abboud
	FA Ahmed Kheir
	Fin Abdul Magid Ahmed
12 Nov 63	*Fin* Said Mamoun Biheiry
30 Oct 64	*PM* Serr al-Khatim Khalifa
	FA Mohamed Ahmed Mahgoub
	Fin Mubarak Zarrouk

18 Feb 65	Khalifa resigns and forms a new government on 23 Feb 65 with the above posts unchanged	
2 June 65	Khalifa government resigns	
10 June 65	Mohamed Ahmed Mahgoub elected PM	
17 June 65	*FA*	Mohamed Ibrahim Khalil
	Fin	Ibrahim al-Mufti
27 July 66	*PM*	Sadiq al-Mahdi
31 July 66	*FA*	Ibrahim al-Mufti
	Fin	Hamza Mirghani
15 May 67	Mahdi resigns	
18 May 67	*PM*	Mohamed Ahmed Mahgoub
29 May 67	*PM/FA*	Mohamed Ahmed Mahgoub
	Fin	Hussein al-Sharif al-Hindi
2 June 68	*FA*	Ali Abdul Rahman al-Amin
25 May 69	Coup	
	PM/FA	Babikar Adwallah
	Fin	Mansour Mahgoub
27 Oct 69	Adwallah resigns	
28 Oct 69	*Pres/PM*	Maj.-Gen. Jaafar Mohamed al-Nemery
	FA	Babikar Adwallah
	Fin	Mansour Mahgoub
23 July 70	*Pres/PM/FA*	Jaafar Mohamed al-Nemery
3 Aug 71	*FA*	Mansour Khaled
8 Apr 72	*Fin*	Musa al-Mabarek (replaces Mohamed Abdul Halim Abdul Rahman, but no date given for the beginning of Rahman's term)
9 Oct 72	*Fin*	Ibrahim Elias
8 May 73	New constitution; presidential government introduced. Cabinet dismissed 7 May 73 and a new one installed 10 May 73:	
	Pres/PM	Jaafar Mohamed al-Nemery
	FA	Mansour Khaled
	Fin	Ibrahim Moneim Mansour
25 Jan 75	*Fin*	Ma'mun Bihairi
	FA	Khaled sacked but not replaced

16 May 75   *FA*   Gamal Mohamed Ahmed

11 Feb 76   *FA*   Mahgoub Makawy

9 Aug 76   *PM*   Rashid al-Tahir Bakr

9 Feb 77   *FA*   Mansour Khaled
             Fin   Sharif al-Khatim Mohamed

10 Sep 77   *Pres/PM/Fin*   Jaafar Mohamed al-Nemery
             FA   Rashid al-Tahir Bakr
             1st V Pres   Abou Kassem Mohamed Ibrahim
             Fin   Osman Hashim Abdul Salam

17 Aug 80   *Fin*   Badr ad-Din Sulaiman

SWAZILAND

6 Sep 68   Independence; government had been elected Apr 67

             PM   Prince Makhosini Dlamini

12 Apr 73   King Sobhuza II announces all parties disbanded, the indepen-
             dence constitution repealed, supreme legislative and execut-
             ive power to be vested in himself and the ministers to
             continue at his discretion as an advisory council. In this
             capacity Prince Makhosini continues in office

19 Jan 76   Prince Makhosini resigns

             PM   Col. Maphevu Diamini

12 Feb 76   *Fin*   Laurence Funwake Simelane

1977   *FA*   Mhlangano Matsebula
             Fin   Robert P. Stephens

1980   *Fin*   J. S. F. Simelane

TANGANYIKA

9 Dec 61   Independence. A PM and Ministers had been appointed after
             the general election of 30 Aug 60:

             PM   Julius K. Nyerere (after independence Pres)
             Fin   Sir Ernest Vasey
             FA   none

22 Jan 62   *PM*   Rashidi M. Kawawa
             Fin   Paul Bomani

12 Mar 63	*FA*	Oscar Kambona
27 Apr 64	Union with Zanzibar to form Tanzania (q.v.)	

TANZANIA

27 Apr 64	Union of Tanganyika (q.v.) and Zanzibar (q.v.) to form new state of Tanzania	
	Pres/PM	Julius K. Nyerere
	FA	Oscar Kambona
	Fin	Paul Bomani
30 Sep 65	*Fin*	Amir H. Jamal
22 Feb 67	*FA*	Hasnu Makame
17 Feb 72	*PM*	Rashidi M. Kawawa
	FA	John Malesela
	Fin	Cleopa Msuya
9 Nov 75	*FA*	Ibrahim Kaduma
	Fin	Amir Jamal
13 Feb 77	*PM*	Edward Sokoine
	FA	Benjamin Mkapa
	Fin	Edwin Mtei
Nov 78	*Fin*	Amir H. Jamal

TOGO

24 Aug 56	Independence within the French Community	
16 Sep 56	Cabinet government introduced	
	PM	Nicholas Grunitzky
	FA	none
	Fin	unknown
27 Apr 60	Full independence	
	Pres/PM	Sylvanus Olympio
13 Jan 63	Pres Olympio murdered	
16 Jan 63	*Pres/PM/FA*	Nicholas Grunitzky
	Fin	Antoine Meatchi
16 May 63	*FA*	Georges Apedoamah

13 Jan 67	Army coup. Government set up under
	Pres/FA Col. Kléber Dadjo *Fin* Benoît Bedou
14 Apr 67	Government dissolved and new government set up:
	Pres Lt-Col. Étienne Eyadéma *FA* Joachim Hunlede *Fin* Boukari Djobo
4 Aug 69	*Fin* Jean Tévi
21 Aug 73	*Fin* Edouard Kodjo
Mar 75	The cabinet (having taken African forenames some time previously) appears as
	Pres/PM Gen. Gnassingbe Eyadema *FA* Ayi Houenou Hunlede *Fin* Alien Kodjo
6 Sep 76	*FA* Edem Kodjo *Fin* Yaou Grunitzky
1979	*FA* Anani Akakpo-Ahianyo *Fin* Teti Tere Benissan

TUNISIA

17 Aug 50	*PM* Mohamed Chenik (appointed six years ahead of full independence)
28 Mar 52	Chenik dismissed *PM* Salaheddin Baccouche
12 Apr 52	Baccouche forms a cabinet, but this does not include a minister of FA or Fin – both portfolios still handled by the French administration
18 Jan 54	Baccouche resigns
2 Mar 54	*PM* Mohamed Salah Mzali
7 Aug 54	*PM* Tahar Ben Ammar
17 Sep 55	*Fin* Hedi Nouira
20 Mar 56	Independence
10 Apr 56	*PM/FA* Habib Ben Ali Bourguiba *Fin* Hedi Nouira

25 July 57		Bourguiba also becomes head of state
30 July 57	*FA*	Sadok Mokkadem
30 Dec 58	*Fin*	Ahmed Mestiri
16 Aug 62	*FA*	Mongi Slim
11 Nov 64	*PM*	Bahi Ladgham (PM's title changes to 'President of the Republic', under Pres Bourguiba. He retains most of the functions of a PM)
	FA	Habib Bourguiba Jr
	Fin	Ahmed Ben Salah
8 Sep 69	*Fin*	Abderrazak Rassaa
7 Nov 69		Post of PM revived
12–17 June 70		Cabinet reshuffle
	FA	Mohamed Masmoudi
1 Nov 70	*Interim PM*	Hedi Nouira (later confirmed in office)
6 Nov 70	*FA*	Mohamed Masmoudi
	Fin	Abderrazak Rassaa
26 Oct 71		Cabinet resigns
29 Oct 71		Cabinet reformed
	Fin	Mohamed Fitouri
14 Jan 74	*FA*	Habib Chatti
26–27 Dec 77	*Fin*	Abdelaziz Mathari

UGANDA

1 Mar 62		Independence
	PM	Benedicto Kiwanuka
	Fin	Lawrence Sebalu
30 Apr 62	*PM/FA*	A. Milton Obote
	Fin	A. K. Sempa
24 Aug 64	*FA*	Sam Odaka
	Fin	L. Kalule-Settala
25 Jan 71		Army coup

2 Feb 71	Council of Ministers formed:
	Head Gen. Idi Amin *FA* Wanume Kibedi *Fin* E. B. Wakhweya
29 Apr 73	Kibedi dismissed
Early May 73	*FA* (acting) Paul Etiang
10 Oct 73	*FA* Lt-Col. Michael Ondoga
19 Feb 74	*FA* Elizabeth Bagaya
28 Nov 74	Miss Bagaya dismissed
	Pres/FA Idi Amin
18 Jan 75	Wakhweya resigns
29 Jan 75	*FA* Lt-Col. Juma Oris Abdallah
20 Feb 75	*Fin* (acting) A. C. K. Oboth-Ojumbi
6 Apr 77	M. S. Kiyingi retires as Fin Minister, but no date given for the beginning of his term
Jan 78	Reference to Brig. Moses Ali as Fin Minister
14 Apr 79	*Pres* Yusaf Lule *FA* Otema Alimadi *Fin* Lawrence Sebalu
20 June 79	Pres Lule suspended
	Pres/FA Godfrey Binaisa *Fin* Jack Sentengi
18 May 80	Military Commission under Paulo Muwanga
1980	*Pres/FA/interim Fin* A. Milton Obote

UPPER VOLTA

5 Aug 60	Independence
	Pres/PM Maurice Yameogo (appointed Oct 58 on the death of PM Ouezzin Coulibaly)
3 Jan 61	*FA* Lompolo Koné
4 Jan 66	Yameogo overthrown

7 Jan 66	*Pres/PM/FA*	Lt-Col. (later Gen.) Sangoulé Lamizana
	Fin	Tiemoko Marc Garango
6 Apr 67	*FA*	Malick Zomore
13 Feb 71	*PM*	Gérard Kango Ouedraogo
22 Feb 71	*FA*	Joseph Issou Conombo
8 Feb 74	Government dismissed by Pres Lamizana	
11 Feb 74	*Pres/PM*	Sangoulé Lamizana
	FA	Capt. Seye Zerbo
29 Jan 76	Government dissolved	
9 Feb 76	*FA*	Alfred Kabore
	Fin	Sango Mamadou
23 July 76	*Fin*	Capt. Léonard Kalmogo
14 Jan 77	*FA*	Moussa Kargougou
July 78	*PM*	Joseph Issou Conombo

ZAÏRE (formerly REPUBLIC OF THE CONGO)

30 June 60	Independence	
24 June 60	*PM*	Patrice Lumumba
	FA	Justin Bomboko
	Fin	Pascal Nkayi
11 Sep 60	Joseph Ileo appointed PM by Pres Kasavubu, but Lumumba refuses to give up office	
14 Sep. 60	Coup by Col. Joseph Désiŕe Mobutu	
9 Feb 61	Pres Kasavubu finally succeeds in getting Ileo into office as PM	
12 Feb 61	Lumumba murdered	
Aug 61	*PM*	Cyril Adoula
	FA	Auguste Mavika-Kalanda
	Fin	Emmanuel Bamba
1 Dec 63	Mavika-Kalanda arrested	
	PM/FA	Cyril Adoula
2 Mar 64	Parliament suspended by Pres Kasavubu	

30 Jun 64   Adoula resigns, and is asked to head a caretaker government preparing for elections under a new constitution

10 July 64   *PM/FA*   Moïse Tshombe
             Fin   Dominique Ndinga

12 Oct 65   Tshombe government dismissed

             PM   Evariste Kimba

19 Oct 65   Kimba forms his cabinet:

             FA   Cléophas Kamitatu
             Fin   Jean Litho

18 Dec 65   *FA*   Joseph Kulumba

14 Sep 66   *FA*   Justin Bomboko

26 Oct 66   *Pres/PM* Gen. Joseph Désiré Mobutu (replaces Gen. Mulamba, but no date given for the beginning of Mulamba's term)

5 Oct 67   *Fin*   Paul Mushiete

17 Aug 68   *Fin*   Victor Nendaka

1 Aug 69   *FA*   Cyril Adoula
             Fin   Louis Namwisi

7 Dec 70   *FA*   Mario Cardoso

21 Feb 72   *FA*   Jean Nguza (Nguza Karl I Bond)
             Fin   M. Barute (Barute wa Ndwale)

8 Mar 73   *FA*   Umba Di Lutete

7 Jan 75   *FA*   Bula Mandungu (said to have replaced Batwanyele Losembe, but no date for beginning of his term)
             Fin   Bofossa W'amb'ea Nkoso

4 Feb 76   *FA*   Nguza Karl I Bond

23 Feb 77   Reorganisation: Nguza becomes also chairman of the Political, Economic and Financial Committee and thus supervises Bofassa's Fin Department

1 July 77   Executive Council deemed to have resigned; new officers appointed:

             PM ('*First Commissioner*')   Mpinga Kasenga

13 Aug 77   Nguza arrested and dismissed; temporary successor Engulu Baanganpongo Bakolele Lokanga

19 Aug 77	*FA*	Umba Di Lutete
	Fin	Kiakwama Kia Kiziki
13 Dec 77	*Fin*	Emony Mondanga
18 Jan 80	*FA*	Nguza Karl I Bond
	Fin	Namwisi Ma Nkoy

ZAMBIA (formerly NORTHERN RHODESIA)

23 Jan 64	Pre-independence cabinet:	
	PM	Kenneth David Kaunda
	Fin	Arthur Wina
	FA	none
23 Oct 64	Independence	
	Pres/PM	Kenneth David Kaunda
24 Sep 64	*FA*	Simon Mwanza Kapwepwe
7 Sep 67	*FA*	Reuben Kamanga
	Fin	Elijah Mudenda
23 Dec 68	*FA*	not known
25 Aug 69	*Pres/PM*	Kenneth David Kaunda
Dec 69	*FA*	Elijah Mudenda
Mar 70	Reference to Moto Nkama as FA Minister	
7 Oct 70	*FA*	Elijah Mudenda
	Fin	John Mwanakatwe
28 Aug 73	*PM* (under new constitution)	Mainza Chona
10 Dec 73	*FA*	Vernon Mwaanga
	Fin	Alexander Chikwanda
1 Dec 75	*Fin*	Luke Mwananshiku
10 May 76	*FA*	Siteke Mwale
May 76	*Fin*	John Mwanakatwe
24 Apr 77	*PM*	Elijah Mudenda
20 May 77	*PM*	Mainza Chona
2 June 80	*PM*	Daniel M. Lisulo
	FA	Wilson M. Chakulya
	Fin	Kebby Musokotwane

ZANZIBAR

24 Jun 63	Government elected to manage the run-up to independence

PM   Sheikh Mohamed Shamte Hamadi
Fin   Sheikh Juma Aley

9 Dec 63	Independence

FA   Sheikh Ali Muhsin

12 Jan 64	The Sultan and government overthrown. New government installed:

PM   Sheikh Abdallah Kassim Hanga
FA   Sheikh Mohamed Abdul Rahman 'Babu'
Fin   Hasnu Makame

27 Apr 64	Union with Tanganyika to form Tanzania (q.v.)

ZIMBABWE (formerly RHODESIA, q. v.)

18 Apr 80	Independence

Pres   Canaan Banana
PM   Robert Gabriel Mugabe
Fin   Enos Mkala
FA   Simon Nzenda
Home Affairs   Joshua M. N. Nkomo (to Jan 1981)

4 CONSTITUTIONS AND PARLIAMENTS

ALGERIA

In 1945 Algeria was regarded as an integral part of France. The northern territories, where most of the sizable European (*colon*) minority lived, were considered metropolitan areas. Administration was by a governor-general assisted by Consultative and Superior Councils; three senators and 10 deputies represented the territory in Paris. In 1944 60,000 Muslims were granted French citizenship and thus the right to vote.

The Algerian Statute of 1947 created an Algerian Assembly. The 120 members were elected by two electoral colleges, one Muslim, the other European; representatives were also elected to the French National Assembly, the Council of the Republic, and the Assembly of the French Union.

A war against France began in 1954 and a nationalist government-in-exile was formed. In 1958 Muslims were given full voting rights and a large majority was recorded as supporting the new constitution for a French Fifth Republic. A referendum in 1961 held in both France and Algeria accepted the right of Algeria to self-determination. In 1962 Algerian–French peace talks led to the formation of an interim provisional government in Algeria. The same year the country became an independent republic. In 1963 a new constitution declared Algeria to be a Popular and Democratic Republic under an executive president and a National Assembly elected from a single party.

A military coup in 1965 suspended the National Assembly and a 26- (later 22-) member Revolutionary Council ruled the country. Elections took place for the 261-member National Assembly in 1977. Under a new constitution approved by referendum in 1977 an executive president was to be elected for six years; legislative powers lay with a National People's Assembly elected for five years from a single party list. An amendment to the constitution in 1979 reduced the presidential term to five years and obliged the President to appoint a prime minister.

ANGOLA

By the Organic Charter incorporated into the Portuguese constitution of 1933, the colony of Angola was declared to be an integral part of Portugal. The colony was subject to decrees from the Colonial (later Overseas) Ministry in Lisbon and was administered directly by a governor-general.

In 1958 Angola was designated an overseas province and given a measure of local autonomy. The Governor-General was assisted by a Provincial Council and also a Government Council. A 36-member Legislative Council was established in 1953 with a majority of its members drawn from various interest groups in the territory. In 1963 advisory economic and social councils were set up consisting of seven *ex officio* members and eight elected from various corporate bodies. The Organic Law of 1972 enlarged the Legislative Council to 53 members, of whom 32 were elected by direct suffrage. Seven representatives were also elected to the National Assembly in Lisbon. After a long guerrilla war against the Portuguese and a military coup in Lisbon which ended the dictatorship, Angola was proclaimed an independent people's republic in November 1975. Under the 1976 constitution an executive president presided over a Council of Ministers and also the Council of the Revolution, a temporary body established until a People's Assembly could be elected. The Popular Movement for the Liberation of Angola (MPLA) is the only legal party.

BENIN (DAHOMEY until 1977)

In 1945 Dahomey was a colony of French West Africa administered by a governor. By the constitution of the Fourth Republic, 1946, it became an overseas territory of the French Union within the structure of French West Africa administered from Dakar. A territorial assembly of 30 members was established, elected on a double electoral-college system. A narrow franchise elected representatives to the French National Assembly and the Council of the Republic in Paris and also to the Assembly of the French Union. Representatives from Dahomey were also elected to the Grand Council at Dakar, which had certain powers over the federal budget of French West Africa.

The *loi cadre* of 1956 provided for a larger measure of self-government. An Executive Council was created responsible to an enlarged territorial assembly of 60 members. The territorial assembly had more extensive powers and was elected by universal adult suffrage. In 1958 the French Fourth Republic collapsed and under the new de Gaulle constitution of the Fifth Republic Dahomey became a self-governing member of the French Community. In 1959 a constitution similar to that of the French Fifth Republic was adopted. An independent republic was proclaimed in 1960. Under a new constitution an executive president ruled with a Council of Ministers drawn from a single-chamber National Assembly. A military coup in 1963 dissolved the National Assembly and abrogated the constitution. In 1964 a new constitution provided for a single-party state and a 42-member Assembly; the same year the army again took power and dissolved the Assembly and governed through a Committee of National Renovation. A further military coup in 1967 established a Military Revolutionary Council. A constitution was introduced in 1968 which provided for a one-party state and an executive president elected for a five-year term. The constitution was suspended by the army in 1969 and a three-man military directorate was appointed to run the country. A fifth military coup occurred in 1972. Discussions for a new constitution began in 1977 and proposals were made for the National Council of Revolution to be disbanded and for a National Revolutionary Assembly consisting of People's Commissioners to be directly elected; the Assembly would in turn elect the President.

BOTSWANA (BECHUANALAND until 1966)

The territory became a British protectorate in 1885. It was governed by the eight major chiefs, with a British commissioner, under the direction of the High Commissioner for British Southern Africa, with authority to issue proclamations. Chiefly powers were slightly limited in the 1930s and their views represented through the African Advisory Council. The Resident Commissioner was also advised by a European Council and a joint body. Chiefs' powers were, for the first time under colonial rule, comprehensively defined by the African Administration Proclamation, 1954, and an attempt to democratise these powers was made by establishing African local councils in 1957. The almost autocratic powers of the chiefs were further limited with the introduction of universal adult suffrage in 1966.

A constitution was granted in 1961 which provided for a Legislative Council with an elected majority. African members were indirectly elected; European and Asian members were directly elected by communal voting. There was an Executive Council with an official majority and unofficial members drawn from the Legislative Council. An African Council was set up to replace the old advisory council of chiefs, and this elected from among its own members the African members of the Legislative Council. The protectorate became independent as a republic in 1966, with a constitution drafted in 1965 and still in force with minor amendments. Executive power is vested in the President, who is responsible to the National Assembly and an *ex officio* member of it. The legislature has one chamber, the Assembly, which has 36 members and a majority elected on adult suffrage. There is also a House of Chiefs to advise the government; it is composed of chiefs of the eight principal tribes and elected representatives of the sub-chiefs.

BURUNDI (RUANDA-URUNDI until 1962)

Burundi, a former German territory, was administered as part of Ruanda-Urundi by Belgium, first as a League of Nations mandate and then, after 1946, as a United Nations trust territory. The territory was ruled by a vice-governor-general directly responsible to the Minister of Colonies in Brussels.

An Advisory Council was created in 1947 consisting of officials and three persons representing the interests of Africans. In 1960 the first elections were held for municipal councils. In 1961 an interim government was hastily formed of representatives from the municipal governments, who constituted a Legislative Assembly. The Hutu king (Mwami) Mwambutsa IV was confirmed as ruler while the Belgians retained reserve powers over foreign affairs, defence, finance, and law and order. Burundi became an independent state in 1962 with a new constitution which provided for a Legislative Assembly of 33 members and a Senate of 16 members.

In 1966 the King was deposed by the army and the constitution suspended. A republic was proclaimed and Burundi was declared a one-party state under a president, who chaired the National Council of Revolution. A Supreme Council of Revolution of 30 members was set up in 1971.

The new constitution of 1974 confirmed Burundi as a one-party state. In 1978 the office of prime minister was abolished and the President became head of the government. He chairs the 11-member Executive Committee and is responsible to the Supreme Council.

CAMEROON

The territory was formerly German but was divided between France and Britain after the First World War, and was administered by both states first as League of Nations mandates and then, after 1946, as United Nations trust territories. The British ruled Northern and Southern Cameroons while the French administered the largest part of the territory.

Under the British, Northern Cameroons was administered as part of Northern Nigeria and eventually represented in the Nigerian federal legislature. The Southern Cameroons was governed by a commissioner subject to the Governor (later Governor-General) of Nigeria. In 1955 Southern Cameroons was given a Legislative Council with a majority of representatives drawn from native authorities; the executive was presided over by the Commissioner and consisted of two *ex officio* members of the Legislative Council and four members of the Legislative Council selected by the Governor-General. In 1958 the executive had an unofficial majority led by a prime minister; the Governor-General of Nigeria became the High Commissioner for Southern Cameroons.

French Cameroon was an associated territory administered by a high commissioner. A Consultative Economic and Social Council of 34 members was established in 1942. In 1945 this was succeeded by a territorial assembly, which was elected by a double electoral-college system; by 1952 the Assembly had 50 members. Elections on a similar basis sent four deputies to the French National Assembly, three senators to the Council of the Republic and five members to the Assembly of the French Union. In 1956 a larger measure of self-government was granted and the enlarged territorial assembly was elected by direct universal suffrage. The Commissioner worked in consultation with the Executive Council, over which he presided.

A serious revolt broke out in French Cameroon in 1957 and lasted until 1962. In 1959 the territory was given full internal autonomy; in 1960 Cameroon became independent and a new constitution established a unitary state under a presidential system of government.

In 1961 Northern Cameroons joined Nigeria; by a referendum the people of Southern Cameroons elected to join the Cameroon Republic, which by constitutional amendment became a federal republic. The former Republic of Cameroon was then known as Eastern Cameroon and the former British territory of Southern Cameroons became known as Western Cameroon. Local legislative and administrative bodies were maintained in each state.

In 1972 a new constitution established Cameroon as a unitary state with an executive president elected for five years; the executive is separate from the National Assembly of 120 members. The constitution was amended in 1975.

CAPE VERDE ISLANDS

In 1946 the Cape Verde Islands formed an overseas province of Portugal administered by a governor. He was assisted by a Government Council composed of officials. By the Organic Act 1963 a Legislative Council was established; its 18 members were partially elected; by 1973 it consisted of 22 members. Representatives were also elected to the National Assembly and Corporate Chamber in Lisbon.

At the end of 1974 power was transferred to a transitional government headed by a Portuguese high commissioner. The islands became an independent republic in 1975 with a president and a National People's Assembly of 56 deputies, all drawn from a single party. The aim of the government is eventual unification with Guinea-Bissau.

CENTRAL AFRICAN REPUBLIC
(UBANGI-CHARI until 1958)

The territory was a colony administered by a lieutenant-governor as part of French Equatorial Africa. The lieutenant-governor was assisted by a nominated Administrative Council. By the constitution of the French Fourth Republic Ubangi-Chari became an overseas territory ruled by a governor and with a territorial assembly. This was elected on a very limited franchise by a double electoral-college system and in 1946 consisted of 25 members. Representatives elected on a similar basis were sent to the Grand Council at Brazzaville, the French National Assembly and the Council of the Republic in Paris, and also to the Assembly of the French Union at Versailles.

In 1951 the electorate was increased and the territorial assembly enlarged to consist of 40 members; by 1956 it had 45 members. In 1957, under the *loi cadre* of 1956, the territory was given internal autonomy; the territorial assembly was elected by universal adult suffrage. During the constitutional referendum of 1958 the territory elected to become a self-governing republic within the French Community with a president and a National Assembly of 50 elected members. In late 1958 Ubangi-Chari became the Central African Republic, which in 1960 became an independent state, with a constitution which provided for a president, a Council of Ministers and an elected Assembly of 50 members.

A military coup led by Col. Bokassa in 1965 abrogated the constitution and dissolved the National Assembly, establishing a military regime under a Revolutionary Council. A new constitution in 1976 proclaimed the state as the Central African Empire, with Bokassa as Emperor. In 1979 Bokassa was overthrown and the state reverted to its former title of the Central African Republic.

CHAD

In 1945 Chad was a colony ruled by a lieutenant-governor and administered as part of French Equatorial Africa. The lieutenant-governor was assisted by an Administrative Council composed of officials.

By the constitution of the French Fourth Republic of 1946 Chad was designated an overseas territory under a governor and given a territorial assembly. The assembly of 30 members was elected on a narrow franchise by a double electoral-college system; representatives were also elected in a similar way to the Grand Council in Brazzaville, the National Assembly and Council of the Republic in Paris, and the Assembly of the French Union in Versailles. The franchise was increased in 1951 and the territorial assembly enlarged to 45 members.

Under the *loi cadre* of 1956 the double electoral-college system was abandoned and a responsible government was elected by universal adult suffrage. An Executive Council was appointed, presided over by the Governor and responsible to the territorial assembly.

In 1958 Chad accepted the de Gaulle constitution and became an autonomous republic within the French Community. In 1960 independence was achieved with a constitution which provided for an executive president and a National Assembly. An amended constitution introduced in 1964 established a single-party state, a Council of Ministers appointed by an executive president, and a National Assembly of 105 members.

A military coup in 1975 suspended the constitution and established a Supreme Military Council of nine members. In the same year a new provisional constitution was adopted by which the President is chosen by the nine members of the Supreme Military Council. The President presides over the Council of Ministers and has supreme executive and legislative powers.

COMORO ISLANDS

A group of islands in the Indian Ocean which formed a French colony. Up to 1946 the islands were administered as part of Madagascar. By the constitution of the Fourth Republic they were separated from Madagascar and received a degree of autonomy with a General Council and one representative in the French National Assembly and one in the Council of the Republic. The franchise was limited.

In the constitutional changes of 1956 and 1958 the Comoros remained an overseas territory of France under a high commissioner. Internal autonomy was granted in 1968, with a Council of Government presided over by a prime minister and a Chamber of Deputies; the French High Commissioner retained reserve powers. The franchise was based on proficiency in French and was thus limited.

In 1974 a referendum held separately on each of the four islands supported independence. However, the vote on the island of Mayotte had a majority against any break with France. The Chamber of Deputies made a unilateral declaration of independence and reformed itself as a National Assembly with a president and an Executive Council. Mayotte remained under French control, while the other three islands became an independent republic, which was recognised by France in 1976.

In 1975 a coup overthrew the President of the Republic, abolished the National Assembly and established a National Revolutionary Council with a Revolutionary Executive Council. In 1976 the Revolutionary Council was superseded by a National Institutional Council. A further coup in 1978 led to the adoption of a federal-style constitution and a Federal Assembly of 39 members. The aim of the Comoros is to incorporate Mayotte within the republic. Mayotte, in a referendum in 1976, voted to remain an overseas territory of France. In 1980 it became an overseas department ruled by a prefect and an elected General Council of 17 members; it is represented by one member each in the French National Assembly and Council of the Republic.

CONGO (MIDDLE CONGO until 1958)

In 1945 Middle Congo was a colony administered by a lieutenant-governor as part of French Equatorial Africa. In 1946, under the terms of the constitution of the Fourth Republic, Middle Congo became an overseas territory ruled by a governor, and with a territorial assembly. The assembly of 30 members was elected on a double electoral-college system; representatives elected on a similar basis were sent to the Grand Council at Brazzaville, the French National Assembly and Council of the Republic in Paris, and also to the Assembly of the French Union at Versailles. The franchise was widened in 1951 and the territorial assembly increased to 37 members; by 1956 it consisted of 45 members.

By the *loi cadre* of 1956 the territory received responsible government with the assembly elected by universal adult suffrage. Between 1958 and 1959 eleven constitutional laws established the framework of government. Congo accepted the de Gaulle constitution of 1958 and became an autonomous republic within the French Community. In 1960 it became an independent state as the Republic of Congo.

In 1963 the President was forced to resign and the National Assembly was dissolved and the constitution suspended. A new constitution was adopted following a referendum and this provided for a two-man executive. In 1968 a military coup abrogated the constitution, dissolved the National Assembly and established the National Council of the Revolution with its president as head of state. A new constitution introduced in 1970 provided for a one-party state and the country was renamed the Congo People's Republic. A new constitution approved by referendum in 1973 established an Executive Council of State, a People's National Assembly of 115 members, with the chairman of the ruling party as President. In 1977 the constitution was abolished and replaced by an Acte Fondemental with the Party Military Committee as the chief organ of government.

DJIBOUTI (FRENCH SOMALILAND until 1967; FRENCH TERRITORY OF THE AFARS AND ISSAS until 1977)

In 1957 French Somaliland was given a measure of autonomy. The Representative Council was replaced by a territorial assembly of 32 members elected by direct universal suffrage. The French Governor presided over a Council of Ministers, which was responsible to the assembly. In the constitutional referendum of 1958 the population voted to continue the connection with France.

A referendum based on a restricted franchise in 1967 voted to maintain an association with France as an overseas territory; French Somaliland was renamed the French Territory of the Afars and Issas. The National Assembly was reconstituted as a Chamber of Deputies with 40 seats, and the Council of Ministers was presided over by a chairman who was head of government. The Governor was renamed High Commissioner and retained reserve powers. The territory was represented in the National Assembly and Council of the Republic by one representative each.

In 1974 the territory was given increased powers over internal security. Djibouti became an independent republic in 1977. The government is headed by a president and the Chamber of Deputies has 65 members. The Chamber of Deputies was charged with drafting a new constitution in 1977.

EGYPT

Egypt in 1945 was an independent kingdom with a government based on the constitution of 1923. This provided for a two-chamber legislature, a Senate of

180 members, of whom two-fifths were nominated by the King and the rest elected, and a Chamber of Deputies with 319 elected members.

By the terms of the Anglo-Egyptian Treaty of 1936 Britain had the right to maintain troops in the country to garrison and defend the Suez Canal. During the Second World War British troops effectively occupied Egypt and controlled its government.

In 1952 the royal government of King Farouk was overthrown by a military coup, a nine-man Revolutionary Command Council assumed power and the constitution was abolished. In 1953 the monarchy was abolished and Egypt became a republic. Lt-Col. Nasser assumed control of the Military Council in 1954 and became President in 1956, following an election in which voting was compulsory. British troops finally evacuated the Canal Zone in June 1956. A provisional constitution was introduced in 1956 which provided for an executive president. This was approved by plebiscite and Nasser was elected President.

In 1958 Egypt joined with Syria to form the United Arab Republic. A provisional constitution superseded that of 1956 and established presidential government and a National Assembly elected from the existing Egyptian and Syrian parliaments. There was to be a central cabinet and regional councils. A military coup in Syria in 1961 led that country to leave the union, but Egypt retained the title of the United Arab Republic.

President Nasser in 1961 announced plans for a new constitution for Egypt. An elected National Congress of Popular Forces met in the same year and approved President Nasser's National Charter embodying the aims and ideas of the Egyptian Revolution, and creating the Arab Socialist Union, which was to be the sole representative of the Egyptian people. The constitution of 1964 defined Egypt as a democratic socialist state. The National Assembly was to consist of 360 members elected by universal suffrage; the President could appoint a further 10 members to the Assembly. The Assembly would nominate the President, who had to be confirmed in office by plebiscite.

In 1971 a new and permanent constitution was introduced, based substantially on the constitution of 1964. The President had to be nominated by two-thirds of the People's Assembly and to serve for six years. The legislative body, the People's Assembly, was to be elected for five years and consist of no less than 350 members; the President had power to appoint 10 additional members. Beginning in 1977, political parties were permitted to function, but they faced considerable restrictions on their activities.

EQUATORIAL GUINEA (SPANISH GUINEA until 1968)

Equatorial Guinea consists of two territories, the mainland area of Guinea formerly known as Rio Muni, and the island of Fernando Po and adjacent islands. In 1945 the territory was a Spanish colony administered by a governor-general based in Fernando Po; he was assisted by a nominated council and responsible to the Colonial Ministry in Madrid.

In 1959 Equatorial Guinea was made an integral part of Spain and entitled the Equatorial Region of Spain; it consisted of two provinces. Representatives from the territory were elected to the Spanish Cortes. Reforms to government introduced in 1963 created a joint General Assembly of elected deputies and a cabinet of eight members under a president nominated by Madrid. The Governor-General became a high commissioner with reserve powers over police, defence and foreign relations.

In 1968 the two provinces became the independent republic of Equatorial Guinea. The independence constitution provided for presidential government with a National Assembly and provincial councils for the mainland and Fernando Po. A new constitution of 1973 ended provincial autonomy and the government came under the arbitrary control of President Nguema. He was overthrown by a coup in 1979 and a Supreme Military Council of 10 army officers formed a government with executive and legislative powers.

ETHIOPIA

Ethiopia was an empire governed by the constitution of 1931, as restored in 1942 following the defeat of the Italians in East Africa. The Emperor had a dominant role in government with power to appoint the cabinet and members of the upper house of legislature, the House of Notables. The lower house, the Chamber of Deputies, was formally a nominated body but after 1943 its members were indirectly elected by nobles and local chiefs. In 1955 the constitution was reformed and the Chamber of Deputies of 250 members was elected by adult suffrage every four years; the House of Notables then consisted of up to 125 members. In 1966 the appointed Prime Minister was allowed to choose his own cabinet.

Eritrea, a former Italian colony under British military administration from 1942 to 1952, was federated with Ethiopia under the Ethiopian crown in December 1952. Under the constitution the government of Eritrea had executive and legislative powers in domestic affairs. The Chief Executive was elected by, but not responsible to, the Constituent Assembly. The single-chamber Assembly was elected by all adult males. In 1962 Ethiopia proclaimed Eritrea part of a unitary Ethiopian state. Since 1961 Eritrean nationalist forces have fought against Ethiopia.

In 1974 an Armed Forces Co-ordinating Committee seized power, deposed the Emperor, suspended parliament and the constitution, and appointed a Provisional Military Administrative Council. Ethiopia was declared a republic.

FRENCH EQUATORIAL AFRICA

The Federation of French Equatorial Africa was established in 1910. In 1945 it consisted of the four territories of Gabon, Middle Congo, Ubangi-Chari and

Chad, each administered by a lieutenant-governor advised by a council, and subject to the Governor-General in Brazzaville. By the constitution of the French Fourth Republic of 1946, each territory was designated an overseas territory under a governor. Territorial assemblies were established which exercised control over local budgets. They were elected on a double electoral-college system from a limited franchise; the first college consisted of French citizens, the second of non-citizens. Seven deputies were elected to the French National Assembly, nine senators to the Council of the Republic, and seven councillors to the Assembly of the French Union. Five members from each territorial assembly were sent to form the Grand Council in Brazzaville.

In 1951 the electorate was increased and the territorial assemblies enlarged; the Chad assembly had 45 members, Middle Congo 37, Ubangi-Chari 40, and Gabon 37.

By the *loi cadre* of 1956 the territories were granted internal self-government. The dual electoral system was ended and the enlarged territorial assemblies elected by universal adult suffrage. The Governor presided over the executive councils, which were in effect embryonic cabinets, and acted on the advice of the Prime Minister.

In the constitutional referendum of 1958 all four territories voted to become autonomous republics within the French Community. In 1960 they became independent republics and the Federation ceased to exist.

FRENCH WEST AFRICA

The territories of French West Africa were organised in a federation in 1904. In 1945 it consisted of seven colonies: Senegal, Mauritania, Soudan, Guinea, Dahomey, Niger and the Ivory Coast. Upper Volta was separated from the Ivory Coast and constituted a separate territory in 1947.

By the constitution of the Fourth Republic, 1946, the colonies were designated overseas territories. Each territory was ruled by a governor subject to the High Commissioner of the Federation in Dakar. The High Commissioner was answerable to the Minister of Overseas France and to the French parliament. He was assisted by two advisory councils, the Disputes Council, composed of five official members, and the Government Council. The governor in each territory (except Mauritania) was aided by a secretary-general and an advisory privy council.

In each territory assemblies, known as general councils, were established with powers over the local budget. Senegal retained its pre-war Colonial Council. The assemblies were elected by limited franchise on a double electoral-college system, the first college consisting of French citizens, and the second of non-citizens. Senegal was the exception with a single-college system. Five representatives from each assembly were sent to a 40-member advisory Grand Council in Dakar. The West African territories also sent 13 (eventually 20) elected representatives to the

French National Assembly (of 622 members), and a similar number of senators to the Council of the Republic. French West Africa was represented by 27 councillors in the Assembly of the French Union, which met at Versailles. Deputies to the National Assembly were elected on a single roll; senators by dual roll. In 1951 the franchise was extended and the territorial assemblies enlarged.

The *loi cadre* of 1956 granted internal autonomy to each territory. The double electoral system was ended and universal adult suffrage introduced. The territorial assemblies were enlarged (Senegal, Guinea, Ivory Coast, Niger and Dahomey to 60 members, Mauritania to 34, Soudan and Upper Volta to 70) and given a wider measure of legislative power. The executive councils, which were in effect embryo cabinets, were drawn from within and outside the assemblies; the governor presided over meetings of the executive council but was effectively guided by the vice-president or prime minister. The Grand Council in Dakar continued to exist but the reforms of 1956 had limited its powers.

Following the constitutional referendum of 1958 seven of the West African territories voted to become autonomous republics within the French Community. Guinea alone voted to become an independent sovereign republic. The autonomous republics had complete executive and legislative control over internal affairs, but matters such as defence, foreign affairs, currency and higher education were reserved to the Executive Council of the Community.

In 1959 the French government accepted that a state could become independent but remain a member of the French Community. The French West African territories all became independent in 1960.

GABON

In 1945 Gabon was a French colony governed by a lieutenant-governor and administered as part of French Equatorial Africa. By the constitution of the Fourth Republic Gabon became an overseas territory under a governor. A territorial assembly of 30 members was established, elected on the double electoral-college system. Representatives to the Grand Council at Brazzaville, the French National Assembly and the Council of the Republic, and also the Assembly of the French Union were elected on a similar basis. The franchise was widened in 1951 and the territorial assembly enlarged to 37 members.

Under the *loi cadre* of 1956 Gabon received, in the following year, a measure of internal self-government with an enlarged territorial assembly of 40 members elected by a single electorate. In the constitutional referendum of 1958 Gabon voted to become an autonomous republic within the French Community. Two years later the country became an independent state.

A provisional constitution was adopted in 1960 which provided for an executive president and an elected single-chamber National Assembly. The constitution was revised in 1961, 1967 and 1975. The National Assembly has 70 members and both President and Assembly are elected for a seven-year period. The Council of Ministers is appointed by the President.

THE GAMBIA

The Gambia in 1945 consisted of a British Crown colony and a protectorate administered by a governor under the 1888 constitution as modified in 1902. The Executive and Legislative Councils were composed of nominated official and unofficial members appointed by the Governor.

In 1946 the Executive Council was widened to include three nominated unofficial members, including the elected member from the Legislative Council. The Legislative Council had its first elected representative, from the colony, three *ex officio* members and several nominated official and unofficial members appointed by the Governor. In 1951 a second elected representative from the Colony was added to the Legislative Council.

By the constitution of 1954 the Executive Council had an unofficial majority, with two to three unofficial members in charge of government departments. The Legislative Council had a majority of elected members, although seven out of the 11 were elected by chiefs and divisional councils in the Protectorate. The franchise was given to all males aged over 25 years in the Colony, and to all male property-owners in the Protectorate.

In 1960 a new constitution was promulgated following a general election with universal adult suffrage. It provided for a House of Representatives of 27 elected members, three nominated and four official. The Executive Council consisted of four officials and six ministers appointed from among the elected and nominated members of the House. The first chief minister was appointed in 1961; the title was changed to prime minister in 1962. Internal self-government was achieved in 1963 and full independence in 1965. The House of Representatives now had 32 elected members, four nominated non-voting members and four chiefs elected by the Chiefs in Assembly.

The Gambia became a republic in 1970, following a referendum.

GHANA (GOLD COAST until 1957)

In 1945 the Gold Coast consisted of three territories, the Gold Coast Colony, Ashanti and the Northern Territories. The whole territory was administered by a British governor, while chief commissioners had local executive power in Ashanti and the Northern Territories. The two chief commissioners were official members of the nominated Executive Council, which also included five African unofficial members appointed in 1942–3. The jurisdiction of the Executive Council extended to Ashanti and the Northern Territories (since 1934). The Legislative Council operated only for the Colony. It consisted of 15 official members, five unofficial Europeans, six chiefs representing the provincial councils, and three municipal representatives elected on a limited franchise. In the Colony there were three provincial councils of chiefs and a Joint Provincial Council. Ashanti had a Confederacy Council, established in 1935. A Northern Territories Provincial Council was established in 1946.

The Burns constitution of 1946 provided that a central representative government should rule over Ashanti as well as the Colony. The Legislative Council was given an elected African majority and consisted of six official members, six unofficial members nominated by the Governor (three African and three European) and 18 elected members, of whom nine were elected by the Joint Provincial Council, four by municipalities in the Colony, four by the Ashanti Confederacy Council, and one by the municipality of Kumasi in Ashanti. The Executive Council had three unofficial members and eight official, of whom one was nominated, and the Governor still had reserve powers of veto and emergency action.

In 1950 a new constitution enlarged the Legislative Assembly (as the Legislative Council was now called) and its members were mainly elected by popular vote, either direct or indirect, over the whole country. There was a speaker, six special members elected by commercial and mining interests, three officials, 33 members elected from the Colony, 18 from Ashanti, 19 from the Northern Territories, and five municipal members. A further 37 members were elected indirectly by the territorial councils. The Executive Council had a majority of Africans drawn from the Legislative Assembly as ministers in charge of government departments. The office of prime minister was created in 1952.

The constitution of 1954 provided the basis for independence in 1957. This created a single-chamber legislature with an eight-member cabinet of wholly African membership. The Assembly was entirely elected by adult suffrage in 104 single-member constituencies on a population basis. It was presided over by a speaker. The Governor still had reserve powers over defence and external affairs and might ensure the passing of any bill essential to public order.

Ghana became independent in March 1957 and comprised the former Gold Coast Colony and the trusteeship territory of Togoland. Regional Assemblies were created in 1957 as a concession to federal sentiment, but were dissolved in the following year.

A republican constitution came into force in 1960, with a president as head of state. The President had extensive powers, including the right to appoint and dismiss civil servants and dismiss the Chief Justice. A referendum approved the new constitution. In 1964 a further referendum supported the introduction of a single-party state. In early 1966 there was a military coup and the constitution was suspended by the newly formed National Liberation Council; ministers were dismissed, parliament suspended and all parties banned. A Presidential Commission was set up under a new constitution for the Second Republic in 1969; it had three members and was dissolved in 1970, its place being taken by a president. Political parties were reinstated in 1969 and a Council of State of 12 members was established, together with the reinstated Legislative Assembly.

In 1972 the armed forces took over power from the civil government and established the National Redemption Council, suspending the constitution of 1969, abolishing the office of president and dissolving the Legislative Assembly. The National Redemption Council was replaced in 1975 by a Supreme Military

Council, which became the highest legislative and administrative authority, with the head of state as its chairman; all other members were *ex officio*. The National Redemption Council was then reconstituted as a subordinate body, also composed of *ex officio* members. Government departments were headed not by ministers but by administrative commissioners.

The Supreme Military Council announced that elections for a new civilian government would take place in 1979, but it was overthrown by a junior officers coup in the middle of that year. An Armed Forces Revolutionary Council was formed, but after the elections it surrendered power to a newly formed civilian government. A new constitution prepared by a Constituent Assembly was promulgated in 1979; it provided for an executive president elected by adult suffrage, and a unicameral legislature of 140 elected members.

GUINEA

In 1945 Guinea was a French colony ruled by a lieutenant-governor and administered as part of French West Africa. Under the constitution of the Fourth Republic of 1946 it became an overseas territory ruled by a governor. A territorial assembly with 40 members was established, elected on a double electoral-college system. Representatives were sent to the Grand Council in Dakar, and elected to the French National Assembly and the Council of the Republic, and also the Assembly of the French Union at Versailles. The franchise was extended in 1951 and the territorial assembly progressively enlarged so that by 1956 it numbered 60 members.

In the constitutional referendum of 1958 Guinea was the only French African territory to reject de Gaulle's proposal for a French Community. As a result Guinea became an independent republic in October of that year. The independence constitution declared the country to be a democratic, secular and social republic, and the Parti Democratique de Guinée to be the sole party. It provided for an executive president elected for seven years, and a single-chamber National Assembly of 150 deputies elected for five years by universal adult suffrage. The President appoints ministers by decree and is responsible to the National Assembly. The constitution was amended in 1963.

GUINEA-BISSAU (PORTUGUESE GUINEA until 1974)

In 1945 Guinea was a Portuguese colony administered directly by a governor responsible to the Colonial Ministry in Lisbon. The Governor was assisted by a Government Council composed of officials. The territory was designated an overseas province of Portugal in 1951. The Organic Act of 1963 established a Legislative Council which had advisory and legislative powers; it consisted of *ex officio* members and 11 elected members representing a limited franchise. The franchise was slightly extended in 1968. Representatives from the province were elected on a similar basis to the National Assembly and Corporate Chamber in Lisbon.

A nationalist revolt led by the Partido Africano da Independência da Guiné e Cabo Verde (PAIGC) broke out in 1963. By the early 1970s the guerrilla army of the PAIGC controlled a large part of Guinea. In 1973 they proclaimed the territory an independent republic. Following the military coup in Lisbon in 1974 the Portuguese government recognised the independence of Guinea-Bissau.

Under the draft constitution of 1973 the PAIGC is the only permitted party. Government is by a National People's Assembly; executive power is vested in a Council of State of 15 members elected for a period of three years by the Assembly from its members. The President of the Council of State is head of state. A Revolutionary Council was established following a coup in November 1980.

IVORY COAST

In 1945 the Ivory Coast was a French colony ruled by a lieutenant-governor and administered as part of French West Africa. The region of Upper Volta was included with Ivory Coast but separated from it by decree in 1947. By the constitution of the Fourth Republic in 1946 Guinea was designated an overseas territory and ruled by a governor. A territorial assembly was established with 45 members elected by a double electoral-college system. Representatives were sent to the Grand Council at Dakar, and elected to the French National Assembly and Council of the Republic in Paris, and also to the Assembly of the French Union at Versailles. The franchise was extended in 1951 and the territorial assembly enlarged; by 1956 it consisted of 60 members.

Under the *loi cadre* of 1956 the territory received internal self-government. The double electoral-college system was ended and the new territorial assembly was elected by universal adult suffrage. In the constitutional referendum of 1958 the Ivory Coast voted to become an autonomous republic within the French Community. A constitution adopted in 1959 provided for an executive presidential system of government and a National Assembly. This was replaced by a new constitution in 1960, subsequently modified in 1971 and 1975. This provided for a president elected for a period of five years with power to appoint a Council of Ministers not drawn from the Assembly and answerable only to him. The National Assembly of 120 members is elected for five years at the same time as the President. All members of the National Assembly belong to the Parti Démocratique de la Côte d'Ivoire (PDCI).

KENYA

Kenya in 1945 was a British Crown colony and a protectorate (along the coast) administered by a governor. He was assisted by an Executive Council consisting of eight *ex officio* members and four nominated unofficial members (three Europeans and one Asian). In 1947 the 'membership' system was introduced, with groups of departments being made the specific responsibility of members of the Executive Council. The Legislative Council consisted of a speaker, 18 elected members (11 Europeans, five Asians, one Arab) and a nominated African member appointed in 1944; a second African nominated member was added in 1947.

In 1948 a Legislative Council with an unofficial majority was introduced; this included four nominated African members selected from a list submitted through local native councils. European settlers exercised considerable economic power and political influence through the Executive and Legislative Councils; their aim was to preserve white dominance in Kenya.

The Legislative Council was enlarged under the constitutional changes implemented in 1952 to 20 members and 21 elected members of whom 14 were Europeans, and six nominated African members. An African was also nominated to the Executive Council. There were separate electoral rolls for Europeans and Asians based on property and educational qualifications.

From 1952 to 1956 the 'Mau Mau' peasant rising in central Kenya brought about a declaration of a state of emergency and a ban on African political party activity. The temporary Lyttelton constitution was introduced in 1954 and provided for a 14-member Council of Ministers, of whom eight were to be *ex officio* and six appointed by the Governor. In 1957 African membership of the Legislative Council was increased to eight, elected on a qualified franchise in eight constituencies.

By the Lennox-Boyd constitution of 1958 the Legislative Council was increased substantially. It consisted of a speaker, six *ex officio* members, 37 nominated members, 36 elected members (14 Africans, 14 Europeans, six Asians, two Arabs), and 12 'specially elected members' (four Africans, four Europeans, four Asians) chosen by the Legislative Council acting as an electoral college. The Council of Ministers had 16 members, including two Africans. Africans boycotted the Council of Ministers and the Legislative Council and demanded more rapid constitutional advance.

Following the Lancaster House Conference, 1960, the Legislative Council was increased to 65 members with an effective African majority; the council consisted of 33 openly elected seats, 10 seats reserved for Europeans and 10 reserved for Asians; the 12 specially elected members were maintained. The 12-man Council of Ministers comprised four officials and four Africans, three Europeans and one Asian; in addition there were nine parliamentary secretaries.

A second constitutional conference at Lancaster House in 1962 agreed on a strong central government with federal provisions for regional governments. After elections in 1963 Kenya received responsible government under a majority-party prime minister. The constitution provided for a two-chamber legislature, a Senate, and a House of Representatives of 129 members, which included three seats reserved for Europeans. At the end of 1963 Kenya became independent and in 1964 a republic with an executive president.

In 1966 the House of Representatives and the Senate were amalgamated into a single National Assembly. By a constitutional amendment in 1969 Kenya became a single-party state. Executive power rests with the President, Vice-President and cabinet; the National Assembly consists of 158 representatives elected for five years, 12 members nominated by the President, and two *ex officio* members.

LESOTHO (BASUTOLAND until 1966)

From 1884 Basutoland was directly administered by a commissioner as a representative of the British Crown; he was under the direction of the High Commissioner for British Southern Africa, in whom legislative power was vested and by whom it could be exercised by proclamation. The supreme native authority was the Paramount Chief. A Basutoland Native Council, established in 1903, consisting largely of chiefs nominated by the Paramount, was purely an advisory body without legislative power. This system of parallel rule remained largely unchanged for fifty years. In 1946–7 a National Treasury and also native treasuries were established and chiefs were paid a regular salary. The number of chiefs was also reduced. By 1950 the Basutoland National Council had 100 members presided over *ex-officio* by the Resident Commissioner. The Council consisted of the Paramount Chief, five members nominated by the Resident Commissioner, and 94 members nominated by the Paramount Chief, of whom 36 were elected by district councils and six by various associations. The Council became more representative in 1948, when the Paramount Chief agreed to consult it over new laws and taxes. The constitution of 1959 provided for a more representative Basutoland National Council of 80 members, half of them elected from among members of district councils. The district councils were in turn elected on a common-roll franchise. The other half of the National Council was composed of chiefs, members nominated by the Paramount Chief and official members. There was an Executive Council with advisory powers, half of the members being unofficial members of the National Council. The country became independent in 1966 as the Kingdom of Lesotho, with the Paramount Chief as King. Parliament consisted of a 60-member National Assembly and a Senate, the former being elected on universal adult suffrage and the latter composed of 22 chiefs and 11 members nominated by the King.

The constitution was suspended between 1970 and 1973, when parliamentary government was restored. In 1973 an 86-member interim National Assembly was established to draw up a new constitution.

LIBERIA

Liberia is an independent republic established in 1847. The constitution promulgated in that year was modelled after that of the United States. Executive power rested with the President, who was elected by universal suffrage for an eight-year term, the President could be re-elected for a further four-year term. Legislative power was vested in two houses, the Senate of 18 members, and the House of Representatives, consisting of 71 members. The House of Representatives was elected for four years and the Senate for six years. A number of amendments were made to the constitution.

A military coup in March 1980 overthrew the government and established a People's Redemption Council. Executive power was vested in a Head of State and in a Cabinet of 17 members subject to the PRC.

LIBYAN ARAB REPUBLIC (LIBYA until 1969)

Libya was formerly an Italian colony. From 1943 until 1949 it was under French and British military administration, the French controlling the province of Fezzan, and the British the provinces of Cyrenaica and Tripolitania. In 1949 the British recognised the ruler of the Senussi as the Amir of Cyrenaica, and he became king of the independent state of Libya which was established in 1951.

The constitution of 1951 established a monarchy with a federal system of government. The King was supreme head of state. The federal government consisted of a Council of Ministers appointed by the King but responsible to the Chamber of Deputies, the lower elected legislative house, consisting of 55 members. The upper legislative house was the Senate, which had 24 members, eight from each province. The king had powers to nominate half the senators and to veto legislation from the Chamber of Deputies. The three provinces were each administered by a governor assisted by an executive and legislative council. In 1963 the provincial councils were dissolved and the country became a unitary state organised into 10 administrative districts.

The King was deposed by an army coup in 1969. A republic was proclaimed and the country renamed the Libyan Arab Republic. A Revolutionary Command Council was established which governed the country with the assistance of a largely civilian cabinet of ministers.

In 1977 a new constitution was introduced and the name of the country was changed to the Popular Libyan Socialist Arab Jamahiriya (*Jamahiriya* meaning 'state of the masses'). The Revolutionary Command Council and the cabinet were abolished. A General People's Congress appointed the former President, Col. Gadaffi, head of state. Under the terms of the constitution the Congress assisted by a General Secretariat formed a Popular Legislature; executive functions are in the hands of a General People's Committee of 26 members.

MADAGASCAR (MALAGASY REPUBLIC)

In 1946 Madagascar was designated an overseas territory within the French Union. The island was ruled by a governor-general until 1946 and thereafter by a high commissioner. He was assisted by a Government Council and a territorial assembly of 60 members established by the constitution of the Fourth Republic. The territorial assembly was elected on a double electoral-college system; Madagascar also elected on a similar basis five deputies to the French National Assembly, five senators to the Council of the Republic, and six representatives to the Assembly of the French Union.

In 1947 a serious revolt broke out in the island which was suppressed with great loss of life. The franchise was extended in 1951 and the territorial assembly enlarged. By the *loi cadre* of 1956 universal adult suffrage was introduced and the island received internal autonomy in 1957. In the constitutional referendum of 1958 Madagascar voted to become an autonomous republic within the French Community. A new constitution was promulgated in 1959, and amended in 1960, which provided for a National Assembly of 107 elected members and a Senate of 52 members. Executive power was vested in the President, who appointed ministers.

The army took over full powers in 1972 and a constitutional law gave Maj.-Gen. Ramantsoa full presidential powers for a period of five years. The legislative bodies were suspended and the President was assisted by a Higher Institutional Council and a People's National Development Council. In 1975 a National Military Directorate assumed executive power. A new constitution was approved by referendum in 1975. This provided for executive power to rest with a president elected for seven years and the Supreme Revolutionary Council; legislative authority resided with a National People's Assembly elected for five years.

MALAWI (NYASALAND until 1964)

Nyasaland was a British protectorate (proclaimed 1907) administered by a governor, who was assisted by Executive and Legislative Councils, both nominated. Local legislation was by ordinance and the Governor had the right of veto. African provincial councils were established in each of the three provinces in 1944 and 1945. These councils were advisory and composed of chiefs under the presidency of the Provincial Commissioner. An African Protectorate Council established in 1946 had advisory powers.

The constitution of 1949 allowed all communities in Nyasaland to be represented in the Legislative Council. Federation with Southern Rhodesia and Northern Rhodesia was imposed in 1953 and lasted till 1963. The constitution was altered in 1956 and the Legislative Council was changed. Nominated unofficial members no longer sat in the legislature, which now consisted of 12 officials, and six European and five African unofficial members.

A constitution granted in 1960 provided for a Legislative Council of 28 elected, three official and two nominated members. There were two electoral rolls – 20 members were elected on the lower roll and eight on the upper, the electors having different qualifications. The Executive Council had five officials chosen from among the elected members of the Legislative Council.

Self-government with a ministerial system was introduced in 1963 for all internal affairs; the Legislative Council was renamed the Legislative Assembly. By the constitution of 1964 Nyasaland became the independent state of Malawi. The Legislative Assembly consisted of 53 members, of whom 50 were elected by an adult franchise and three were European members elected on a special roll. In 1966 Malawi became a republic with a president as head of state; he is also head of the government and of the one political party. By a new constitution of 1966 Malawi became a republic with an executive president, who is the leader of the sole party and acts as prime minister. The unicameral legislature consists of 87 members, of whom up to 15 can be nominated by the President.

MALI (FRENCH SOUDAN until 1959; FEDERATION OF MALI 1959–60)

In 1945 the French Soudan was governed by a lieutenant-governor and administered as part of French West Africa. In 1946, in accordance with the terms of the constitution of the Fourth Republic, a territorial assembly was established. This consisted of 50 members and was elected on a double electoral-college system. Representatives were also sent to the Grand Council at Dakar, and elected to the French National Assembly and Council of the Republic, and the Assembly of the French Union. The franchise was extended in 1951 and representation in the territorial assembly enlarged to 70 members by 1956. Under the *loi cadre* of 1956 the territory was given increased internal self-government and the territorial assembly elected by universal adult suffrage.

In 1958 the Soudan voted in the constitutional referendum to become an autonomous republic within the French Community. At a conference at Bamako in 1958 representatives from four of the French West African territories proposed the creation of a federation. Dahomey and Upper Volta decided against joining the federation, which was formed in 1959 by the Soudan and Senegal and named the Mali Federation. France recognised the independence of the federation in 1960. Shortly after independence the federation broke up, with the former Soudan retaining the name of Mali.

The constitution of the former federation was adapted to Mali. This provided for presidential government with a National Assembly of 80 members. In 1968 President Keita dissolved the National Assembly by decree and assumed full legislative powers. Later that year he was overthrown by a military coup, which established a 14-man Military Committee of National Liberation. In 1974 a referendum was held on a new constitution, but despite an overwhelming vote of approval the military government announced it would continue to govern for a further five years. The constitution of 1974 proposed an elected president and a single-chamber National Assembly elected on a single-party basis. In 1979 a

Constitutional Congress of 137 members (104 civilians, 27 military, and six representatives from youth and women's organisations) formed a national political party, the Union Démocratique du Peuple Malien (UDPM).

MAURITANIA

In 1945 Mauritania was a French colony administered by a lieutenant-governor and administered as part of French West Africa. By the constitution of the Fourth Republic a territorial assembly was established elected by a single electoral roll; representatives were sent to the Grand Council at Dakar, and elected to the French National Assembly and Council of the Republic, and the Assembly of the French Union. The franchise was extended in 1951 and the territorial assembly enlarged; in 1956 it consisted of 34 members.

In 1957 the territory received internal self-government under the terms of the *loi cadre* of the previous year. In the constitutional referendum of 1958 Mauritania voted to become an autonomous republic within the French Community. The territorial assembly became the Legislative Assembly in 1959 and adopted a new constitution.

The constitution promulgated in 1961, a modification of that of 1959, declared Mauritania to be an Islamic republic. An executive president headed the government, assisted by a council of 16 ministers appointed by him; the National Assembly had 70 members and was elected by universal adult suffrage for five years. After 1964 all members of the National Assembly were drawn from one party.

In 1976 part of the former Spanish territory of Western Sahara was added to the republic and seven representatives added to the National Assembly. A military coup in 1978 overthrew the government, suspended the constitution and established a Military Committee of National Recovery. A Military Committee for National Salvation took over executive powers in 1979. A constitutional charter was adopted which established a prime minister responsible to the Military Committee; the prime minister as head of government could not simultaneously be head of state. Mauritania relinquished control of the southern portion of Western Sahara in 1979.

MAURITIUS

Under the constitution of 1885 Mauritius was a colony ruled by a governor and an Executive Council appointed by him; there was a legislature (the Council of Government) of 27 members, 10 of them elected on a limited franchise.

The constitution of 1947 provided for an Executive Council of four officials, two appointed members and four members elected by the Legislative Council. The Legislative Council consisted of three *ex officio* members, 12 nominated members and 19 members elected on the basis of 'simple literacy'. The constitution of 1958 provided for a Legislative Council of 40 members elected from single-member constituencies and 12 nominated members. Universal adult suffrage was introduced. The constitution was revised in 1964 to provide for a Council of Ministers presided over by the Governor.

Internal self-government was achieved in 1967 and under the revised constitution the Legislative Assembly was enlarged to 70 members. Responsible ministerial government was introduced and the island became an independent state within the Commonwealth in 1968. A constitutional amendment in 1969 provided for a cabinet of up to 20 ministers presided over by a prime minister, and a legislature of a speaker, 62 elected members, and eight additional members.

MOROCCO

In 1945 Morocco was a sultanate but divided into three territories: a French protectorate over most of the country, a Spanish protectorate in the north, and the international zone of Tangier. The enclaves of Ceuta and Melilla were Spanish state territories and remained so in 1980.

Under the French protectorate the Sultan was a nominal ruler; real power lay with the French representative, the Resident-General, who acted as the Sultan's foreign minister. The Sultan's authority extended to all three areas of Morocco; as reorganised in 1947 it comprised a council, or Makhzan, of 60 members, presided over by the Grand Vizier; delegates from the council were attached to the French heads of the five main government departments. A Government Council, established in 1919, represented the interests of French settlers and a small number of Moroccans, and dealt with financial and economic affairs.

The Spanish protectorate was administered by a high commissioner. From 1941 to 1945 the Spanish suppressed the international administration in Tangier but this was reinstated at the end of the Second World War and Spanish troops withdrew. The International Committee of Control consisted of representatives for Belgium, France, Italy, Netherlands, Portugal, Spain, the United Kingdom and the United States; its structure was reformed in 1953.

In an attempt to curb growing nationalist unrest in Morocco, the French sent the Sultan into exile from 1953 to 1955. In 1956 the French agreed to Moroccan independence; the Spanish protectorate and Tangier were integrated with the newly-independent kingdom of Morocco. Spanish Ifni was ceded to Morocco in 1969 and the northern half of Spanish Western Sahara in 1976.

From 1956 to 1960 Morocco was an absolute monarchy with royal government exercised through a three-member Crown Council and a National Consultative Assembly of 76 nominated members. A constitution approved by referendum and introduced in 1962 declared the country to be a democratic and social monarchy and a Muslim state. A two-chamber elected parliament was established which had limited legislative power and was subject to royal veto.

The House of Representatives with 144 members was directly elected for four years. The House of Councillors was indirectly elected, two-thirds of its members coming from an electoral college composed of the recently created provincial councils, and one-third being drawn from members of various economic and social interest groups.

A new constitution was approved by referendum in 1972. This provided for a constitutional monarchy and a single-chamber legislature of 264 deputies, 176 deputies by general election and 88 deputies by direct vote through an electoral college representing various councils and economic interests. The King was the head of state with power to appoint the Prime Minister and other ministers and to dissolve the National Assembly.

MOZAMBIQUE

Mozambique was declared an integral part of Portugal by the Organic Charter incorporated into the constitution of 1933. The colony was subject to decrees from the Colonial (later Overseas) Ministry in Lisbon and administered directly by a governor-general.

In 1958 Mozambique was designated an overseas province and given a measure of local autonomy. The Governor-General was assisted by a Provincial and a Government Council. The Organic Act of 1953, modified in 1963, established a Legislative Council of 29 members; there were two *ex officio* members and the remaining members were elected on a narrow franchise by a mixture of direct suffrage and from various economic and social interest groups. Advisory economic and social councils were set up in 1963 consisting of seven *ex officio* members and eight elected members representing the interests of various corporate groups. Seven representatives from Mozambique were sent to the National Assembly in Lisbon.

From 1964 to 1974 the nationalist party Frelimo waged an armed struggle against the Portuguese in Mozambique. Following the military coup in Lisbon in 1974 a transitional government was established under a high commissioner. Mozambique became an independent republic in June 1975.

By the constitution of 1975 executive powers are vested in a president who presides over the People's Assembly; a Council of Ministers is answerable to the president. Considerable powers rest with the Central Committee of Frelimo, the only permitted political party, and also a 15-member Permanent Commission of the Assembly. The legislative function lies with the People's Assembly, which consists of up to 210 elected members.

NAMIBIA (SOUTH WEST AFRICA)

South West Africa was a former German colony administered by South Africa as a League of Nations mandate. In 1946 South Africa refused to submit the territory to United Nations trusteeship. The status of South West Africa was contested and in 1966 the United Nations terminated the mandate; in 1971 the International Court of Justice ruled that South Africa's presence in the territory was illegal. The United Nations referred to the territory as Namibia.

In 1945 the Administrator of the territory was assisted by an Advisory Council and a Legislative Assembly of 12 elected and six nominated members. The South West Africa Amendment Act, 1949, abolished the Advisory Council and introduced a wholly elected Legislative Assembly of 18 members. The Executive Council had four members chosen from the legislature. South West Africa was represented in the South African House of Assembly by six members and in the Senate by four members, two of whom were elected and two nominated by the Governor-General of South Africa. The franchise was restricted to registered voters, who were all white. After 1950 apartheid policies were introduced into the country; in 1966 the apartheid and security laws of South Africa were applied to the territory retroactively to 1950. African nationalists of the South West African People's Organisation (SWAPO) began a guerrilla war against the South African presence in 1966 and this intensified throughout the 1970s.

Following the Odendaal Report of 1964 South Africa began to divide Namibia into 'homelands'; the first was created in 1968 in Ovamboland, which received executive and legislative councils. In 1969 South Africa transferred most of the administrative functions of the Legislative Assembly to the appropriate government departments in South Africa and Namibia became virtually a fifth province of the Republic.

In 1973 the South African government established an Advisory Council to discuss a constitution for Namibia; it rejected United Nations attempts to alter the status of Namibia. The withdrawal of Portugal from Angola in 1975 put pressure on South Africa to seek an internal solution. A constitutional conference, the Turnhalle Conference of 1975–7, attempted to establish a transitional government leading to an independent Namibia which would remain sympathetic to South Africa. A draft constitution of 1977 appointed an administrator-general to organise elections for a Constituent Assembly in preparation for independence. South Africa rejected a proposal for United Nations supervised elections. The elections of 1978, based on adult suffrage, were boycotted by SWAPO. Following the elections the 50-member Constituent Assembly constituted itself as the National Assembly with legislative powers over Namibian affairs. Executive power was retained by the Administrator-General assisted by an Executive Council of 12 drawn from the National Assembly. SWAPO forces continued to fight against the new government and South African forces occupying the country.

NIGER

In 1945 Niger was a colony ruled by a lieutenant-governor and administered as part of French West Africa. By the constitution of the Fourth Republic of 1946

Niger was designated an overseas territory and placed under a governor. A territorial assembly was created and representatives were elected by a double electoral-college system to the Assembly, and also to the Grand Council at Dakar, the French National Assembly and Council of the Republic, and the Assembly of the French Union. The franchise was increased in 1951 and the territorial assembly enlarged from 30 members to 50 members.

In 1957 the double electoral-college system of voting was replaced by universal adult suffrage and Niger was given internal self-government. In the constitutional referendum of 1958 the territory voted to become an autonomous republic within the French Community. The first constitution was framed in 1959 and replaced with another when Niger became independent in 1960. This provided for an executive president elected for five years by universal adult suffrage. The President was assisted by a Council of Ministers, who were responsible to him. A single-chamber National Assembly of 60 members, all from a single party, was elected for five years.

In 1974 the constitution was suspended following a military coup. Executive and legislative powers were taken over by a group of army officers who constituted themselves as a Supreme Military Council. A predominantly civilian cabinet was established in 1976.

NIGERIA

In 1945 Nigeria was administered by the constitution of 1922. This provided for an Executive Council of official members, to which two unofficial African members were added in 1943, and a Legislative Council consisting of 26 official members, 15 nominated unofficial members, and three members elected from Lagos and one from Calabar.

The Richards constitution of 1946 extended the authority of the Legislative Council to the whole of Nigeria, and established under it a house of chiefs and a house of assembly for the Northern province; these together were called the Northern Regional Council. The Western and Eastern provinces were created and given houses of assembly, which formed links between the native rulers and the Legislative Council; they were advisory bodies with a majority of unofficial members chosen by the native authorities.

Under the McPherson constitution of 1951 the Legislative Council was replaced by a House of Representatives which had a majority of members elected indirectly. The regional houses of assembly were given powers in local legislation, and the Western province gained its own house of chiefs. Elections were through electoral colleges; electors in the primary election needed residence and tax qualifications to elect members of a divisional college which in turn elected to provincial colleges. The provincial colleges elected members to each regional house of assembly, which then elected from among its own members those who would represent it in the House of Representatives. The Central Executive

Council became a council of ministers drawn from the regions on the advice of regional legislatures. Officials remained in charge of defence, justice and finance. Ministers of the regions were nominated by regional lieutenant-governors with the approval of the houses of assembly.

By the 1954 Lyttelton constitution Nigeria became a federation. The Governor was replaced by a Governor-General and the regional lieutenant-governors by governors. There was a federal House of Representatives with a speaker, 184 elected members, three officials and six special members. The federal Council of Ministers had authority over all matters on which the House of Representatives might legislate. The House of Representatives had exclusive power in external affairs, migration, citizenship, defence, external trade, customs and excise, currency, banks, loans, mining and communications. There was then a concurrent list, on which federal law prevailed in case of conflict. Elections to the House of Representatives varied with the regions. In the North there were indirect elections, with franchise confined to adult male taxpayers. In the West there were direct elections, as also in the East and in Lagos, based on adult suffrage. The Southern Cameroons were at this time a region of the federation with a house of assembly of mainly elected members and an executive council with an unofficial majority. In 1961 the region joined the Republic of Cameroon.

In 1960 there were further constitutional changes as preparation for independence. The federal House of Representatives was elected in single-member constituencies, and a Senate was established with revisionary powers; its members were nominated by regional governments with the approval of the majority in each regional parliament, and there were four members for Lagos and four appointed by the Governor-General. The regional parliaments consisted of a house of chiefs, an elected house of assembly (five appointed members serving in the Northern regional house) and an executive council of prime minister and other ministers. Full independence followed in October 1960, and Nigeria became a republic in 1963.

In 1966 the government was overthrown by a military coup, which was in turn suppressed by the head of the army, Gen. Aguiyi-Ironsi, who then suspended the constitution and set up a Supreme Military Council. He abolished all political parties and tribal associations and dissolved the federal system of government. He was in turn overthrown in July 1966 and the federal system was restored in September as the Federal Military Government. A constitutional decree of 1967 placed all executive and legislative powers with the Supreme Military Council, which was composed of regional military governors and the heads of the armed forces. A federal Executive Council was also formed from military and civilian commissioners.

In 1967 the republic was divided into 12 states; six in the former Northern Region, three in the former Eastern Region, one in the West, a Mid-West state and a state of Lagos. Following this, the military governor of the Eastern Region states seceded from the federation and renamed the region the Republic of Biafra; this led to civil war, which ended with federal victory in 1970.

In 1976 the number of states was increased from 12 to 19. A draft constitution of 1976 provided for a return to civilian government within three years; there was to be an elected National Assembly and an executive president. In 1977 a 230-member Constituent Assembly was inaugurated to discuss the draft constitution. Up to 1979 central government remained a military government; local government was by native authorities of local-government bodies controlled by state legislation. In 1979 elections took place and a civilian government headed by a president took over from the military government.

FEDERATION OF RHODESIA AND NYASALAND

The federation was created in 1953 from the British territories of Southern Rhodesia, Northern Rhodesia and Nyasaland, and lasted until 1963. Britain retained ultimate responsibility for external affairs. Defence, immigration, European education, European agriculture and health became the responsibility of the new federal legislature, which sat in the Southern Rhodesian capital of Salisbury.

The federation had a governor-general and a unicameral assembly elected on two common rolls with qualified franchise. In 1960 there were 44 seats for elected members of any race, eight for Africans, four for specially elected Africans and three for Europeans responsible for African interests. The constitution provided for an African Affairs Board as a standing committee of the Assembly. It consisted of the three Europeans representing African interests and one specially elected African member from each territory. It had power to make representations to the Federal Assembly, assist a territorial government when asked to, and require any measure which it thought discriminatory to be reserved to the crown. The Federal Assembly had a majority returned by roll voters in constituencies and a minority returned by roll voters in electoral districts. Both franchises were qualified by property and educational standards.

RWANDA (RUANDA-URUNDI until 1962)

Ruanda, a former German territory, was administered as part of Ruanda-Urundi by Belgium, first as a League of Nations mandate and then, after 1946, as a United Nations trust territory. The territory was ruled by a vice-governor-general directly responsible to the Minister of Colonies in Brussels. An Advisory Council was set up in 1947 consisting of officials and three persons representing the interests of Africans.

The first elections held in the country were in 1960 for municipal councils. In 1959 the Belgians announced that Rwanda was to become independent, and representatives of the municipal councils were hastily convened into the Rwanda Council of 48 members, which constituted a national government in October

1960. A state of civil war existed throughout the country between the Hutu majority and the Tutsi feudal minority, who opposed the prospect of a government in the hands of the Hutu.

In 1961 the Tutsi king was deposed and a republic established. Internal self-government was achieved in early 1962 and the country was proclaimed an independent state in July the same year. The constitution of 1962 provided for an executive presidential government elected for four years, assisted by a council of 12 ministers. The National Assembly was to consist of 47 members elected by universal suffrage every four years.

A military coup in 1973 led to a change in the executive functions of the constitution: under the Second Republic supreme authority was in the hands of the Committee of Peace and National Unity. In 1975 Rwanda was declared to be a one-party state led by the Mouvement Révolutionnaire National pour le Développement (MRND).

ST HELENA, ASCENSION ISLAND AND TRISTAN DA CUNHA

St Helena and its dependencies Tristan and Ascension form a Crown colony administered by Britain. In 1945 St Helena was administered by a governor assisted by an Executive Council of five members and an Advisory Council of six unofficial members chosen to represent all sections of the community.

A government representative was responsible for Ascension, while Tristan had a chief with three administrative officers; the chief was chairman of the island council. An administrator was appointed in 1948 and he chairs the island council of six nominated and 15 elected members.

In 1967 St Helena received a Legislative Council consisting of the Governor, two official members and 12 elected members; government departments were run by committees of the Council, whose chairmen, together with the two official members, form the Governor's Executive Council.

SÃO TOMÉ AND PRINCIPE

The islands of São Tomé and Principe, together with the fort of São João Baptista de Ajuda on the coast of Dahomey, formed in 1945 an overseas province of Portugal. They were administered by a governor directly responsible to Lisbon, who was assisted by a Government Council composed of officials. The fort of São João Baptista was taken over by Dahomey in 1960.

By the Organic Act of 1963 a Legislative Assembly was established composed of 10 elected and three *ex officio* members; the province was also represented in the National Assembly and the Corporative Chamber in Lisbon.

The military coup in Lisbon in 1974 led to negotiations between nationalists from the islands and the new Portuguese government. A transitional government was formed in São Tomé under a high commissioner and in 1975 the islands became an independent republic. By the constitution of 1975 executive power lies with the President and his ministers, who are responsible to the People's Assembly. The People's Assembly is elected for four years and draws its 22 members from the sole party, the Movement for Liberation of São Tomé and Principe.

SENEGAL

Senegal was a colony administered as part of French West Africa. In 1946 the constitution of the Fourth Republic transformed the pre-war Colonial Council into a territorial assembly of 50 members. The franchise was limited and based on a single electoral roll. Representatives were also sent to the Grand Council in Dakar, and elected to the French National Assembly and the Council of the Republic, and the Assembly of the French Union.

The franchise was extended in 1951. By the *loi cadre* of 1956 Senegal received internal self-government; the assembly was enlarged to 60 members and elected by universal adult suffrage. An Executive Council, presided over by the Governor, functioned as an embryo cabinet. In 1958 the territory voted to become an autonomous republic within the French Community. Senegal joined with the Soudan to form the Mali Federation in 1959 but separated to become an independent republic in the following year.

The constitution of 1959 provided for a National Assembly of 80 members. A revised constitution of 1960 introduced a government with executive power divided between a president and a prime minister. The President was elected for seven years and he appointed the Prime Minister, who held executive power subject to the National Assembly.

In 1963 a referendum approved a new constitution, subsequently amended in 1967. This provided for an executive president elected for four years by universal suffrage; he appointed the 15 ministers and two secretaries of state who formed the Government Council and who were responsible to him. The National Assembly of 100 members was elected for five years. The constitution was amended in 1970 and the office of prime minister re-created. Although the country is a *de facto* one-party state the constitution permits other parties to function.

SEYCHELLES

The islands were ruled by a governor assisted by an Executive Council and a Legislative Council with a majority of official members. In 1948 four elected members were added to the Legislative Council of six official and two nominated unofficial members; the franchise was based on property, income and educational qualifications. In 1960 the Legislative Council was reconstituted with a presiding governor, four *ex officio* members, five elected members and three nominated members, one of whom was unofficial. The Executive Council had a similar structure.

In 1970 a new constitution provided for a Legislative Assembly of 15 elected members, three *ex officio* members and a speaker. Internal self-government was achieved in 1975 and independence in 1976. The 1976 constitution provided for executive power to be held by the President and a prime minister responsible to an elected National Assembly of 25 members.

In 1977 a coup ousted the President and the National Assembly was suspended. The constitution was reintroduced but modified to give full executive powers to the President.

SIERRA LEONE

Sierra Leone consisted of two territories, the Colony, which extended along the littoral, and the Protectorate in the hinterland. Both Colony and Protectorate were administered by a governor assisted by a single executive and legislature.

In 1945 the Legislative Council had 11 official members and 10 unofficial members, of whom three were elected for a five-year term on a limited (male) franchise from the Colony; there was no franchise in the Protectorate. The Executive Council was increased in 1943 to include two African unofficial members (one a chief), who were drawn from the Legislative Council; another member was added in 1948. In 1946 district councils and a Protectorate Assembly were established in the Protectorate; the Assembly was composed of 26 paramount chiefs, 11 official members and three nominated members (one Creole and two Protectorate Africans).

Under the constitution of 1951 the Executive Council had an unofficial majority and the Legislative Council a large elected majority, members being elected by the Protectorate for the first time. Seven members were elected from the Colony and 12 by the district councils of the Protectorate; two were elected by the Protectorate Assembly; two were nominated by the Governor; and seven were *ex officio* members. The Governor had an Executive Council of four official members and six unofficial members appointed from among the unofficial members of the Legislative Council. The Protectorate was administered by a chief commissioner responsible to the Governor, and, although it was represented in the Legislative Council, it retained the Protectorate Assembly. This now consisted of representatives from each district council and six members nominated by the Governor to represent other interests; it met in an advisory capacity.

In 1952 departments of government were assigned as the special responsibility of certain members of the executive. In 1953 a full ministerial system was introduced, the ministers all being elected members of the Legislative Council. A chief minister was appointed in 1954.

A new constitution in 1956 replaced the Legislative Council with a House of Representatives which had a speaker, four official members, 14 directly elected from the Colony and 25 directly elected from the Protectorate, 12 paramount chiefs elected by district councils in the Protectorate, and two nominated members with no voting rights.

In 1958 the executive was made collectively responsible to the legislature. The government consisted of at least seven elected ministers appointed on the advice of the Chief Minister. The Governor retained his responsibility for 'peace and good government', external affairs, defence, internal security, police and public service. In 1960 he ceased to preside over the executive and was replaced by the Chief Minister; he also transferred to the ministers his powers on police and internal security. The territory became fully independent in 1961.

Under the constitution of the independent state the Queen was represented by a governor-general appointed on the advice of the Prime Minister. There was a House of Representatives of not less than 60 members elected from constituencies established by an electoral commission.

In March 1967 there were two successive military coups, the first of which overthrew the newly elected government and the second of which proclaimed the National Reformation Council; the Council consisted of eight members. In April 1968 it was in turn overthrown by non-commissioned officers of the army and police force, who formed the Anti-Corruption Revolutionary Movement. This movement appointed an interim council, and constitutional government was restored on 26 April.

In 1971 the state became a republic under the President as head of state; he was also head of the cabinet. A new constitution, approved by referendum in 1978, declared Sierra Leone to be a single-party state. The executive president was elected for seven years by members of the National Delegates Conference of the All-People's Congress (APC), the sole party. The House of Representatives consisted of 60 elected members, whose nominations were endorsed by the Central Committee of the APC.

SOMALIA

In 1945 Somalia was divided into two territories. British Somaliland in the north was a protectorate but under wartime military administration, which lasted to 1948. Civil government was then resumed under a governor who had sole legislative and executive authority. A Legislative Council was established in 1957, with an official majority and six appointed members. In 1959 it was enlarged to include 12 elected members and 17 appointed members. The next year it became the Legislative Assembly, with 33 elected members.

Italian Somalia in the south was occupied by British forces in 1941 and placed under military administration until 1949. The territory then passed under British Foreign Office administration until 1950, when Italy resumed control as trustee for the United Nations. The trusteeship was governed by a UN Advisory Council with representatives from Egypt, Colombia and the Philippines; advisory or departmental bodies were mainly under Somalis. A territorial council of 35 members appointed by the trusteeship administration had to be consulted by the Italians on all important matters relating to the territory. Following elections in 1956 the territorial council was replaced by a Legislative Assembly of 70 elected members; this was enlarged to 90 members in 1959. A constitution for the territory was drafted by the Assembly between 1957 and 1960.

In 1960 British Somaliland became an independent republic. Six days later it merged with Italian Somalia when that territory also became independent, to form the Somali Republic. The president of the southern legislature was proclaimed provisional head of state and the two legislatures were united at Mogadishu to form a single-chamber National Assembly of 123 members, 33 from the north and 90 from the more populous south.

The constitution of the former trust territory was adopted by referendum in 1961 as the constitution for the unified republic. This provided for a president elected by the National Assembly and a prime minister as head of government; the National Assembly was elected for five years.

A military coup in 1969 suspended the constitution and dismissed the National Assembly. The new government which assumed power consisted of a 73-member Supreme Revolutionary Council. In 1976 the Council was replaced by a civilian government. Somalia is a single-party state with the Central Committee of the Somali Socialist Revolutionary Party having considerable executive powers.

SOUTH AFRICA

South Africa was established as a Union in 1910 from the four self-governing territories of Cape Colony, Natal, Orange Free State and the Transvaal. In 1945 it was a sovereign state within the Commonwealth governed by a governor-general appointed by the Crown and exercising executive power in conjunction with a cabinet drawn from the legislature. Legislative power was vested in a House of Assembly of 153 elected members, and a Senate of 48 members. The Senate consisted of members elected by the members of the provincial councils and those nominated by the Governor-General.

Money bills had to originate in the lower house; the Senate's powers to block them were restricted, as they could still be passed on recommendation from the Governor-General. Each province after Union was administered by a provincial council elected for three years, each council having an executive committee presided over by an administrator appointed by the Governor-General. The term was later extended to five years.

Members of the Union parliament had to be white, but this did not apply to members of the provincial council. The franchise was restricted to whites except in Cape Province, where a small number of Africans and Coloureds had the vote. The Coloureds voted on the common roll until 1956, when they were placed on a separate roll and could elect four white representatives to the Assembly and one to the Senate. Africans in the Cape were placed on a separate roll by the Representation of Natives Act 1936; by this they could elect three white representatives to the Assembly. Africans in the rest of the Union elected three white senators through electoral colleges. An African Representative Council was set up in 1936. Under the policies of apartheid all African representation in the Assembly was abolished in 1959 and replaced by a system of regional and territorial Bantu authorities. Coloured representation in the Assembly was ended in 1969.

A referendum was held in 1960 to decide whether the Union should become a republic; it was restricted to white voters. The Republic came into being in 1961 with a president as head of state, elected by an electoral college for seven years. The executive consists of the State President and the cabinet. The Senate now comprises 51 members, of whom 45 are elected and eight nominated by the State President to represent each of the four provinces. The House of Assembly has 159 members elected for five years. From 1949 to 1977 representatives from South West Africa, or Namibia, were elected to both the Senate and the House of Assembly. South Africa left the Commonwealth in 1961.

The Promotion of Bantu Self-Government Act was passed in 1959 and provided for the establishment of self-governing ethnic states for Africans. Under this and further legislation implementing apartheid all Africans within the Republic were to be deprived of their South African citizenship and to become citizens of 10 independent black states. The first of these to be created was Transkei in 1976; Bophuthatswana followed in 1977, and Venda in 1979. None of these 'independent' states has gained any international recognition.

TRANSKEI

Under the constitution of Transkei the President is elected for seven years; the President appoints the Executive Council. The legislature is a unicameral chamber composed of 74 chiefs and paramount chiefs, and 50 members elected on a franchise restricted to those aged 25 years and over.

BOPHUTHATSWANA and VENDA

The constitution provides for a president and an Executive Council of 12 ministers. The Legislative Assembly has 96 members, of whom 48 are appointed and 48 elected. The constitution of Venda is very similar, with a president and a Legislative Assembly of 42 elected and 42 nominated members.

SPANISH SAHARA

The Spanish occupation of the Western Sahara began in 1860 and the interior was finally conquered and annexed in 1934. The enclave of Ifni was effectively occupied by Spanish forces in 1932–3.

Until 1958 both territories were regarded as colonies and administered jointly by a military regime. In 1958 the two territories were formed into separate provinces and a new system of administration established under the 'Fundamental Laws of Spain'. Each province was under a governor-general, who in practice was always a military man. Local elected councils met under a president. In Spanish Sahara in 1963 the council consisted of seven Spaniards and seven Saharan representatives; the council was responsible for 12 government departments. Three representatives were elected to the Cortes in Madrid. A General Tribal Assembly to represent all Saharans was set up in 1967. It had 82 members and was to be elected every four years. In 1973 the Assembly was increased to 102 members.

Morocco and Mauritania both claimed large parts of the territory and from 1956 onwards a Moroccan-backed guerrilla movement fought against the Spanish authorities. A northern strip of Spanish Sahara was ceded to Morocco in 1958 and Ifni was returned in 1969. In 1976 the Spanish withdrew from the territory, which by agreement was divided between Morocco and Mauritania. A Saharan independence movement, Polisario, began a guerrilla war against both the occupying Moroccan and Mauritanian forces and proclaimed a Saharan Arab Democratic Republic. In 1979 Mauritania withdrew from the southern part of the territory, which was then occupied by the army of Morocco.

SUDAN (ANGLO-EGYPTIAN SUDAN until 1955)

The Sudan was an Anglo-Egyptian condominium established in 1899. The Anglo-Egyptian Treaty of 1936 confirmed a joint administration under a British governor-general. Britain effectively controlled the territory.

In 1944 an Advisory Council was established for northern Sudan. It was composed of 18 Sudanese elected or nominated from the provincial councils that already existed in the six northern provinces, eight other Sudanese nominated by the Governor-General, and two members elected by the Chamber of Commerce.

Executive and Legislative Councils were set up in 1944. The Governor-General's Council ceased to exist and was superseded by the Executive Council of 12–18 members, of whom half had to be Sudanese. A Sudanese chief minister was appointed; the Governor-General retained the power of veto. The Legislative Assembly represented the whole of the Sudan, with 52 members elected directly and indirectly to represent the north and 13 members elected by the southern provincial councils. The franchise was limited.

In 1952 the Self-Government Statute was passed. This established a Council of

Ministers composed entirely of Sudanese and responsible to a two-chamber legislature; the legislative body consisted of a House of Representatives with 97 seats, of which 68 were elected directly, and the Senate, with 30 elected members and 20 members nominated by the Governor-General. The Governor-General acted on the advice of the Prime Minister and had reserve powers over defence and foreign affairs.

The new constitution was intended as transitional, leading to independence. A major problem was Egypt's claim to the Sudan and its refusal to accept constitutional advancement for the territory. Political changes in Egypt in 1952 led to the Anglo-Egyptian Agreement of 1953, which guaranteed Sudan's right to self-determination. Another problem for the Sudan was the provinces of the south, which under British administration had for years been treated separately from the northern provinces; many southerners demanded a federal government. In 1955 a revolt broke out in the southern provinces and this continued until 1972.

In 1956 the Sudan became an independent republic. A transitional constitution was introduced which continued the parliamentary system but transferred the Governor-General's powers to a Supreme Commission of five Sudanese, including one southerner. A military coup took over power and suspended the constitution in 1958. A 12-man Supreme Council of the Armed Forces became the supreme constitutional authority, with Gen. Abboud as President; a seven-member Council of Ministers headed government departments. Gen. Abboud resigned as President in 1964 and his place was taken by a five-member Council of Sovereignty; the Supreme Council was replaced by a civilian cabinet. In 1965 parliamentary government was reintroduced, with a president elected by the Constituent Assembly.

A second army coup in 1969 suspended the constitution and placed government in the hands of a 10-man Revolutionary Council and a cabinet of 21 members. In 1973 a new constitution with an executive president was introduced; a 304-member National People's Assembly was to be elected every four years, with up to 10 per cent of its members appointed by the President. A regional constitution for the southern Sudan provided for a regional executive headed by a president and a 60-member Regional People's Assembly responsible for a wide range of local affairs.

SWAZILAND

Swaziland was a British protectorate administered by a high commissioner who had power to make laws by proclamation. The High Commissioner was represented in the territory by a resident commissioner. Native administration was in the hands of chiefs and their councils; ultimate authority in native affairs lay with the National Council, or Libandla, and an inner or privy council, the Liqoqo. The Resident Commissioner was advised by the Council through the paramount chief, the Ngwenyama, and by a special standing committee in his dealings with Swazi affairs.

In 1950 the traditional system was reformed with the creation of a Swazi National Treasury and also a High Court and lower African courts. A European Advisory Council (created 1921) consisted of elected representatives of the small European community to advise on European affairs.

In 1963 a new constitution established an Executive Council of three *ex officio* members and five elected members presided over by the British-appointed Commissioner; a 24-member Legislative Council was also created, composed of 16 elected members, five of whom had to be white, and eight nominated members. The Legislative Council had powers of legislation over minerals, and mineral ownership was formally vested in the Ngwenyama on behalf of the Swazi nation.

In 1967 the country achieved internal self-government as a protected state with the Ngwenyama as King and head of state. The legislature was a House of Assembly of 24 elected and six nominated members, and a Senate composed of 12 members, six elected by the House of Assembly and six appointed by the King. The House of Assembly was elected by universal adult suffrage. Swaziland became an independent kingdom in 1968.

In 1973 the King assumed supreme power and repealed the constitution. In 1977 he announced the abolition of the system of parliamentary government and its replacement by traditional tribal institutions known as Tinkhundla.

TANGANYIKA/TANZANIA

Tanganyika came under effective British control in 1919 and was administered as a League of Nations mandate. A governor headed the administration, assisted by an Executive Council of nominated members. In 1945 the Legislative Council (established 1926) was enlarged to seven official, eight *ex officio* and up to 14 unofficial members (seven Europeans, four Africans, three Asians). The League of Nations agreement was replaced by a United Nations trusteeship in 1946.

In 1948 the member system was introduced into the Executive Council – that is to say, each department of government was the responsibility of one member of the council. A speaker was appointed to the Legislative Council in 1953.

The constitution of 1953 provided for 31 official members and 30 unofficial in the Legislative Council, the latter being 10 Africans, 10 Asians and 10 Europeans, all nominated after consultation with the bodies they represented. The members of the Executive Council with responsibility for departments became ministers in 1957. The first elections to the Legislative Council were held in 1955–9; each constituency elected one African, one Asian and one European member. Voters were all over 21 with an educational or property qualification. Unofficial members were appointed as ministers from 1959. The tripartite system of voting ended in 1959 and in the elections of the following year for the

71-member Legislative Council 50 seats were open to members of any race, 11 were reserved for Asians, and 10 for Europeans.

The constitution of 1960 provided for an elected majority in the Legislative Council and ministers responsible to parliament. In 1961 internal self-government was introduced, with the withdrawal of official members from the Council of Ministers and restriction of the powers of the Governor. The National Assembly had 71 members elected on a common roll and some nominated members. Full independence was attained in December 1961, when the trusteeship agreement with the UN came to an end. A republican constitution with the President as head of state was adopted in 1962. In 1964 Zanzibar joined Tanganyika to form the united republic Tanzania.

An interim constitution for Tanzania was adopted in 1965. It provided for a National Assembly of 107 elected members from Tanganyika, 10 appointed members, 15 members elected by the Assembly after nomination by various national interests, 20 regional commissioners, up to 32 members of the Zanzibar Revolutionary Council, and up to 20 other Zanzibari members appointed by the President after consultation with the President of Zanzibar. The number of members elected from Tanganyika was later reduced to 96. There is only one political party. In 1977 a permanent constitution was adopted; it is an amended version of the 1965 draft constitution.

TOGO

Togo was a former German colony administered by France as a League of Nations mandate and then, after 1946, as a trust territory of the United Nations. By the constitution of the Fourth Republic Togo was designated an associated territory ruled by a commissioner and separate from the Federation of French West Africa. A territorial assembly was established with powers over the budget; in 1952 it consisted of 30 members elected by a single electoral roll. Togo was represented in the French National Assembly by one deputy, in the Council of the Republic by two senators, and in the Assembly of the French Union by one member.

By statute in 1955 Togo became an autonomous republic within the French Union. The Legislative Assembly was elected by universal adult suffrage and had considerable power over internal affairs; there was an elected executive presided over by a prime minister responsible to the legislature. These changes were promulgated in a constitution approved by referendum in 1956.

In 1960 the trusteeship was ended and Togo became an independent republic with a provisional constitution. A new constitution of 1961 established an executive president, elected for seven years, and a weak National Assembly. A military coup in 1963 suspended the constitution. The same year another constitution was promulgated, which provided for an executive president elected for five years and a weak National Assembly.

A second army coup in 1967 suspended the constitution. A Committee of

National Reconciliation was established and Colonel Eyadéma became a plebiscitary president with executive and legislative powers heading a government composed of army officers and civilians.

TUNISIA

Tunisia became a French protectorate in 1881. Although there were indigenous institutions under the Bey of Tunis, effective executive power was by the decrees of 1943–4 exercised through the French Resident-General.

In 1945 a Legislative Assembly in which European settlers and Tunisians were equally represented was established; the government of the protectorate comprised six Tunisian ministers and six French directors. The powerful settler lobby wanted the system of co-sovereignty under French control to continue, while the Tunisian nationalists demanded internal autonomy and the restoration of sovereignty.

In 1951 the French established a Tunisian cabinet headed by a prime minister. Settler opposition to this led to French repression of the Tunisian government and an insurrection among the nationalists from 1952 to 1955. In 1954 the French promised internal autonomy, which was granted in 1955. The country was administered by a high commissioner through an elected Constituent Assembly of 98 members. In 1956 Tunisia became an independent state; the Constituent Assembly deposed the Bey and a republic was proclaimed in 1957, with Habib Bourguiba as executive president.

Under the constitution promulgated in 1959 the country is ruled by an executive president and a National Assembly, elected simultaneously for five years. The President is assisted by a Council of State and also by an Economic and Social Council; the National Assembly has 90 members.

UGANDA

The territory was a British protectorate administered by a governor. Native rulers with rights regulated by treaty had some powers over their subjects; the province of Buganda was recognised as a native kingdom under its Kabaka, who was assisted by a council of ministers and an assembly, the Lukiiko.

In 1946 the Executive Council consisted of the Governor plus seven official members and one nominated unofficial member; the Legislative Council consisted of nine official and nine nominated unofficial members, including three Africans. The Legislative Council was enlarged at various times from 1949 to 1954 and by that date included 14 Africans elected from the newly formed district councils and the Lukiiko. A constitution introduced in 1955 provided for ministers in the Executive Council.

In 1958 the Legislative Council was given a majority elected on an extended franchise, and the Executive Council became a Council of Ministers with a non-official majority. In 1961 internal self-government was introduced with federal status for Buganda. There was a National Assembly entirely elected on universal adult suffrage, and full responsible government. The Governor retained responsibility for external affairs, defence and security pending full independence, which followed in 1962. In 1963 the constitution was amended to provide Buganda with its own head of state; at the same time the Governor-General was replaced by a president elected by the National Assembly for a five-year term.

In early 1966 Prime Minister Milton Obote suspended the constitution and assumed all executive powers; a few weeks later he abrogated the constitution. In 1967 Uganda became a republic with executive authority vested in the President assisted by a cabinet of ministers. The power and status of all the kingdoms were reduced and the country was organised into four regions, one of which was Buganda.

In 1971 President Obote was overthrown by Gen. Amin, who set up a military government. In 1978 President Amin announced the formation of an advisory United National Forum; it was to consist of about 1000 members and only to meet occasionally. In 1979 President Amin was overthrown following a Tanzanian-backed invasion of Uganda. The victorious Uganda National Liberation Front established a provisional government under President Lule. He was dismissed after a few weeks and President Binaisa assumed power, with executive functions in the hands of a National Consultative Council. Following elections President Milton Obote came into office in 1980.

UPPER VOLTA

In 1945 Upper Volta was a region of the French colony of Ivory Coast. In 1947 it was constituted a separate overseas territory under a governor and administered as part of French West Africa. In 1948 a territorial assembly of 50 members was established. The franchise was limited and based on a double electoral-college system; five representatives from the assembly went to the Grand Council in Dakar, and representatives were also elected to the French National Assembly and the Council of the Republic, and the Assembly of the French Union at Versailles.

In 1951 the franchise was extended. By the *loi cadre* of 1956 Upper Volta became a self-governing territory; the double electoral system was ended and the enlarged territorial assembly of 70 seats was elected by universal adult suffrage. In the constitutional referendum of 1958 Upper Volta voted to become an autonomous republic within the French Community. In 1960 it became an independent republic.

A constitution adopted in 1960 provided for an executive president and a unicameral national assembly. Following a bloodless coup by the military in 1966 the constitution was suspended. A military government under Gen. Lamizana ruled the country. A new constitution was approved by referendum in

1969 and introduced in the following year. This provided for an elected National Assembly under a civilian prime minister, but President Lamizana was to remain President for a further five years.

A confrontation between the Prime Minister and the National Assembly in 1974 led the army to suspend the constitution and dissolve the legislature. Legislative functions were taken over by a 65-man Consultative Council for National Renewal, which was composed of civilians and military officers. Widespread opposition to military rule forced President Lamizana in 1976 to set up a Constitutional Commission, which recommended an executive president and political activity by no more than three parties. A draft constitution was introduced in 1977 and approved by referendum; the President and National Assembly were to be elected for five years, and the 57 seats in the National Assembly were to be contested by three political parties.

ZAÏRE (BELGIAN CONGO until 1960; then REPUBLIC OF THE CONGO until 1971)

The administration of the Belgian Congo was based upon the Charte Coloniale of 1908, which centralised executive and legislative control in the hands of the Governor-General subject to the Minister of Colonies. The Council of Government was reorganised in 1947 with a non-official majority, but its functions remained purely advisory. By 1951 the Council included eight African members representing African interests. By 1955 the Council consisted of the Governor-General, the Vice-Governor-General, the six provincial governors, the commander of the *Force publique*, up to six unofficial notables nominated by the Governor-General, 16 members representing various commercial and settler associations, and the eight Africans representing African interests. A standing committee of the Council held quarterly meetings. Each of the six provinces was administered by a governor assisted by an advisory provincial council.

Until 1958 the only elections held in the country were those on a limited franchise for municipal governments. Following serious riots in the Congo in 1959 the Belgians announced constitutional reforms. An interim constitution of 1960 proposed a federal parliamentary government with a two-chamber legislature, the House of Representatives based upon direct and proportional representation, and a Senate with equal representation from each of the six provinces. The President was to be elected by a congress of parliament; the Prime Minister was to be appointed by the President and his cabinet had to include at least one minister from each province. Provincial assemblies were also proposed.

The Belgian Congo became independent in June 1960. Shortly after independence serious disturbances broke out in various parts of the country and the *Force publique* mutinied. In September 1960 the Army announced that it was 'neutralising' all politicians; it installed a College of Commissioners to govern the country. The province of Katanga attempted to secede and the Congo went into a constitutional crisis with rival claimants to central government authority. The constitution of 1962 provided for a constitutional president, a prime minister, and a federal structure of 21 provinces with local and restricted powers. President Kasavubu dissolved parliament and suspended the constitution in 1963 and granted the Prime Minister full legislative powers.

A new constitution was introduced in 1964 which reduced the powers of the legislature but increased those of the head of state. A military coup led by Gen. Mobutu in 1965 briefly suspended the National Assembly and then governed through it by presidential decree. A national referendum in 1967 approved a new constitution, the third since independence, which was further revised in 1971, 1974, and 1977, and promulgated in 1978. This provided for an executive president elected for seven years, and a single-chamber National Legislative Council of 268 deputies. The President was to be leader of the sole political party, the Mouvement Populaire de la Révolution (MPR), and would be assisted by a National Executive Council consisting of state commissioners, who would also be heads of government departments.

ZAMBIA (NORTHERN RHODESIA until 1964)

In 1945 the British protectorate of Northern Rhodesia was administered by a governor assisted by an Executive Council of five official and three nominated unofficial members. The Legislative Council consisted of nine official members, eight elected members, three unofficial members appointed to represent African interests, and two nominated unofficial members. By 1948 the number of unofficial members on the Executive Council had been increased to four or five and the Governor was obliged to regard the unanimous advice of the unofficial members as the advice of the Executive, even if the officials disagreed. He had either to accept it or to refer his rejection to the Secretary of State. In 1949 two unofficial members held ministerial portfolios.

In 1953 Northern Rhodesia became part of the Federation of Rhodesia and Nyasaland despite widespread African protests. Britain retained ultimate responsibility for external affairs, while defence, immigration, European education, European agriculture and health were transferred to a new federal legislature. Northern Rhodesia continued as a protectorate, and its government retained control over African affairs, local government, housing, police, internal security, industrial relations, lands, mining and irrigation.

By 1955 the Legislative Council had been enlarged to 26 members. It consisted of eight official and 12 elected members, plus two nominated by the Governor to represent African interests, and four Africans elected by the African Representative Council (established 1945–6). The constitution of 1960 was an attempt by the British Secretary of State to balance power between the African majority and the small white minority. It provided for a Legislative Council with an elected majority – 12 members elected by European constituencies, six by special African constituencies, two to seats reserved for Africans and two to seats reserved for Europeans. There was a franchise on a common roll with qualifications. Ministers were to be appointed to the Executive Council on the advice of the lower house.

The federation came to an end in 1963. Northern Rhodesia became the independent republic of Zambia in 1964, after ten months of internal self-government. The constitution provided for a president, to be elected for the first term by the Legislative Assembly but thereafter by the electorate at each general election. There is a single-chamber parliament, the National Assembly of 110 members; the government is led in the Assembly by the Vice-President, appointed by the President. Since 1972 Zambia has been a one-party state.

A new constitution was introduced in 1973. This provided for an executive president elected by popular vote; the President would appoint a prime minister. The Central Committee of the ruling United National Independence Party (UNIP) has greater powers than the cabinet; of its 28 members 25 are elected at the UNIP General Conference, and three are nominated by the President. The cabinet is appointed by the President. The National Assembly consists of 125 elected members all drawn from the UNIP. There is also a House of Chiefs, with 27 members representing each province in the country.

ZANZIBAR

Zanzibar was a sultanate and a British protectorate administered by a British Resident. Executive and Legislative Councils were established in 1926. The Executive Council, of which the British Resident was chairman, continued as an entirely official body until 1956; the Legislative Council in 1945 consisted of three *ex officio* and five official members, with six unofficial members appointed to represent the various communities. Arabs received the largest representation in the Legislative Council, although they did not constitute the majority of the island population. In 1956 the membership of the Executive Council was altered to allow more Zanzibari representatives; the Legislative Council was expanded and six of its 12 unofficial members were to be elected.

A new constitution of 1960 opened the franchise to women on the same qualifications of property and education as applied to men. The Legislative Council now had 22 elected members, three *ex officio* and up to five nominated members, and was presided over by a speaker. The Executive Council had three *ex officio* members and five unofficial members, including a chief minister. In 1962 the Executive Council was replaced by a Council of Ministers, the franchise was widened by the removal of property and educational qualifications, and the official members were removed from both the Executive and the Legislative Councils. Full ministerial government was introduced, as a preliminary to independent status, achieved in December 1963, when the Legislative Council was replaced by a National Assembly.

In 1964 the sultanate was abolished by a revolution and the People's Republic of Zanzibar established. Zanzibar joined with Tanganyika to form a united republic which was named Tanzania; it retained its own executive and legislature. The First Vice-President of the united republic is the head of the executive in Zanzibar under the title of President of Zanzibar.

ZIMBABWE (SOUTHERN RHODESIA until 1965; RHODESIA until 1978; ZIMBABWE–RHODESIA, 1978–80)

By the constitution of 1923 Southern Rhodesia became a self-governing colony with internal autonomy except in legislation affecting the African population and mining royalties. A governor appointed by the Crown administered the country through an Executive Council drawn from and responsible to the single-chamber Legislative Assembly, which in 1946 had 30 members, all white and elected on a restricted franchise.

The Federation of Rhodesia and Nyasaland was formed in 1953. Britain retained ultimate responsibility for external affairs; defence, immigration, European education, European agriculture and health were transferred to the new federal legislature. Salisbury, the capital of Southern Rhodesia, became the federal capital. Southern Rhodesia continued to have the status of a self-governing colony. It retained control over African affairs, local government, housing, police, internal security, industrial relations, lands, mining and irrigation.

The constitution of 1961 transferred to Southern Rhodesia some powers still vested in the British government and included the Declaration of Rights. It created the Governor's Council, consisting of the Prime Minister and up to 11 ministers, to replace the Executive Council. The constitution stated that certain of its basic provisions might not be altered without majority approval by each of the four main races voting separately in referendum, *or* the approval of the British government, which could refuse to give a decision if it was thought a referendum desirable. The only reserved powers remaining related to the Sovereign and the Governor, international obligations and loans under Colonial Stock Acts. The Legislative Assembly was enlarged to 65 members – 50 seats reserved to Europeans voting on the upper roll, and 15 to Africans on the lower roll.

In 1963 the Federation came to an end. Southern Rhodesia reverted to the status of a self-governing colony but took additional powers over matters previously transferred to the federal government in 1953.

In 1965 the Prime Minister of Rhodesia declared a state of emergency, overriding normal constitutional safeguards, and issued a unilateral declaration of independence. His government was dismissed by the Governor, but continued to carry on effective internal administration. The British government reasserted its formal responsibility for Rhodesia and passed an enabling bill which gave it power to deal with the situation by orders-in-council. In 1969 a new constitution was passed in Rhodesia which declared the country to be a republic. The constitution further provided for a president elected for five years and a bicameral legislature consisting of a House of Assembly and a Senate. The House of Assembly had 66 members, 50 elected by a white roll and 16 by an African roll; the Senate had 23 members. The British government declared the constitution illegal. Attempts to reach an agreement (which would allow legal independence under agreed conditions) were made in 1966, 1968, 1970–2, 1974, 1975 and 1976.

African nationalist forces began a guerrilla war in north-east Rhodesia in 1972. From 1973 onwards the white government under Ian Smith discussed a possible internal settlement with other African nationalist leaders. Negotiations failed and the war escalated. In 1977 both the Smith government and the guerrilla leaders rejected an Anglo-American proposal for a constitutional settlement. In the following year a transitional government was formed by the white ruling party and African nationalists not involved in the guerrilla war. This provided for executive power to be shared between the white Prime Minister and three African ministers, who would take turns to chair the Executive Council. The Council of Ministers was equally divided between European and African ministers, who were similarly to share the role of chairman. The state was renamed Zimbabwe–Rhodesia and the transitional government set about drafting a constitution on the basis of majority rule and adult suffrage.

The constitution of 1979 provided for a 100-seat House of Assembly; 28 seats were reserved for whites, 20 being elected and eight chosen by the 92 elected members of the House from among white members of the former House of Assembly. The Senate consisted of 30 members, 10 white and 10 black senators elected by the House of Assembly, and 10 senators elected by chiefs. In May 1979 Bishop Muzorewa became Prime Minister of Zimbabwe–Rhodesia. His government failed to receive international recognition or to bring about the lifting of economic sanctions, and the guerrilla war in the country intensified. These events forced the transitional government to agree to constitutional talks in London with the British government; the nationalist groups in the guerrilla war also agreed to participate in the talks.

At the Lancaster House talks in London it was finally agreed by all parties that Britain would resume responsibility for Rhodesia and supervise elections to produce a government which would then rapidly lead the country to legal independence. A British governor was installed in Salisbury late in 1979. Under the constitution agreed in London the new state of Zimbabwe was to be a republic with a president as constitutional head of state. Executive power was to rest with the Prime Minister and Executive Council, responsible to the House of Assembly of 100 members. 20 of the seats in the House were to be reserved for white electors, the rest having no racial restrictions. There was to be a Senate of 40 members chosen by various electoral colleges.

Elections were held in early 1980 and the nationalist groups which had been involved in the guerrilla war won an overwhelming majority. In April, Robert Mugabe became Prime Minister at the head of a coalition government and Zimbabwe was declared an independent republic within the Commonwealth.

5 POLITICAL PARTIES

ALGERIA

Front de Libération Nationale (FLN)
Founded in November 1954, it led the movement for independence from France. Dedicated to socialism, non-alignment and pan-Arabism, it is the only party with legal status. Since independence the party has been split many times over economic and ideological policies. The party congress nominates candidates to be president of the republic, and the FLN organises mass movements for women and young people.

Unofficial and illegal opposition comes from:

Front des Forces Socialistes (FFS)
This organisation led the Kabylia revolt against President Ben Bella in 1963–4.

Organisation Clandestine de la Révolution Algérienne (OCRA)
Founded in 1966, the OCRA supported the imprisoned Ben Bella as lawful president.

Mouvement Démocratique du Renouveau Algérien (MDRA)
Founded in 1967, the MDRA supported Krim Belkacem, who was implicated in an anti-government conspiracy of that year.

Parti de l'Avant Garde Socialiste (PAGS)
Founded in 1965, the PAGS consisted of communist and Marxist critics of the FLN. Formerly called the Organisation de la Résistance Populaire, it was allied with the French Communist Party. All its leaders were imprisoned.

Parti Communiste Algérien (PCA)
Banned in 1963, the PCA works underground and through Algerians overseas.

Other small parties: *Conseil National pour la Défense de la Révolution*; *Parti de la Révolution Socialiste*; *Rassemblement Unitaire des Revolutionnaires*, formed in 1967.

WESTERN SAHARA

Frente Popular para La Liberacion de Sakiet el Hamra y Rio de Oro (Polisario)
Founded in 1973, the Polisario has fought for the independence of the Western

Sahara, first from Spain and later from Morocco and Mauritania. Based in Algeria, it forms the government of the self-proclaimed Saharan Arab Democratic Republic.

ANGOLA

Political institutions inside Angola were those of metropolitan Portugal until independence.

Movimento Popular de Libertação de Angola (MPLA)
Formed in 1957 by the merger of several militant nationalist groups, the MPLA was based in Zambia and led by Agostinho Neto. In the civil war which followed independence from Portugal in 1974 the MPLA was victorious and it now forms the government. A new name, the Marxist–Leninist Angola Workers' Party was proposed in 1977. All other parties have been banned.

Frente Nacional de Libertação de Angola (FNLA)
Formed in 1962 by the merger of two earlier groups, the FNLA established a government-in-exile under Roberto Holden in Kinshasa, Zaïre. Active in northern Angola, it was strongly anti-communist.

União Nacional para a Independencia Total de Angola (UNITA)
Formed in 1966, UNITA was based in south-eastern Angola. Since the MPLA's victory in 1976, UNITA has continued a guerrilla war against the Angolan government and has received support from South Africa.

Frente de Libertação de Enclave de Cabinda (FLEC)
Formed in 1963, the FLEC fights a guerrilla war in Cabinda from bases in Zaïre, but it has been plagued by repeated splits in its leadership.

Movimento para a Libertação de Cabinda (Molica)
An offshoot of the FLEC.

BENIN (formerly DAHOMEY)

Parti de la Révolution Populaire du Benin (PRPB)
Formed in 1975, the PRPB is the country's only legal party and has a Marxist–Leninist programme.

Before 1975, political parties did not take firm root in the country, owing to government policies in successive periods of military rule. All political parties were banned in 1965, and the constitution of 1968 envisaged the establishment of a one-party political system.

Union pour le Renouveau du Dahomey (URD)
Formed in 1968, it organised support for the military-backed government of
Émile Derlin Zinsou.

Front pour la Libération du Dahomey
The illegal opposition party, implicated in an abortive coup of 1977.

BOTSWANA

Botswana Democratic Party (BDP)
The ruling party of Sir Seretse Khama, it is the strongest party in Botswana,
favouring close relations with South Africa and Western-style democracy.

Botswana Peoples' Party (BPP)
Until 1969 the principal minority party, advocating pan-Africanist policies and
social democracy.

Botswana National Front (BNF)
A left-wing pro-communist party formed after the 1965 elections, it polled the
second largest number of votes in the 1969 and 1974 elections.

Botswana Independence Party (BIP)
Formed in 1965, the BIP is a small opposition party with similar policies to the
BPP.

BURUNDI

Parti de l'Unité et du Progrès National du Burundi (Uprona)
Formed before independence, Uprona won the elections of 1961 and 1965 and
became Burundi's only legal political party. Dominated by the Tutsi ruling tribe
and by ex-President Micombero, the party stressed national unity with social and
economic progress.

24 parties contested the pre-independence elections of 1961, but all are now
banned. Unofficial opposition centres on:

Parti du Peuple (PP)
The party of the numerically dominant Hutu tribe, it was implicated in the
abortive coup of 1965.

Parti Démocratique Chrétien (PDC)
A Tutsi party, it was discredited for its complicity in the assassination of Prime
Minister Prince Louis Rwagasore in 1961.

CAMEROON

Union Nationale Camerounaise (UNC)
The one-party system of Western Cameroon was extended to Eastern Cameroon in 1966, when all parties merged to form the UNC. The party sponsors organisations of women, young people and trade unionists. Its policy is pan-Africanist and combines the encouragement of private initiative with a positive leading role for the state.

Before 1966, the major parties were:

Union Camerounaise
Based in Eastern Cameroon.

Kamerun National Democratic Party
Founded in 1951 by Vice-President Foncha, it was based in the west of the country.

Kamerun United National Congress
Based in the west.

Kamerun People's Party
Based in the west.

After 1966, illegal opposition centred on

Union des Populations Camerounaises (UPC)
A pro-Chinese Communist group, banned in 1966 but active among Cameroon émigrés. The party was finally crushed in 1971.

CAPE VERDE ISLANDS

Partido Africano da Independencia da Guiné e Cabo Verde (PAIGC)
Founded in 1956 and based in Conakry, Guinea, the PAIGC was the liberation movement in Guinea-Bissau and the Cape Verde Islands until independence. The PAIGC seeks the reunion of Guinea-Bissau and the Cape Verde Islands and the Comisão National de Cabo Verde da PAIGC is the republic's only legal political party.

CENTRAL AFRICAN REPUBLIC

Mouvement d'Évolution Social en Afrique Noire (MESAN)
Founded before independence by Barthélemy Boganda, the MESAN became the Central African Republic's single political party under the regime of President

David Dacko. All other parties were banned in 1962. The new military government of 1966 under Col. J. B. Bokassa took over the MESAN as an instrument of political control and to rally support for Bokassa, who was crowned Emperor in 1977. All other parties remain banned.

CHAD

All political parties were banned in 1975.

Mouvement National pour la Révolution Culturelle et Sociale, formerly the *Parti Progressiste Tchadien (PPT)*
Founded in the late 1950s as the local division of the Ivory-Coast-based Rassemblement Démocratique Africain, the PPT was based among the Sara community in southern Chad. In 1962 the PPT became Chad's only legal political party, and the party adopted its new name in 1973.

Clandestine opposition parties of the Muslim north include *Parti National Africain*; *Union Nationale Tchadienne*; *Mouvement Socialiste Africain*.

Front de la Libération Nationale Tchadien (Frolinat)
The government's major adversary in civil war, Frolinat controls much of eastern Chad and is led by Dr Abba Siddick.

Front de la Libération Tchadienne (FLT)
Formerly part of the guerrilla opposition, the FLT supports the 1975 government.

Mouvement Démocratique pour la Renouvellement de Tchad (MDRT)
Formerly an opposition party based in Paris, the MDRT welcomed the 1975 government.

COMORO ISLANDS

Front National Uni (FNU)
Formed by the major opposition parties after independence the FNU provided the government from 1975 until the coup of May 1978.

Mouvement de Libération Nationale des Comores (Helinocom)
Active against the French in the 1960s, it was led by Abdou Bakari Boina.

On Mayotte, which remains under French rule, the *Mouvement Populaire Mahorais* is the major party. It wants departmental status for the island.

CONGO

Parti Congolais du Travail (PCT), formerly the *Mouvement National Révolutionaire (MNR)*
Established by the then President Massemba-Débat, the MNR became the country's only legal party in 1963, devoted to a programme of 'scientific socialism'. A new name was adopted in 1969, after the army took power.

Opposition parties were banned in 1963, but until then the main parties were the *Union pour la Défense des Intérêts Africains (UDIA,* the party of ex-President Youlou) and the *Mouvement Socialist Africain (MSA).*

DJIBOUTI

Rassemblement Populaire L'Indépendance (RPI)
The coalition which won the 1977 election, it comprises the *Front de la Libération de la Côte des Somalies (FLCS),* which was founded in 1963 and from its base in Mogadishu, Somalia, fought for independence from France; and the *Ligue Populaire Africaine pour l'Indépendance (LPAI),* which provides the major component of the government.

Union Nationale pour l'Indépendance (UNI)
Founded in 1975, the UNI is the major party of the Afar opposition. A breakaway group joined the RPI for the 1977 elections.

Mouvement pour la Libération de Djibouti (MLD)
Founded in 1964, the MLD is an illegal Afar party based in Ethiopia.

Mouvement Populaire de Libération (MPL)
Another Afar party, the MPL has a Marxist–Leninist policy.

EGYPT

Arab Socialist Union (ASU)
Established in 1962 by President Nasser as the country's only legal political party, the ASU was charged with the safeguarding and development of Egypt's programme of Arab socialism. The party underwent reorganisation in 1968, and ASU membership rose to 5 million. The ASU lost its monopoly and its dominant position in 1976, and is now just a watch dog for the other political parties.
  The ASU was the successor to two other parties sponsored by Nasser, the National Liberation Rally and the National Union. All Egypt's old political parties were banned when the monarchy was destroyed in 1953.

Arab Socialist Party (ASP)
Founded in 1976, this centrist party supported President Sadat. It won 280 seats in the 1976 parliamentary elections.

Liberal Socialist Party (LSP)
Founded in 1976, the LSP supports private enterprise and liberalisation. It won 12 parliamentary seats in the 1976 elections.

National Progressive Unionist Party (NPUP)
Founded in 1976, the NPUP is the permitted left-wing party. It won two seats in the 1976 elections.

New Wafd Party
Founded in 1978, it takes up the traditions of the old Wafd party and has the support of 24 members of the ASP, LSP and NPUP parties. Formed after World War I, the Wafd was the main nationalist party and dominated Egyptian politics. It stood for independence from Britain and constitutionalism rather than autocratic rule by the King, but pursued a pragmatic policy of compromise.

A number of parties active before 1952 remain banned. These include the *Communist Party of Egypt* and the *Muslim Brotherhood*, which was founded in 1928 and led anti-British demonstrations in the 1940s.

EQUATORIAL GUINEA

Partido Unico Nacional de los Trabajadores (PUNT)
Established in 1970 through the merger of all existing parties, the PUNT is led by the President.

Alianza Nacional de Restoracion Democratica (ANRD)
Founded in 1974 and based in Geneva, the ANRD forms the opposition to the present regime and publishes *La Voz del Pueblo*.

The political parties which proliferated before and just after independence were:

Movimento de Union Nacional de Guinea Ecuatorial (MUNGE)
Founded in 1964, the MUNGE represented the traditionalist right wing of the mainland people.

Movimento Nacional de Liberacion de la Guinea Ecuatorial (Monalige)
Formerly part of the nationalist guerrilla movement, based on the mainland, Monalige helped form the first independent government but soon fell foul of President Francisco Macias Nguema.

Idea Popular de la Guinea Ecuatorial (IPCE)
A third mainland party, the IPCE stood on the left wing.

Union Democratica Fernandina (UDF)
Based in Fernando Po, the UDF wanted loose federation with Rio Muni.

Union Bubi
The second party of Fernando Po, it helped form the first independent government.

ETHIOPIA and ERITREA

No political parties were allowed to exist before 1974 under the Haile Selassie government.

Provisional Office for Mass Organisational Affairs
Promoted in 1977 by the military government (Dergue) to politicise the people and help found a revolutionary party.

Seded (Revolutionary Flame)
Since 1977 the main government-supported party.

Malerid (Marxist–Leninist Organisation), *Eech-At* (Revolutionary Movement for the Oppressed) and *Wozader* (Labour League)
Supported by the government.

Other parties are illegal. These include:

Mesan (*Me'ei Sone*) (All-Ethiopia Socialist Movement)
Supported by the Dergue until 1977, it continued to be strong among trade unionists.

Ethiopian Democratic Union (EDU)
Founded in 1975, the EDU is the conservative anti-Marxist party, engaged in guerrilla resistance to the Dergue in some provinces.

Ethiopian People's Revolutionary Party (EPRP)
Formed in 1972, the Marxist EPRP stands for a return to civilian rule, and its Ethiopian People's Revolutionary Army organises urban guerrillas in opposition to the Dergue.

Afar Liberation Front (ALF)
A separatist guerrilla group near Djibouti.

Eritrean Liberation Parties
A united front launched in 1977 to embrace the *Eritrean Liberation Front* (*ELF*), which was founded in 1958, maintains the (Muslim) Eritrean Liberation Army,

and is based in Beirut, Lebanon; the *Eritrean People's Liberation Front* (*EPLF*), which was founded in 1970 as a Marxist party with Muslim and Christian support, and maintains the Eritrean People's Liberation Army; and the *Eritrean Liberation Front – Popular Liberation Forces* (*ELF–PLF*), a breakaway from the EPLF.

Oromo Liberation Front (OLF)
A separatist group in one province.

Somali Abo Liberation Front
Another separatist group.

Somali Fatherland Liberation Front (SFLF)
Founded in 1975 as the Western Somali Liberation Front, the SFLF is based in Mogadishu, Somalia. It failed in its attempt in 1977–8 to unite the Ogaden region with Somalia.

Tigre People's Liberation Front (TPLF)
A separatist movement in one province.

GABON

Parti Démocratique Gabonais (PDG)
Founded in 1968 by President Bongo as Gabon's only legal political party, the PDG was the successor to the ruling Bloc Démocratique Gabonais (BDG). This itself was part of the Rassemblement Démocratique Africain, based in the Ivory Coast. The BDG and PDG have been consistently pro-French and stand for no protest or dissent in the country.

Clandestine opposition centred on:

Union Démocratique et Sociale Gabonaise (UDSG)
An affiliate of the Senegal-based Parti du Regroupment Africain, the UDSG was banned in 1964 and its leader imprisoned.

Mouvement de la Révolution Gabonaise (MRG)
This party opposed the PDG in the 1967 elections.

THE GAMBIA

People's Progressive Party (PPP)
Founded in 1958, it merged with the Gambia Congress Party in 1968. From 1965 it was the governing party and advocated closer economic and cultural links with Senegal.

The Gambia remains a multi-party democracy, and opposition parties include the *United Party* (founded in 1952), the *Progressive People's Alliance* (founded in 1968), the *National Convention Party* (founded in 1975) and the *National Liberation Party* (founded in 1975). The opposition parties combined for the April 1977 election.

GHANA

Military rulers from 1966 to 1969 and after 1972 all political parties banned.

United Gold Coast Convention (UGCC)
Formed in 1947 by the intelligentsia, notably the lawyer Dr J. B. Danquah. The first political organisation to talk in practical terms of self-government 'in the shortest possible time'. Kwame N. Nkrumah was briefly the general secretary. Defeated in the general election of 1951 and dissolved in the next year.

Convention People's Party (CPP)
Formed in 1949 by Kwame N. Nkrumah, Prime Minister and later President of Ghana, the CPP became the country's only legal political party in 1964.

National Liberation Movement (NLM)
An Ashanti-based party formed in 1954 which demanded a 'federation' for Ghana.

United Party (UP)
Established in 1956 by a merger of various opposition parties, principally the Northern People's Party and the NLM. It opposed Nkrumah's government but was effectively banned when Ghana became a one-party state.

Progress Party (PP)
Founded in 1969 and led by Dr Busia, it won the 1969 elections and formed the government until 1972.

National Alliance of Liberals (NAL)
The main opposition party in the 1969 elections.

(Three other parties contested the 1969 elections.)

Justice Party
Founded in 1970 by the merger of the NAL with the United Nationalist Party and the All People's Republican Party.

After several years of military rule political parties were formed for the elections of 1979.

People's National Party
Won 71 of the 140 seats in all regions of the country and formed the government under Dr Limann as president.

Popular Front Party
Secured 42 seats, mostly in Ashanti and Brong-Ahafo regions.

(Several other parties contested the elections.)

GUINEA

Parti Démocratique de Guinée (PDG)
Founded in 1947 as an affiliate of the Rassemblement Démocratique Africain, the PDG was first based on Guinea's well organised, pro-communist trade-union ' movement. It is the country's only legal political party. Led by President Sékou Touré, it is organised on democratic centralist principles with an array of affiliated mass organisations.

Front de Libération Nationale de Guinée
Formed by Guinean exiles in 1966, it was based in France, Senegal and the Ivory Coast.

GUINEA-BISSAU

Partido Africano da Independencia da Guiné e Cabo Verde (PAIGC)
Formed in 1956 and based in Conakry, Guinea, the PAIGC undertook political campaigning and guerrilla struggle for the liberation of Guinea-Bissau and the Cape Verde Islands from Portuguese rule. It is the country's only legal party and stands for eventual reunion with the Cape Verde Islands.

Front de Lutte pour l'Indépendance de la Guinée (Fling)
A rival to the PAIGC, it was based in Dakar, Senegal, during the war of independence.

IVORY COAST

Parti Démocratique de la Côte d'Ivoire (PDCI)
Formed in 1946 as the main affiliate of the Rassemblement Démocratique Africain, the PDCI has been the country's only political party since independence. Led by President Houphouët-Boigny, the party was reorganised after an abortive coup in 1963 and takes a pro-French political stance.

Rassemblement Démocratique Africain (RDA)
Established in 1944, the RDA was an international political party with branches

in most of France's former colonies in West Africa. Based in the Ivory Coast, its leading light was Félix Houphouët-Boigny.

KENYA

Kenya African National Union (KANU)
Formed in 1960 and based on Kikuyu support, KANU later absorbed the non-Kikuyu Kenya African Democratic Union (KADU) and the African People's Party (APP). Its leaders, the late Jomo Kenyatta and Tom Mboya, stressed 'African socialism', racial harmony and centralised government. In 1969 KANU became Kenya's only legal political party.

Kenya People's Union (KPU)
The main opposition party, banned in 1969, was led by Oginga Odinga. Formed in 1969 by former members of KANU, the KPU was socialist, anti-Western and based on support from the Luo tribe.

LESOTHO

Basutoland National Party (BNP)
Formed in 1959 and led by Chief Leabua Jonathan, the conservative BNP formed Lesotho's government, which favours free enterprise and co-operation with South Africa. It claims 80,500 members.

Basutoland Congress Party (BCP)
Founded in 1952, the BCP is the main opposition party. It favours non-alignment, is strongly anti-apartheid and pan-Africanist. It claims 75,000 members. The party's militant wing is led from outside Lesotho by Ntsu Mokhehle.

Marematiou Freedom Party (MFP)
This royalist party was formed in 1962 and claims 50,000 members.

United Democratic Party
A breakaway from the BNP, it was formed in 1967.

LIBERIA

True Whig Party (TWP)
Prior to the 1980 coup the only legal political party. The TWP had held power

continuously since 1878. The party stresses national development and cultural integration of the Americo-Liberian community and the indigenous population.

Opposition parties and dissident groups have been fragmented and short-lived.

LIBYA

Arab Socialist Union (ASU)
Formed in 1971 as the country's sole political party. In 1975 the General National Congress of the ASU became the country's General People's Congress, which produced a new national constitution.

All political parties were banned in 1952 and before the 1969 revolution there were no legally constituted political parties, but several clandestine organisations existed; e.g. the *Baath Party*, the *Arab Nationalist Party*, and the *Muslim Brotherhood*.

MADAGASCAR (MALAGASY REPUBLIC)

Front National pour la Défense de la Révolution Socialiste Malgache
Founded in 1977 to rally pro-government political parties. All opposition parties had been banned in 1975. The Front incorporates:

Avant-garde de la Révolution Malgache (Arema)
Formed in 1976 as the mainstay of the revolution, the Arema forms the nucleus of the Front National.

Élan Populaire pour l'Unité Nationale (VONJY)
A nationalist party formed in 1973.

Parti du Congress de l'Indépendance de Madagascar (AKFM)
The pro-Soviet party, established in 1958.

UDECMA–KMTP
A Christian Democrat party formed in 1977.

Other independent parties include:

Mouvement National pour l'Indépendance de Madagascar (Monima)
An anti-French radical socialist party, it withdrew from the Front National in 1977.

MFM
Extreme left-wing party which supports the government.

Parti Social Démocratique (PSD)
Founded by Philibert Tsiranana in 1956, the PSD was the ruling party from 1959

to 1972. Non-Marxist but committed to Christian Socialist principles, the PSD drew its strength from the coastal tribes and its policy was pro-French.

Mouvement pour la Rénouvation Nationale (Morena)
A small left-wing and Catholic opposition party.

MALAWI

Malawi Congress Party (MCP)
Malawi's only authorised political party, the MCP was founded in 1959 to succeed the Nyasaland African National Congress. Life President Dr Hastings Banda's policy is strongly pro-Western, multi-racial and with emphasis on internal development.

There is little organised opposition. Henry Chimpembere (a former Minister of Education) led an unsuccessful revolt in 1965.

MALI

Union Démocratique du Peuple Malien (UDPM)
Founded in 1976 as the country's sole political party, the UDPM is a democratic centralist structure.

Between 1968 and 1974 all political parties were banned by the military government. These parties included:

Union Soudanaise (US)
Founded after the Second World War as an affiliate of the Rassemblement Démocratique Africain (see Ivory Coast), this party supported the Keita government of 1960–8 and controlled the press, trade unions and other social institutions.

MAURITANIA

Parti du Peuple Mauritanien (PPM)
Founded in 1961, through the merger of the Parti du Regroupement Mauritanien, the Union Nationale Mauritanienne, Nahda and the Union des Socialistes Musulmans Mauritaniens, the PPM became the country's only legal political party in 1964. Its policy combined moderate socialism and a non-aligned foreign policy.

There is no organised opposition.

MAURITIUS

Mauritius Labour Party (MLP)
The governing party, led by Sir Seewoosagur Ramgoolam, enjoys strong urban trade-union support, plus rural Hindu agricultural votes. It led the drive for independence.

Muslim Committee of Action (MCA)
Led by those Muslims who believe they can gain most by communal action, it is part of the governing coalition.

Parti Mauritien Social-Démocratique (PMSD)
The leading Francophile opposition party gains support from the Creole middle-class and Franco-Mauritian landowners and was originally opposed to independence. Part of the government coalition after 1976.

Mauritian Militant Movement (MMM)
The leading Marxist party, and the largest single party in the legislative assembly since 1976.

Mauritian Militant Movement – Social Progress (MMM–SP)
An opposition party formed from the MMM.

Independent Forward Bloc (IFB)
Founded 1958, this is a small party based on Hindu farm-labourer support.

Independence Party (IP)
A short-lived coalition of the MLP, IFB and the MCA, in 1967–9.

Mauritius People's Progressive Party (MPPP)
The Mauritian affiliate of the Afro-Asian People's Solidarity Organisation since 1963.

Republican Centre Party
Founded in 1972.

Mauritian Democratic Union (MDU)
An offshoot of the PMSD.

MOROCCO

Istiqlal
Founded in 1943, the Istiqlal led the struggle for independence but split in 1959 and lost power in 1963. It stands for equal rights, better living standards and the

absorption of the Western Sahara and Mauritania. Istiqlal is represented in the 1977 government of national unity.

Mouvement Populaire (MP)
Formed in 1957, it is the pro-royalist Berber party, shared in the government of 1963–5 and dominates the constitutional government formed in 1977.

Mouvement Populaire Constitutionnel et Démocratique (MPCD)
Breakaway from the Mouvement Populaire.

Parti de l'Action
Formed in 1974, it calls for democracy and progress.

Parti Démocratique Constitutionnel (PDC)

Parti Démocrate de l'Indépendance (PDI)
A left-wing offshoot from the Istiqlal, now defunct.

Parti du Progrès et du Socialisme (PPS)
Formed in 1974 to succeed the Parti Marocain de la Libération et du Socialisme (PMLS). A pro-Soviet communist party, the PPS replaces the banned Parti Communiste Marocain, and PMLS leaders were arrested in 1969. It won one seat in the 1977 general elections.

Parti Libéral Progressiste (PLP)
Formed in 1974, it stands for free enterprise and individual rights.

Parti Socialiste Démocratique (PSD)
A small party which shared in government 1963–5.

Union Nationale des Forces Populaires, Casablanca (UNFP)
Formed in 1959 as a left-wing offshoot of Istiqlal, the UNFP campaigned for the restoration of constitutional rule and a programme of social and economic change. Its leader, Ben Barka, disappeared in France in 1965. It has suffered government harrassment and internal disagreements. The Rabat UNFP was banned in 1973 and many party leaders were arrested. It remains in opposition.

Union Socialiste des Forces Populaires (USFP)
A breakaway from the UNFP, formed in 1974 from the banned Rabat section.

MOZAMBIQUE

Frente de Libertação de Moçambique (Frelimo)
Formed in 1962 by the merger of various small nationalist parties: the Unido

Democratica Nacional de Moçambique (Udenamo), the Mozambique African Nationalist Union (MANU) and the União Africana de Moçambique Independente (Unami). Frelimo was first led by Eduardo Mondlane from Dar es Salaam in Tanzania, until Mondlane's assassination in 1969. The Frelimo styles itself as Marxist–Leninist and is Mozambique's only legal party.

Comite Revolutionario de Moçambique (Coremo)
A small nationalist group based in Zambia in the 1960s.

NAMIBIA

Democratic Turnhalle Alliance
Formed in 1977, it represents whites and some African delegations to the Turnhalle Conference. It is sponsored by South Africa to lead a multi-racial independent Namibia.

Namibia National Front
An umbrella body for ten African groups, including the SWANU.

National Democratic Unity Organisation (NDUO)
The party of the Herero people.

National Democratic Party
An Ovambo grouping.

South West Africa Coloured People's Organisation
Founded in 1959.

South West Africa National Union (SWANU)
Founded in 1959, the SWANU was supported by South Africa's African National Congress.

South West Africa National United Front (SWANUF)
A guerrilla force formed in 1964.

South West Africa People's Organisation (SWAPO)
Founded in 1958 as the Ovambo People's Organisation and strongest among the Ovambo tribe, the SWAPO is the main nationalist movement and has organised a guerrilla war for independence. Based in Tanzania and later in Zambia, SWAPO is backed by the Organisation of African Unity (OAU) and receives aid and arms from the Eastern-bloc communist countries. Its programme is Marxist–Leninist, and leadership of the exiled wing rests with Sam Nujoma. An internal faction operates inside Namibia.

Under South African government, the major parties for white voters were:

National Party (NP)
A branch of South Africa's ruling party which dominated the territory's representation in the South African parliament.

Federal Party of South West Africa, formerly the *United National South West Africa Party*
Formed in 1927 as an all-white opposition party, independent from parties in South Africa.

White Republican Party
Founded in 1977 as a breakaway from the National Party, the party supports the Democratic Turnhalle Alliance.

NIGER

Parti Progressiste Nigérien (PPN)
Formed in 1946 as an affiliate of the Rassemblement Démocratique Africain (see Ivory Coast), the PPN became Niger's only legal party in 1959. Its policy was generally pro-French and conservative.

Sawaba (Freedom) Party
Founded as the Union Démocratique Nigérienne (UDN), the Sawaba was Niger's principal left-wing opposition party until its banning in 1959. It continued illegal subversive activities from abroad.

All political parties were banned in 1974 by the military government.

NIGERIA

In May 1966, the new military rulers banned all existing political parties. These parties were regional and based on particular tribal and sectional loyalties:

Northern People's Congress (NPC)
The predominant party in the Federal Parliament.

National Council of Nigerian Citizens (NCNC)
The main party of the Eastern province, the NCNC collaborated with the NPC.

Nigerian National Democratic Party (NNDP)
An opposition party of the Western Region.

Action Group
An opposition party of the Yoruba people, Western Region.

In October 1975 it was announced that party politics would be resumed in 1978. In 1979 elections were held and the country returned to civilian rule. Only parties with a nationwide organisation were able to register, i.e. regionally-based parties were excluded.

Greater Nigeria People's Party (GNPP)
Essentially a conservative party which stressed national unity; led by a Northerner.

National Party of Nigeria (NPN)
Formed by representatives of all the pre-1966 political parties drawn from all areas of the country. Polled 33 per cent of the votes in the elections of July–August 1979 with Alhaji Shehu Shagari becoming President of Nigeria.

Nigerian People's Party (NPP)
Established in 1978 but then split into various factions after disputes over personalities, leadership and finance. Led by the veteran nationalist leader Dr Nnamdi Azikiwe. Polled just over 16 per cent of votes in 1979 elections.

People's Redemption Party (PRP)
Slightly left of centre party with policy of 'democratic humanism' and a 'socialist democracy'.

Unity Party of Nigeria (UPN)
Founded by Chief Obafami Owolowo. Proclaimed itself a democratic socialist party which was in fact just left of centre. Gained 29 per cent of the votes in the 1979 elections.

RWANDA

Mouvement Révolutionnaire National pour le Développement (MRND)
Formed in 1975 as the sole political party, it seeks to remove inter-tribal conflict and promote national unity and development.

Mouvement Démocratique Républicain, formerly the Parti de l'Emancipation Hutu (Parmehutu)
Founded in 1959 to succeed the Mouvement Social Hutu, the Parmehutu was the only legal political party representing the country's dominant tribe. It was replaced by the MRND.

Union Nationale Ruandaise (UNR)
The party of the minority Tutsi tribe was virtually eliminated in the 1960s.

ST HELENA, ASCENSION ISLAND AND TRISTAN DA CUNHA

St Helena Progressive Party
The dominant party, formed in 1973.

St Helena Labour Party
It advocates free enterprise and opposes British development plans. Its leader was banned from the island in 1975.

SÃO TOMÉ AND PRINCIPE

Movimento de Liberacão de São Tomé e Principe
Formed in 1972, this is the country's only legal party. Its policy stresses non-alignment and agrarian and social reform.

Comissão de Liberacão de São Tomé e Principe
Led by Tomas Medeiros, this was the main underground nationalist party seeking independence from Portugal.

SENEGAL

Parti Socialiste Sénégalais (PSS), formerly the *Union Progressiste Sénégalaise (UPS)*
Founded in 1949 by Léopold Sédar Senghor, the UPS was an offshoot of the French Socialist Party. With a moderate, Francophile policy, it has formed the government since 1960. Between 1966 and 1974 Senegal was in effect a one-party state.

Parti de Regroupement Africain-Sénégal (PRA)
A left-wing opposition party, the PRA was absorbed by the UPS in 1966.

Parti Communiste Sénégalais (PCS)
An illegal party, formed in 1965 as an offshoot of the PAI.

Parti Démocratique Sénégalais (PDS)
Founded in 1974, the PDS forms the liberal democratic opposition.

Parti Africain de l'Indépendance (PAI)
Founded originally in 1957 and reorganised in 1976, the PAI forms the Marxist opposition.

Mouvement Républicain Sénégalais (MRS)
Founded in 1977, it forms the right-wing conservative opposition.

Rassemblement National Démocratique (RND)
An illegal progressive party, formed in 1976.

SEYCHELLES

Seychelles Democratic Party
The conservative party, formed in 1963 and led by ex-President James Mancham.

Seychelles People's United Party
The left-wing party, led by Albert René, who became President of the Seychelles in the 1977 coup.

SIERRA LEONE

All-People's Congress (APC)
Formed in 1960 by Siaka Stevens, the APC drew its strength from the Temne people and minor tribes. With a leftist republican programme, it took power in 1968. All its candidates were returned unopposed in the 1973 elections. It is expected that the APC will become the country's only legal party.

Sierra Leone People's Party (SLPP)
Formed in 1951, it was the country's first political party. Dominant until 1967, the SLPP was based on support from the Mende tribe. Led by Milton and Albert Margai, the party was temporarily split from 1958 to 1961.

Democratic National Party (DNP)
Opposition party.

United National Alliance
Coalition of the SLPP and the DNP in the 1977 elections.

People's National Party
Short-lived break-away party from SLPP formed by Milton Margai and Siaka Stevens. It was badly defeated in the District Council elections of 1959.

SOMALIA

Somali Socialist Revolutionary Party (SSRP)
Formed in 1976 as the country's sole political party. The Central Committee of the SSRP forms the government.

Somali Democratic Action Front (Sodaf)
The illegal opposition party, which advocates democratic elections and peace with Ethiopia.

Political parties which were banned in 1969 by the new military government included:

Somali Youth League (SYL)
The government party since independence in 1960, the SYL was strongly nationalist and irredentist towards Somali minorities in Ethiopia, Kenya and Djibouti. It relied heavily on Eastern-bloc communist aid.

Other parties remained legal under the SYL, and a total of 63 minority parties and groups fought in the 1969 elections (before the military takeover). Most supported the SYL government. These included *Somali National Congress (SNC)*, an offshoot from the SYL and other parties in 1963, which took a radical line in foreign policy; *Somali African National Union (SANU)*; *Liberal Somali Youth Party (PLGS)*; *Independent Constitutional Somali Party (DHMS)*; *Somali Democratic Union*, strongly left-wing; *Democratic Action People's Party (MPAD)*, strongly critical of the SYL in 1969.

SOUTH AFRICA

African National Congress (ANC)
Formed in 1912, the ANC stands for a non-racial society and co-operation with left-wing and liberal organisations of other races. Led by Nelson Mandela (imprisoned for life), it was banned in 1960 and its activities are directed from Zambia.

Black People's Convention (BPC)
Founded in 1972, as an all-African and non-tribal organisation, it was banned in 1976.

Black Unity Front (BUF)
Founded in 1976 and led by the Zulu Chief, Buthelezi.

Coloured Labour Party (CLP)
The main party for people of mixed race.

Congress of Democrats
A communist front, banned since 1962.

Democratic National Party (DNP)
Party of the moderate centre.

Herstigte Nasionale Party (HNP)
Founded in 1969 by National Party dissidents of the right wing, the HNP calls for strict application of apartheid, Afrikaans as the national language and a society based on God's laws as defined by Calvin.

Indian National Congress of South Africa (INC)
Formed in 1896, the INC collaborates with the ANC in exile.

Indian Reform Party

Liberal Party (LP)
Founded in 1953, the party broke up in 1968 when new legislation banned political association among members of different racial groups.

National Party (NP)
Formed originally in 1912, the party has held power since 1948; it absorbed many other parties, including the Afrikaner Party. An all-white party, the National Party represents most Afrikaners and a growing number of English-speaking South Africans, and it stands for apartheid and rigorous anti-communism. Its policies are designed to safeguard the white nation in its South African homeland and to lead the black inhabitants to self-government in their homelands or 'bantustans'.

New Republic Party (NRP)
Formed in 1977 by United Party members, it stands for a power-sharing federal government.

Pan-Africanist Congress of Azania (PACA)
Formed in 1959 as a left-wing offshoot of the ANC, it rejects the multi-racial approach. Banned in 1960, it operates from Zambia.

Progressive Federal Party (PEP)
Established in 1977 from the Progressive Reform Party and part of the old United Party, the PFP is a white organisation which advocates a federal constitution with self-governing states based on territorial rather than racial divisions, power-sharing between the races and an end to discriminatory legislation.

Progressive Party (PP)
Formed in 1959 by United Party dissidents, the party favoured enfranchisement for all qualified persons irrespective of race. It gave way to PFP in 1977. The legislation of 1968 forced the party to become all white.

South African Communist Party (SACP)
Illegal since 1950.

South African Party (SAP)
Formed in 1977 by the Independent United Party, the SAP rejects power-sharing and seeks federal government under white leadership.

United Party (UP)
Founded in 1937, the United Party represented most English-speaking white South Africans, and was the main opposition party from 1948 to 1977, when it was dissolved and gave way to the PFP, SAP and NRP.

SUDAN

Sudanese Socialist Union (SSU)
Formed in 1972 as the country's only legal party, the SSU provides the government's power-base in the country.

Sudanese National Front (SNF)
An umbrella for various oppositions groups, including the Umma Party, the Muslim Brotherhood and the right-wing Union of Sharaf al-Hindi. It was banned in 1969, but tolerated after 1977.

Until the dissolution of all political parties by the military government in 1969, the main organisations were:

Democratic Unionist Party (DUP)
The major government party, formed in 1967 from the former National Unionist Party and the Muslim People's Democratic Party.

Islamic Charter Front (Mithaq)
Formed in 1964, the Mithaq organised strict Muslims.

Southern Front
Founded in 1964, it wanted self-determination for the three southern provinces and co-operated with the DUP to achieve that end.

Sudan African National Union (SANU)
A radical party of the southern provinces, it split in 1967.

Sudan Communist Party (SCP)
The party enjoyed strong trade-union and student support, but was banned intermittently in the 1960s. In the 1970s the government was strongly anti-communist.

Sudan Socialist Party (SSP)
Formed in 1967 after the SCP was banned, the SSP acted as a communist front.

Umma Party
A conservative party, based on the Ansar religious brotherhood and the Mahdi family, the Umma was split for two years from 1967 to 1969.

SWAZILAND

On 12 April 1973, all political parties were dissolved and prohibited by King Sobhuza II. Prior to that date, the five main parties were:

Imbokadvo National Movement (INM)
Founded in 1964, it was moderate, sympathetic to white settlers, and dominated the Swazi elections.

Ngwane National Liberatory Congress (NNLC)
Founded in 1962, it opposed the Imbokadvo Movement and was strongly nationalistic and pan-Africanist. In 1971 it split into two factions.

Swaziland Progressive Party (SPP)
Founded in 1929, as the Swazi Progressive Association.

Swaziland United Front (SUF)
Founded in 1962, as an offshoot of the SPP.

United Swaziland Association (USA)
Representing Swaziland's white community, it supported the INM.

TANZANIA (formerly TANGANYIKA and ZANZIBAR)

Chama Cha Mapinduzi (Revolutionary Party of Tanzania) (CCM)
Formed in 1977, the CCM results from a merger of TANU and the ASP, which operated as the only legal parties on the mainland and Zanzibar respectively. The party aims for a socialist democratic state, advocates self-help methods and sponsors mass organisations for women, young people, trade unionists and co-operatives.

Tanganyika African National Union (TANU)
Founded in 1954, TANU led the movement for independence from Britain.

Afro-Shirazi Party (ASP)
Formed in 1956–7, the ASP mobilised Zanzibar's African people and came to power after the coup of 1964. It pursued a socialist programme.

TOGO

Rassemblement du Peuple Togolais (RPT)
Founded in 1969 as the only legal political party, the RPT organises support for the government.

All other political parties were banned after the coup of 1967. The major parties were:

Unité Togolaise (UT)
Led by Togo's first president, Sylvanus Olympio, the party stemmed from the Comité de l'Unité Togolaise. In power from 1960 to 1963, the Unité Togolaise enjoyed strong support from the Ewe tribe and from trade unionists.

Juvento
Originally the youth movement of the Unité Togolaise, Juvento became independent in 1959.

Mouvement Populaire Togolais (MPT)
Formed in 1954 by UDPT dissidents.

Union Démocratique des Populations Togolaises (UDPT)
Led by Togo's second president, Nicolas Grunitzky, the UDPT was formed in 1959 by the merger of the Parti Togolais du Progrès and the Union des Chefs des Populations du Nord. These formed the main opposition to the Unité Togolaise, and were based on tribal support in the central and northern regions.

TUNISIA

Parti Socialiste Destourien (PSD)
Formed in 1934 by Habib Bourguiba as the Neo-Destour Party, the PSD has been Tunisia's ruling party since independence. It is strongly organised among trade unionists, peasants, women, young people, etc, and stands for a programme of moderate socialism. In the 1974 general election there were no candidates from other parties.

Illegal parties include: *Parti Communiste Tunisien (PCT)*, illegal since 1962, the pro-Soviet PCT was strong in student circles; *Front National Progressiste Tunisien (FNPT)*, an umbrella for groups of Nasserites (Union Socialiste Arabe de Tunisie), Baathists (Mouvement Socialiste Arabe de Tunisie) and Yousefistes; *Mouvement de l'Unité Populaire (MUP)*; and *Parti Social Démocratique (PSD)*.

UGANDA

All political parties were banned after the 1971 coup.

Illegal organisation:

Front for National Salvation (Fronasa)
A guerrilla group, founded in 1973, which aimed to depose President Amin.

Former parties:

Democratic Party (DP)
Based on Roman Catholic and Bugandan support and favouring local control and federal government.

Kababa Yekka (KY)
Based in Buganda, it organised support for the Kabaka (King) until his overthrow in 1966.

Uganda National Union (UNU)
Founded in 1969.

Uganda People's Congress (UPC)
Formed in 1960, the UPC shared in government from 1962 to 1966 and then took full powers. Led by Milton Obote, it advocated strong central government, African socialism and non-alignment.

UPPER VOLTA

Political parties were revived in 1977.

Groupement d'Action Populaire (GAP)
This party organises support for General Lamizana as President.

Mouvement des Indépendants du Parti du Regroupement Africain (MI–PRA)

Union Nationale des Indépendants (UNI)

Union Nationale pour la Défense de la Démocratie (UNDD)

Union Progressiste Voltaique (UPV)
The largest party, drawn from the former MLN and dissidents from other parties.

The older parties which were banned between 1974 and 1977 were:

Union Démocratique Voltaique (UDV)
Affiliated to the RDA (see Ivory Coast), the UDV was the dominant party until 1966 and from 1969 to 1974. It is strongest in the eastern and central regions, and its activities were revived in 1977.

Mouvement de Libération Nationale (MLN)
An opposition party.

Parti du Regroupement Africain (PRA)
An opposition party, the PRA wanted a federal state.

Groupement d'Action Populaire (GAP)
A traditionalist and Islamic party.

Parti Africain de l'Indépendance (PAI)
The main left-wing, communist opposition party remained illegal after the revival of political parties in 1977.

ZAÏRE

Mouvement Populaire de la Révolution (MPR)
Formed by President Mobutu in 1967, the MPR became Zaïre's only legal political party, with a policy of national unity, Zaïrean militancy and nationalism. It is generally anti-communist and anti-clerical.

Illegal parties and former parties, banned in 1965, included:

Alliance des Bakongos (Abako)
Led by ex-President Kasavubu.

Mouvement National Congolais (MNC)
The left-wing party led by Congo's first prime minister, Patrice Lumumba.

Confédération des Associations Tribales du Katanga (Conakat)
Led by Moïse Tshombe.

Parti pour la Conscience Nationale (Pacona)
Formed in 1977, the Pacona aims to depose President Mobutu, to restore a two-chamber parliament and the traditional authority of tribal chiefs, and to rehabilitate the Roman Catholic Church.

Parti Révolutionnaire du Peuple (PRP)
Based in eastern Zaïre, the party organises guerrilla resistance to President Mobutu and has a Marxist–Leninist programme.

ZAMBIA

United National Independence Party (UNIP)
Formed in 1959 and led by Kenneth Kaunda, the UNIP became Zambia's only legal party in 1972. Originally the party's strength came from the Bemba-speaking population.

Parties banned since 1972:

African National Congress (ANC)
Founded in 1944 by Harry Nkumbula as a militant nationalist organisation, the ANC fought against the Rhodesian Federation and racial discrimination. It was strongest among the Borotse people. The ANC favoured co-operation with the white-ruled governments of Southern Africa.

United Progress Party (UPP)

United Party
Active among Lozi tribesmen between 1967 and 1968, when it was banned.

National Progress Party (NPP)
The party of Zambia's white minority, the NPP held 10 seats in parliament until 1966.

ZIMBABWE

African National Council (ANC)
Formed in 1971, the ANC organised opposition to the Anglo-Rhodesian settlement proposals. Its leader was Bishop Abel Muzorewa.

African National Council – Sithole (ANC–Sithole)
Formed in 1977 by former militants of the ANC and the ZANU, the party was led by the Revd Ndabaningi Sithole and supported the 'internal settlement' of Zimbabwe's independence.

African National Council – Zimbabwe (ANC–Zimbabwe)
As the internal wing of the ZANU, the party opposed the internal settlement.

African Progressive Party (APP)
Formed in 1974, it wanted a settlement on the basis of the 1971 proposals.

Centre Party (CP)
Formed in 1968, the CP was multi-racial and critical of the Rhodesia Front's discriminatory legislation.

Conservative Alliance of the Republic of Rhodesia
Formed in 1969 by right-wing dissidents of the Rhodesia Front, the party called for separation of the races.

Front for the Liberation of Zimbabwe (Frolizi)
Led by James Chikerema, the Frolizi merged into the Patriotic Front.

National Association of Coloured People

National People's Union (NPU)
A mainly black party formed in 1969, the NPU combined the former United People's Party and the Democratic Party, and it covered those Africans who sat in the Rhodesian parliament.

National Settlement Convention (NSC)
Formed in 1974 from the former African Settlement Convention and the Rhodesian Settlement Forum, the NSC wanted a settlement based on the 1971 proposals.

National Unifying Force (NUF)
Formed in 1977 from the Rhodesia Party, the Centre Party and the National Pledge Association, the NUF supported a multi-racial Zimbabwe and the Anglo-American proposals for a settlement.

Patriotic Front (PF)
The main nationalist umbrella organisation formed in 1976 by the leaders of the ZANU and ZAPU, the Patriotic Front opposed the internal settlement, promoted guerrilla warfare for the liberation of Zimbabwe, and enjoyed the support of the presidents of Angola, Botswana, Mozambique, Tanzania and Zambia. It was based in Mozambique.

People's Movement (PM)
Formed in 1976 and led by Robert Mugabe, it maintained an internal wing in Zimbabwe.

Rhodesian Action Party (RAP)
Formed in 1977 by former members of the Rhodesia Front.

Rhodesia Front (RF)
The white party led by Ian Smith which held power from 1962 with a policy of racial segregation, white supremacy and independence from Britain. In 1977 the Front accepted the principle of universal adult suffrage and began to devise an 'internal settlement'.

Rhodesia Party
Formed in 1972, it was an opposition white party critical of the Rhodesia Front's racially discriminatory laws and supported a qualified franchise and responsible government.

Rhodesian White People's Party
Formed in 1976, it was anti-liberal and anti-Zionist.

Southern Africa Solidarity Conference (Sascon)
A group for those opposed to majority rule and in support of closer links with South Africa.

United African National Council (UANC)
Formed originally in 1971 as the ANC, the UANC was the party of Bishop Abel

Muzorewa which emerged from the nationalists' split in 1975. It supported the 'internal settlement'.

United Conservative Party (UCP)
Formed in 1975, the white right-wing opposition party which wanted separate parliaments for whites and blacks.

United Front against Surrender
Formed in 1972, the party stood for continued white supremacy.

Zimbabwe African National Union (ZANU)
Formed in 1963 after a split in ZAPU, the party is led by Robert Mugabe and until the 1980 settlement was based in Mozambique, from where it organised guerrilla warfare. It formed part of the Patriotic Front and advanced a Marxist—Leninist programme. In the 1980 elections, it won a landslide victory.

Zimbabwe African People's Union (ZAPU)
Formed in 1961, ZAPU was banned in 1964. Led from Zambia by Joshua Nkomo, it promoted guerrilla warfare and formed part of the Patriotic Front.

Zimbabwe Reformed African National Council
Formed in 1976.

Zimbabwe United People's Organisation (ZUPO)
Formed in 1976, the ZUPO is led by Chief Chirau, and supported the 'internal settlement'.

6 TRADE UNIONS

INTRODUCTORY NOTE

The trade unions which exist in each of Africa's 52 states and territories represent only about 5–15 per cent of the population and exclude the vast majority of the peasants and subsistence farmers. The labour movement, however, constitutes an important force in Africa as elsewhere, for after a brief but stormy history the trade unions have secured for themselves in most countries a role in the machinery of government alongside the ruling political parties and other national organisations.

THE COLONIAL LEGACY

African trade unions were formed and developed during the period of European colonial rule, and Britain and France bequeathed to their respective colonies particular patterns of trade unionism modelled on the differing characteristics of their own labour movements but restricted in various ways to meet the needs of colonial government. In the former Portuguese colonies, however, trade unions for Africans were banned, and developments varied in the few territories relatively free from European influence. In certain regions, trade unions have featured further special characteristics, principally the pan-Arab movement in the north and the white-settler influence in southern Africa. The apartheid code restricted the growth of African unions, and the system of migrant labour hindered the development of a lasting relationship between wage-earners and employers, reducing the workers' interest in trade unions.

In Africa as a whole wage-earners constitute only 5–15 per cent of the population and large-scale urbanisation and industrialisation has been confined to a few areas, notably South Africa and mining zones, as in Zaïre and Zambia. Elsewhere the organised work-force is concentrated in several large towns, such as Dakar, Cairo and Lagos. Industrialised agriculture, whilst employing large numbers of people, has been resistant to trade-union organisation, and in the 1970s the trade unions of Africa continued to draw much of their strength from the public-service employees, including 'white collar' workers, and urban labourers, who were the pioneers of African trade unionism.

This began in the late nineteenth century when workers in business houses and government departments organised themselves to defend their interests. There was a strike by harbour workers in Freetown, Sierra Leone, in 1784, and further industrial action by railwaymen and others followed in Nigeria and the Gold Coast (Ghana). At this time, organised labour encountered hostility from both private employers and the colonial officials of Britain and France. Trade unions were formed in Egypt in the 1890s, but in South Africa the unions which appeared were confined to white workers and white miners and government officers had their own unions in other areas. The Nigerian Civil Service Union of 1912 was one of the first unions in tropical Africa to accept African members.

In the British colonies, the unions which were established after World War I and up to the formation of the independent African states in the 1960s tended to be small and relatively ineffective, especially in West Africa, where the 'house union' of just one factory or business was common and national or industry-wide federations were rare. Government legislation at first only covered labour recruitment and contract labour, but in 1930 the London authorities pronounced that trade unions might be formed in the colonies as a natural and legitimate development as social and industrial progress took place. Legislation followed in the various territories providing for the establishment of trade unions, on the British model for internal organisation and accountancy but with compulsory registration and restrictions on strikes in 'essential industries'. The colonial labour advisory committee formed in 1942 and including representatives of the British Trades Union Congress helped to form new unions which would be 'responsible' and non-political. As a result of this policy, there emerged a system of many small, competing unions with only a few strong bodies, such as the federations of teachers, miners and railwaymen. The unions were also weighed down by bureaucracy and government restrictions—for instance, against strikes which might have political overtones. In this context, trade unionists turned to support movements for political independence and for an end to the domination of the labour market by white European expatriates.

In France's African colonies, trade unions appeared first in Tunisia and Algeria, but legal membership was confined to those with French civil status until 1937. Trade unions for Africans were then formed in West African towns, notably Dakar, but remained weak until after the Second World War. In 1952 comprehensive legislation was introduced, strengthening trade-union rights in line with French laws and practice but restricting strike action through a compulsory arbitration system. Union membership in French colonies was divided between branches of the main trade-union national centres in France, and trade-union development reflected the rivalry of these different unions based on conflicting ideologies. Most African trade unionists joined branches of the communist-oriented Confédération Générale du Travail (CGT), whilst the Christian Confédération Française des Travailleurs Croyants (CFTC) and the social-democratic Confédération Générale du Travail – Force Ouvrière (CGT–FO) were much weaker. Railwaymen and some other groups in the work-force had flourishing independent unions, and in the 1950s the African trade-union branches gradually broke their ties with the paternalistic French confederations.

As in English-speaking areas, the demand was for equal status with expatriate labour and freedom from colonial rule. The trade unions and political parties drew together, and in 1956 the breakaway from the CGT was led by Sekou Touré of Guinea. Later that year the Christian trade unionists set up the Confédération Africaine des Travailleurs Croyants (CATC), independent from the CFTC, and the Force Ouvrière unions formed the Confédération Africaine des Syndicats Libres (CASL) in 1958. Meanwhile, however, the left-wing had created the Union Générale des Travailleurs de l'Afrique Noire (UGTAN) in 1957, absorbing the old CGT and various independent unions. The UGTAN began a vigorous anti-colonial policy.

In the newly independent states which emerged in the 1960s, trade unionists found themselves in positions of power – for example, President Sekou Touré in Guinea, President Siaka Stevens in Sierra Leone and Tom Mboya in Kenya. However, the post-colonial period featured a serious clash between trade unions and governments and political parties in several countries, and many union leaders were gaoled and their unions dissolved. Governments which wanted economic growth needed an ordered system of industrial relations, which meant rationalisation and control of the trade unions.

In Ghana, the trade unions were reorganised to form a single trade-union centre with just 24 affiliated industrial federations; strikes were restricted, but unions were awarded the 'closed shop' and 'check-off' agreements whereby membership could be compulsory and employers would be obliged to collect union membership fees from wages. Where trade-union rights to strike and to free collective bargaining are restricted, they have an important role in the fields of social welfare, pensions, housing and education, and trade unionists sit on many of the government planning and consultative committees. In Tanzania a similar system was secured but only after a long struggle between the government and the unions. The pattern has been repeated in most countries, and as late as 1977 the Nigerian government took action to unite the labour movement.

Generally, therefore, the countries of Africa have trade-union organisations which are linked to or sympathetic to the governments: trade unions perform important functions within their relationship to government. Sometimes this relationship breaks down and then the unions may be a focus of opposition to government. Few states in Africa retain the old system of competing unions, but political changes and military coups have often been the occasion for new rules for trade unions and new personnel, and the position of the unions is uncertain in many countries.

THE INTERNATIONAL TRADE UNIONS IN AFRICA

The international affiliations formed by African unions have been a major cause of dispute both between national trade unions and their respective governments and between the trade-union organisations of different African countries. From the early days of trade-union growth, union leaders looked for financial aid to European unions, especially the British TUC and the various French confederations, and to the international trade-union federations. In the 1960s, however, the growth of pan-Africanism brought pressures to break formal links with foreign union organisations, and especially with the social-democratic International Confederation of Free Trade Unions (ICFTU) and the communist World Federation of Trade Unions (WFTU). The non-aligned African countries felt compromised by the activities of the rival global trade unions and international affiliation was often regarded as a submission to neo-colonialism.

In English-speaking Africa, most unions were affiliated to the ICFTU, whilst the WFTU drew its strength from unions in the former French territories. The UGTAN of 1957 was the first autonomous regional organisation of African trade unions, but even this was supported by the WFTU. To serve its members the ICFTU set up its own African Regional Organisation (AFRO) in 1960. In the following year, however, trade unionists in several countries, including Ghana, Guinea, Mali and the United Arab Republic (Egypt), established a new independent body, the All-African Trade Union Federation (AATUF), which excluded all national unions which were affiliated to the ICFTU, the WFTU or the International Federation of Christian Trade Unions, now known as the World Confederation of Labour (WCL). Rejecting the AATUF, members of the AFRO and the WCL's regional organisation then formed their own African Trade Union Confederation (ATUC) in 1962. The AFRO continued to exist, as did the WCL's Union Pan-Africaine des Travailleurs Croyants (UPATAC), later called the Pan-African Workers' Congress (PAWC). After 1965, however, the AFRO was a dormant organisation. In 1965–6 the AFRO had 738,115 members in 21 unions; the ATUC claimed 2.25 million members in 42 unions; the AATUF claimed 3,773,150 members in 31 unions; and the PAWC claimed 187,894 members in affiliated unions.

Apart from these organisations, other agencies have been established to promote trade unions in Africa. The most important among these is the African–American Labour Centre (AALC) based in Lomé, Togo. Financed by United States unions and other funds, this publishes the periodicals *AALC Reporter*, *Labour and Development* and *African Trade Union News*, and it has a wide educational programme. Other agencies are sponsored from West Germany, Singapore and Israel – for example, the Friedrich Ebert Foundation and the Afro-Asian Trade Union Bureau.

The Organisation of African Trade Union Unity (OATUU) was formed in 1973 to end the schism in the African labour movement, and the existing international trade-union organisations on the continent were dissolved. By 1975 those few national unions which had originally held back from the OATUU were admitted to membership, and in 1976 there were 67 affiliated trade-union national centres in 52 countries. Only white unions in Southern Africa remained outside the OATUU, and only seven African states had trade unions which were still affiliated to the ICFTU, WFTU and WCL. The OATUU is independent of these bodies, is recognised by the Organisation of African Unity (OAU) as the sole labour movement in Africa, and has consultative status at the OAU, the United Nations (UN), the International Labour Organisation (ILO) and other UN agencies. The OATUU has its headquarters in Accra, Ghana; its Secretary-General, J. D. Akumu, is from Kenya, and in 1976–7 the President was Alhaji Ali el-Nefishy from the Libya General Federation of Trade Unions. Its main publications are the *Voice of African Trade Union Unity* and *Information Tips*.

NATIONAL TRADE UNIONS

Algeria. The Union Générale des Syndicats Algériens (UGSA) was formed in 1954 out of the local branch of the French CGT, and local branches of the CFTC and the CGT–FO also existed. The Union Générale des Travailleurs Algériens (UGTA), established in 1956, was linked to the National Liberation Front, and after the war of independence and the French withdrawal became Algeria's single trade-union centre. Formerly affiliated to the ICFTU and the AATUF, it is now a member of the OATUU and the International Confederation of Arab Trade Unions (ICATU). The UGTA has about 300,000 members in 12 national industrial federations.

Angola. Under Portuguese rule, independent trade unions for Africans were illegal, and there existed only a number of restricted workers' organisations for Europeans and 'assimilados'. Among these, the largest was the Sindicato Nacionale des Empregados de Comercio e da Industria, with about 50,000 members in sixteen branches. Free collective bargaining and strikes were banned, and in 1973 a UN Commission on Human Rights reported that a form of forced labour existed in Angola (and Mozambique) among Africans.

Rival movements for national independence formed trade-union branches in exile. The Liga General dos Trabalhadores de Angola (LGTA), founded in 1961, was affiliated to the ICFTU, and the Confederacão General dos Trabalhadores de Angola (CGTA) was a member of the WCL: these merged in 1973 as the Centrale Syndicale Angolaise (CSA), supporting the Frente Nacional de Libertaçao de Angola (FNLA). The Union Nacional dos Trabalhadores Angolanos (UNTA), formed in the 1950s, is linked to the Movimento Popular de Libertaçao de Angola (MPLA), and after independence this became the single trade-union national organisation.

Benin (formerly Dahomey). Branches of French unions gave way to four national federations: the Union Nationale des Syndicats des Travailleurs du Dahomey (UNSTD), affiliated to the UGTAN and including most workers; the Union Nationale des Syndicats (UNS); the Union Générale des Travailleurs du Dahomey (UGTD), formed in 1964; and the ICFTU-sponsored Confédération Nationale des Syndicats Libres (CNSL), later the Union Générale des Syndicats du Dahomey (UGSD). However, in 1974 the Union Nationale des Syndicats des Travailleurs du Benin (UNSTB) was created with government aid to replace all other unions. Its component unions are linked to the WFTU's Trade Unions Internationals (TUIs).

Botswana. Though formed originally before independence, the trade unions are not highly developed. The Botswana Trade Union Centre (BTUC) at Gabarone is the OATUU affiliate, but there are four competing unions in Francistown: the Botswana General Workers' Organisation (BGWO), the Botswana Trade Union Congress (BTUC), the Botswana Workers' Union (BWU) and the Francistown African Employees' Union (FAEU). The Botswana Teachers' Union (BTU) had 265 members in 1975.

Burundi. Belgian trade unions formed branches in the country. The Fédération des Syndicats Chrétiens Ouvriers et Paysans, formed in 1958, was supported by workers of the Hutu tribe and in the civil war came under attack from the dominant Tutsi tribe and Uprona party. The Union des Travailleurs du Burundi (UTB), formed in 1967, became the single trade-union national centre.

Cameroon. In colonial days there were several trade-union centres in both the French-controlled and British-ruled parts of the country, and at the time of independence there were about 100 trade unions and some 40,000 union members. The unions have been reduced in number, so that the four recognised bodies in the 1960s formed a single centre in 1971. This was the Syndicat Central Unique (SCU), which is now called the Union Nationale des Travailleurs du Cameroun (UNTC) and is linked to the Union Nationale Camerounaise (UNC), the country's single political party.

Cape Verde Islands. The Sindicatos Cap Verde was formed in 1976 to be the only trade union and it is affiliated to the OATUU.

Central African Republic. Local branches of French confederations existed until after independence, but in 1964 the Union Générale des Travailleurs du Centrafrique (UGTC) was formed as the single trade-union organisation. In 1973 its leaders were replaced by the government.

Chad. The local branches of French unions and of the rival autonomous bodies, the UGTAN, the CATC and the CASL, were dissolved in 1965 when the Union Nationale des Travailleurs du Tchad (UNTT) was created as the single trade union centre, linked to the ruling political party. Although parts of Chad are controlled by guerrilla forces, there are no reports of trade unions in these areas.

Comoro Islands. The Union des Travailleurs des Comores (UTC), formed after independence, was controlled by the government then in power. There are no details of further unions sponsored by the new government of 1978, nor of trade unions on the French island of Mayotte.

Congo. In French Equatorial Africa, the local branches of French unions were replaced by rival autonomous unions, principally the Confédération Générale Africaine du Travail (CGAT) which was formed in 1957 and affiliated to the WFTU. Trade unionists were prominent in the political changes of 1964, when a new single-party constitution was set up and the Confédération Syndicale Congolaise (CSC) was established as the only trade-union centre. There followed conflict between the government and the Catholic Church over the suppression of the Christian trade unions, and in 1976 the CSC trade-union leaders clashed with the government over policies on wages and prices.

Djibouti. Local branches of French trade unions existed in the territory before independence, and the Front de la Libération de la Côte des Somalies (Djibouti) was supported from Somalia. This was the OATUU affiliate.

Egypt. A cigarette workers' union was formed in 1899, and the Union of Employees of International Firms (UEITF) was established four years later. Subsequent unions were linked to the political parties and the nationalist movement, but the first national trade-union organisation, the Egyptian Federation of Workers (EFW) formed in 1921, was short-lived, and so were two further federations established in the 1930s. Trade unions were given recognition in 1942, when 200 unions with 80,000 members were recognised. By 1950 there were 500 unions with 149,424 members, and this proliferation of small organisations weakened the labour movement. Trade unions were reorganised and brought into a single organisation in 1956, when the Egyptian Federation of Labour (EFL) was formed. Trade unions had an important role in the Arab Socialist system of President Nasser. In the 1970s, the EFL had about 2.5 million members in 16 national unions, and it is affiliated to both the OATUU and the ICATU.

Equatorial Guinea. There were no trade unions under Spanish colonial rule, but a National Trade Union Centre sponsored by the government of Life President Francisco Macias Nguema is affiliated to the OATUU.

Ethiopia. Trade unions date from 1947, when the Franco-Ethiopian Railway Union (FERU) was formed, but legal recognition was withheld from unions until 1962. By then, however, other unions and the Ethiopian Labour Union (ELU) had appeared. In 1963 this became the Confederation of Ethiopian Labour Unions (CELU), supported by the ICFTU and with 55,000 members in 108 unions by 1968. After the revolution of 1974, the CELU formed a centre of opposition to the Dergue government and several union leaders were imprisoned. The All-Ethiopian Trade Union (AETU) was established in 1975 to replace the CELU, and the AETU is affiliated to the OATUU. In 1978 the government dismissed the AETU leaders.

Gabon. Local branches of French unions were replaced by branches of the CATC and the UGTAN, and there existed the Confédération Nationale du Travail Gabonaise (CNTG) which was an ICFTU affiliate. After 1964, when the country adopted a single-party political system, the 70 competing unions were absorbed into the Fédération Syndicale Gabonaise (Fesyga), established in 1969. This had both regional and industrial branches, and in 1978 the union changed its name to the Confédération Syndicale Gabonaise (CSG).

Gambia. The general unions formed in the time of British colonial rule still exist under the independent government, and there are two unions from the Gambia affiliated to the OATUU. These are the Gambia Workers' Union (GWU), formed in 1958 and linked to the ICFTU, and the 'Gambia Trades Union Congress'. This is the Gambia Labour Union (GLU), which was formed in 1928 and is the larger national centre, with some 7800 members in four affiliates. It has been associated with the WFTU, and it claims that the rival GWU has been banned.

Ghana. Trade unions date from the 1920s, when the Gold and Silver Smith Association (GSSA), the Carpenters' and Masons' Association (CMA) and others were formed. Local legislation to provide for trade unions was passed by Britain in 1941, and after the Second World War there was a proliferation of small weak local unions, and much rivalry within the Gold Coast Trades Union Congress, formed in 1945. However, trade unionists allied themselves to the fight for national freedom, and after independence the Industrial Relations Act of 1958 brought a reorganisation of the country's trade unions. Mergers among the existing 113 trade unions produced a new system of just 24 industry-wide unions, all of them members of the Ghana Trades Union Congress (GTUC). By 1965, the number of GTUC affiliates had been reduced to 10, but in 1976 there were 17 with a total membership of 394,697. There have been many changes in the GTUC and industrial relations laws since 1958, occasioned by changes in government. The GTUC first had a close relationship with President Nkrumah's Convention People's Party (CPP), and after the military coup of 1966 there was a major reorganisation of trade unions, giving greater independence to the affiliated unions. The revolution of 1972 then brought a partial return to the 1958 system. The GTUC is affiliated to the OATUU, which is based in Accra.

Guinea. Among local branches of the French national confederations, the CGT was the most powerful and its leader, Sekou Touré, began the movement for autonomy from French unions and in 1957 helped to set up the UGTAN. In 1955, the CGT in Guinea had 39,000 members and many also were in Sekou Touré's Parti Démocratique de Guinée (PDG). This is now the single political party, and the CGT, renamed in 1956 the Confédération National des Travailleurs Guinéens (CNTG), is the only trade-union organisation. It has over 100,000 members in 19 federations and national unions; it is affiliated to the OATUU and many of the national unions have been linked to the WFTU's Trade Unions International.

Guinea-Bissau. Trade unions were not formed in the time of Portuguese rule, but the freedom-fighting Partido Africano da Independencia da Guiné e Cabo Verde (PAIGC) established a trade-union arm whilst in exile. This is the União Nacional dos Trabalhadores Guinéenses (UNTG), which is the only trade-union organisation and is affiliated to the OATUU.

Ivory Coast. Local branches of French unions in the 1950s gave way to autonomous unions, among which the Union des Travailleurs du Côte d'Ivoire (UTCI) was the most important. This was linked to Houphouët-Boigny's Parti Démocratique du Côte d'Ivoire, under which the country achieved independence in 1960. By then the link between government and the UTCI had been broken, for the union supported the UGTAN, which was based in Guinea and distrusted by Houphouët-Boigny. Other unions were a centre of opposition to the government, but in 1961 leaders of the four main competing unions meeting under government sponsorship agreed to form a single trade-union centre. This is the Union Générale des Travailleurs de Côte d'Ivoire (UGTCI), which is affiliated to the OATUU.

Kenya. Trade unions were formed after World War II. Although local legislation stressed that they should be non-political, the unions allied themselves to the independence movement. Both the African Workers' Federation (AWF) of 1947 and the later East African Trades Union Congress (EATUC) supported Kenyatta's nationalist party, and the Kenya Federation of Labour (KFL) was led by Tom Mboya, later to be a prominent minister under President Kenyatta. The KFL was affiliated to the ICFTU–AFRO, but the rival Kenya Trades Union Congress (KTUC) of 1959 was hostile to the ICFTU–AFRO and joined the AATUF. Both the KTUC and the Kenya African Workers' Congress (KAWC) of 1965 were short-lived, and after the adoption of a single-party constitution in 1964 the Kenyan trade unions were reorganised into a single national centre. This is the Central Organisation of Trade Unions (COTU), formed in 1965, which has 28 affiliated trade unions.

Lesotho. The few unions formed before independence set up the Basutoland Congress of Trade Unions (BCTU) in 1961 but this did not long survive. The Lesotho Mineworkers' Union (LMU) is an important organisation of Lesotho's migrant workers in South Africa. At the OATUU Lesotho is represented by both the Lesotho Council of Labour (LCL) and the Basutoland Federation of Labour (BFL), but various other unions are active in the country.

Liberia. Trade unions date from 1949, when legislation was passed to allow formation of the Labour Union of Liberia (LUL). However, industrial relations laws were not passed until 1963, strikes were illegal, and the unions organised few workers in the American Firestone Company, which dominated the economy. The Congress of Industrial Organisations (CIO), formed in 1960, remains an important national centre, affiliated to the ICFTU but also to the OATUU. In 1977 the United Mine Workers' Union refused to join a new single trade-union centre, the Liberian Federation of Trade Unions (LFTU), sponsored by President Tolbert. The United Workers' Congress (UWC) was also an OATUU affiliate, and there existed the Labour Congress of Liberia (LCL).

Libya. After the Italian withdrawal in the Second World War, small and weak competing trade unions appeared in Tripoli and Benghazi. Local branches of the Arab Labour Federation (ALF) were rivalled by affiliates of the Federation of Libyan Trade Unions (FLTU), which was a moderate organisation. This was succeeded by the Libyan General Workers' Union (LGWU) in 1952, affiliated to the ICFTU. The LGWU absorbed the Cyrenaican Federation of Trade Unions in 1959 to form the Libyan National Confederation of Trade Unions (LNCTU). After the revolution of 1969, all the competing unions were replaced by the General Federation of Trade Unions (GFTU), established in 1972. This is affiliated to the OATUU and ICATU, and claims 380,000 members in 15 national unions.

Madagascar. Local branches of French confederations survived as separate unions after independence. The Fédération des Syndicats des Travailleurs de Madagascar (Fisema) was an affiliate of the WFTU and claimed 30,000 members. Its rival from the ICFTU was the Confédération des Travailleurs Malgaches (CTM), formed in 1957. However, the largest federation was the Cartel National des Organisations Syndicales de Madagascar (CNOSM), originally set up in 1937 as the Confédération Chretienne des Syndicats Malgaches ('Sekrima'), affiliated to the WCL. It claimed over 40,000 members in 158 unions. Changes in the trade-union movement have been made since the change of government in 1972 and plans for a one-party system were announced in 1975. However, by 1977 Madagascar still had four affiliated unions in the OATUU: the CNOSM, the Fisema, the CTM and the independent Union Syndicale des Travailleurs et Paysans Malgaches.

Malawi. Several small weak unions came into existence after the Second World War, although the local Trade Union Ordinance dates from 1932. Unions are brought together by the Trades Union Congress of Malawi (TUCM), which was formed in 1964 and is affiliated to both the OATUU and the ICFTU. The TUCM claims about 6000 members in seven affiliated unions, but the Teachers' Union of Malawi (TUM) and the Malawi Government Employees' Association (MGEA) are outside the Congress.

Mali. Local branches of French unions existed before independence, and the leader of the large CGT, A. Diallo, remained loyal to the French parent union and to the WFTU when the campaign for autonomous African unions was launched in 1956–7. However, the CGT joined the UGTAN and after independence in 1960 the Union Nationale des Travailleurs du Mali (UNTM) became the single trade-union centre. This was affiliated to the AATUF and the WFTU's Trade Unions International, and is now affiliated to the OATUU.

Mauritania. At the time of independence in 1960, there were four main trade-union centres: branches of the UGTAN and the CATC, also the Union Nationale des Travailleurs Mauritaniens (UNTN) and the Union Républicaine des Travailleurs Mauritaniens (URTM). The labour movement was then integrated into the Union des Travailleurs de Mauritanie (UTM), formed in 1961, which has been close to the ruling Parti du Peuple Mauritanien (PPM). It has 25,000 members in 26 affiliated unions and it is a member of the OATUU and the ICATU.

Mauritius. Rival trade-union national centres developed before independence from Britain and these organisations still exist. The Mauritius Labour Federation (MLF) and the Confédération National du Travail (CNT) are both affiliated to the OATUU, and the CNT, formed in 1960, was previously a member of the WFTU. The Mauritius Confederation of Labour, or Confédération Mauricienne des Travailleurs (CMT), also exists, and was formed in 1946 as the Mauritius Trades Union Congress (MTUC). The Mauritius Labour Congress (MLC), which dates from 1963, is the ICFTU-affiliated union and claims over 32,000 members in 19 unions. In 1975 there was a total of 141 registered trade unions.

Morocco. Though legally forbidden until 1951 to join the branches of French trade unions which were formed in the territory for expatriates, Moroccan workers joined the local CGT, which was called the Union Générale des Syndicats Confédérés du Maroc (UGSCM). However, in the independence struggle autonomous unions were formed without the link to France. There are now two national centres affiliated to the OATUU. The Union Marocaine du Travail (UMT) formed in 1955 was affiliated to the AATUF and is linked to the Union National des Forces Populaires (UNFP) political party. The UMT split in 1960 and the Union Generale des Travailleurs du Maroc (UGTM) then emerged, linked to the Istiqlal party. The UGTM claims about 500,000 members and the UMT some 700,000, and many other workers are organised in various autonomous unions.

Mozambique. Trade unions for Africans were not permitted during Portuguese colonial rule, but *sindicatos* for an elite of black and white workers were permitted. These continued after independence, for the Frente de Libertaçao de

Moçambique (Frelimo) was slow to develop a trade-union movement. By 1976, however, the Mozambique Federation of Trade Unions (MFTU) was established as the country's single trade union organisation, linked to the Frelimo and affiliated to the OATUU.

Namibia. Branches of South African trade unions were formed for the territory's white and coloured workers, but South African laws blocked the development of trade unions for black African workers. The South West Africa People's Organisation (SWAPO) formed a trade-union wing in 1962, and this organisation, called the Union of South West African Workers in Exile, is affiliated to the OATUU and based in Zambia.

Niger. Local branches of French unions, and later of the UGTAN, the CATC and other unions, were replaced in 1960 by a single trade-union national centre. This is the Union Nationale des Travailleurs du Niger (UNTN), which was an ATUC member and is now affiliated to the OATUU. It claims some 15,000 members in 31 unions.

Nigeria. The Nigerian Civil Servants Union (NCSU) was formed in 1912, but no trade-union laws were passed until 1938, when unions existed for teachers, miners, railwaymen and others. There developed a system of numerous unions at factory level, rather ineffective and preoccupied with bitter rivalries between trade-union national federations. In over 2000 trade unions which existed after 1970 there was a total of only about 1 million members.

The United Labour Congress (ULC), the largest of Nigeria's trade-union centres, claimed 600,000 members in 1971 and some 150 affiliated unions. Formed in 1959 as the Trades Union Congress of Nigeria, the ULC derived from an abortive merger with the Nigerian Trade Union Congress (NTUC) in 1962. The ULC was affiliated to the ATUC, the ICFTU and the AFRO, which had its headquarters in Lagos. The major rival to the ULC was the Nigerian Trade Union Federation (NTUF), which was created in 1973 from a merger of the NTUC (1960), the Labour Unity Front (formed in 1963) and a breakaway faction of the ULC. It was affiliated to the AATUF and claimed over 800 member unions. The Nigerian Workers' Council (NWC) was a third national centre, linked to the WCL–PAWC. Other major unions, such as the Nigerian Union of Teachers (NUT), remain independent. The trade unions themselves and successive governments have tried to unite the labour movement, but attempts failed until 1975, when the major organisations agreed to join together in the Nigerian Labour Congress (NLC). With government sponsorship and support, this was developed in the years that followed and all the existing rival unions were reorganised into just 70 national industrial federations affiliated to the NLC.

Rwanda. Local branches were formed by the main socialist and Christian trade unions in Belgium, and in the 1960s there were two main organisations: the

Confédération Générale du Travail du Rwanda (CGTR) and the Union des Travailleurs du Rwanda (UTR), which was a member of the WCL–PAWC. These were replaced by the Syndicat Interprofessionel des Travailleurs du Rwanda (SIPTR) which is the only trade-union organisation. It is affiliated to the OATUU.

St Helena. The St Helena General Workers' Union (St. HGWU), formed in 1958, is the only trade union and has about 900 members.

São Tomé and Principe. The Union Syndicale des Travailleurs de São Tomé and Principe was formed after independence to be the single trade union. It is affiliated to the OATUU.

Senegal. The local branches of French trade unions, formed in Dakar before the Second World War, claimed over 50,000 members by 1956. Fragmentation of the trade unions was exacerbated when the local branches of the CASL, the CATC and autonomous unions were joined by three separate and rival sections of the UGTAN. Various mergers took place involving the CASL and parts of the UGTAN, and after independence there were just two major national centres, the Confédération Nationale des Travailleurs Croyants (CNTC), with about 2500 members, and the more important Union Nationale des Travailleurs Sénégalais (UNTS), which absorbed all the other unions. In 1969 the CNTC disappeared into a new organisation called the Confédération Nationale des Travailleurs Sénégalais (CNTS), which became the only trade-union centre. It is linked to the ruling Union Progressiste Sénégalaise (UPS) political party and is affiliated to the OATUU. However, in the 1970s other more radical trade unions were formed, including the Union des Travailleurs Libres du Sénégal (UTLS), the Union des Syndicats Confédérés du Sénégal (USCS) and the Syndicat Unique des Enseignements du Sénégal (SUDES).

Seychelles. Trade unions developed in the 1960s promoted by the country's political leaders, and after independence there were two national centres affiliated to the OATUU. These were the Seychelles Trades Union Congress (STUC) and the Seychelles Workers' Education Committee (SWEC). A total of 14 unions were registered in 1975. In 1978 the trade unions set up the National Workers' Union (NWU) as the single labour organisation.

Sierra Leone. Industrial action by mechanics and workers in Freetown dates from 1884, but the first trade union was formed by labourers in 1929. In 1942 the eleven registered unions had only 800 members in all, but 60 per cent of wage-earners were union members by 1958. The Sierra Leone Labour Congress (SLLC) was the main trade-union national centre, but this was rivalled by a second organisation affiliated to the ICFTU. In 1976 the two federations merged as the Sierra Leone Labour Congress (SLLC), with about 50,000 members in 22 unions.

Somalia. The Sindicato Lavoratori della Somalia (SLS) was formed in 1949 and became an ICFTU member. Other unions included the Federazione Lavoratori della Somalia (FLS) of 1955 and the Associazione Sindicato Lavoratori della Somalia (ASLS), and there was some modest trade-union activity in the territory of British Somaliland. After independence, trade unions were reorganised and the Somali Workers' Council (SWC) became the country's trade-union centre. It is affiliated to the OATUU and the ICATU. The Somali Federation of Trade Unions (SFTU) also exists.

South Africa. Trade unions for white workers in Cape Colony were formed from 1881, and soon afterwards spread to the mining areas. The Federation of Trade Unions (FTU) was recognised in 1911, and the South African Industrial Federation (SAIF) of 1914 campaigned to protect the interests of white labour against competition from Africans. White Africans' interests are now represented mainly by the South African Confederation of Labour (SACL), formed in 1957, and since 1956 all unions have been organised in accordance with the apartheid policy. A second national centre, the Trade Union Council of South Africa (TUCSA), formed in 1954, embraces unions which have white, racially mixed and black African membership. This amounts to over 200,000 members in about 67 unions, of which five are unregistered. Total union membership in 1974 in the Republic was over 600,000 in 169 registered unions. However, the law has prevented the growth of black African unions, which are not allowed to register and are denied various rights and responsibilities. Black unions date from 1919 when the Industrial and Commercial Workers' Union (ICU) was formed among dockers at the Cape but spread to the Transvaal and became the first mass political movement of black South Africans. More recently the black federations which have struggled for success include the African National Congress (ANC), the Federation of Free African Trade Unions of South Africa (FFATU), and the South African Congress of Trade Unions (SACTU), which was established through the ANC in 1955, and from exile in Zambia is now South Africa's affiliate to the OATUU. Since the early 1960s African trade unions in the Republic have suffered considerable harassment. In 1975 there were just 24 African unions, with only 60,000 members, and the various bodies which were trying to support these and to promote new unions were hard hit by government actions in 1976, when many union leaders and their white advisers in the Urban Training Project (UTP) were banned under the security laws. Since a series of widespread strikes by black workers in 1973 the government has demonstrated its clear hostility to the development of black unions, but there is still much activity in the African townships, often assisted by representatives of various international trade unions, including the ICFTU and several International Trade Secretariats.

Sudan. Trade unions were formed after the Second World War and there were several rival federations in the country. The largest body, the Sudanese

Federation of Workers' Trade Unions (SFWTU), established in 1950, played a major role in the independence movement and was affiliated to the ICATU and the WFTU. By 1968, however, there was a total of 10 competing national centres, and in 1971 the registered trade unions numbered 562. All these unions were replaced in 1971 by a single organisation, the Federation of Sudanese Workers' Unions (FSWU), later called the Sudan Workers' Trade Union Federation (SWTUF). This has 36 affiliated trade unions and 42 affiliated white-collar and professional associations, with 630,000 members in 1976.

Swaziland. The five registered trade unions established the Swaziland Federation of Trade Unions (SFTU) in 1973, but all union activity was banned by the government in the same year.

Tanzania. Trade unions date from 1949 in Tanganyika, and the Tanganyika Federation of Labour (TFL) was formed in 1955. This was affiliated to the ICFTU, and until independence from Britain the unions were close to the Tanganyika African National Union (TANU). Major disputes arose between the ruling party and the trade unions after independence, and in 1964 the TFL was replaced by the National Union of Tanganyika Workers (NUTW), which was closely integrated with the government and collaborated in its policies, whereby priority was given to peasant farmers rather than to urban workers. The NUTW has some 330,000 members in just nine industrial sections, and it is affiliated to the OATUU (formerly to the AATUF). On Zanzibar, the Workers' Department of the Afro-Shirazi Party undertakes trade-union work. It was formed in 1965 to replace all existing trade unions.

Togo. There were local branches of French unions and of the autonomous West African unions in the territory in the 1950s and 1960s, and the UGTAN branch became the Union Nationale de Travailleurs du Togo (UNTT). The rival trade-union centres were replaced in 1973 by the Confédération Nationale des Travailleurs du Togo (CNTT), which is close to the ruling Rassemblement du Peuple Togolais (RPT). The Afro-American Labour Centre (AALC) has its headquarters in Lomé.

Tunisia. Trade unions for French settlers were formed early in the century, but the first autonomous organisation, the Confédération Générale des Travailleurs Tunisiens (CGTT) of 1924, was suppressed by the colonial authorities. Other unions formed in the 1930s were able to play a major role in the struggle for national independence, but the trade-union movement was developed only after the Second World War, when the Union Générale des Travailleurs Tunisiens (UGTT) was formed (1946) and the local CGT became the Union Syndicale des Travailleurs Tunisiens (USTT). The UGTT is now the single trade-union federation, and its links have been to the Neo-Destour Party in Tunisia, and to the ICFTU, ATUC and OATUU. In 1978 there were widespread strikes against the government, and the UGTT general secretary and other union leaders were imprisoned.

Uganda. Trade unions were first formed before the Second World War. These were federated in 1956, when the Uganda Trades Union Congress (UTUC) was formed. In the 1960s this was an ICFTU affiliate, with over 100,000 members in 23 unions. The rival Federation of Uganda Trade Unions (FUTU) of 1964 supported the AATUF. Under the Amin government, trade unions were reorganised into the National Organisation of Trade Unions (NOTU), established in 1973. Several International Trade Secretariats, linked to the ICFTU, claim affiliates in Uganda.

Upper Volta. The local branches of French trade unions became rival national centres after independence, and in 1976 Upper Volta had five affiliated unions in the OATUU, and a sixth centre was established in 1978. The Union Syndicale des Travailleurs Voltaiques (USVT) stems from the French CGT, the UGTAN and the AATUF; it is also affiliated to the WFTU. The Confédération Nationale des Travailleurs Voltaiques (CNTV) was formed in 1956 as a local branch of the CATC and it is affiliated to the WCL. The Organisation Voltaique des Syndicats Libres (OVSL), formerly the Union Nationale des Travailleurs de Haute-Volta, belonged to the ATUC and is an ICFTU affiliate. The Confédération Syndicale Voltaique (CSV) was formed in 1974 from 20 autonomous trade unions and is free from global affiliations. The Union Générale des Travailleurs Voltaiques (UGTV) broke away from the OVSL in 1978. The Union des Forces-Ouvrières Voltaiques (UFOV), formed in 1975, remains very small. Successive attempts since 1966 to unify the trade-union movement have ended in failure.

Zaïre. Belgian trade unions established branches in the territory for white workers, but not until after the Second World War were Africans admitted to membership. The Christian, socialist and liberal unions had local branches, and in 1959 the autonomous Syndicat National des Travailleurs du Congo (SNTC) was formed by Patrice Lumumba. This merged with several other bodies in 1961 to create the Confédération des Syndicats Libres du Congo (CSLC), but this was rivalled by the Christian Union des Travailleurs Congolais (UTC) and the Fédération Générale du Travail du Congo (FGTC). In 1967 all trade unions were reorganised into the Union Nationale des Travailleurs du Zaïre (UNTZ), which is affiliated to the OATUU and embraces just 13 national industrial federations.

Zambia. Trade unions were formed in the 1930s for white workers on the Copper Belt, and these were followed by unions of African labourers in the mines. The many local and independent unions were merged into the Zambia Congress of Trade Unions (ZCTU), which was established in 1965 as the single national centre. The Civil Servants' Union (CSU) and the large Zambian African Mining Union (ZAMU) remain independent, but the government forbids international affiliations other than to the OATUU.

Zimbabwe (formerly Rhodesia). White workers formed unions early in the century, and African unions date from 1927, when the Industrial and Commercial Workers' Union was formed. The law discriminated against African trade unions, and the 1959 Industrial Conciliation Act excluded farm-workers, domestic servants and many government exployees from full trade-union rights. Most unions were racially segregated, but mixed unions did exist. The Zimbabwe African Congress of Unions (ZACU), loyal to the Patriotic Front, was affiliated to the OATUU and based in Zambia. Inside the country there was the Trades Union Congress of Rhodesia (TUCR) for European workers, dating from 1964 and supporting the Rhodesia Front. This had no international affiliation, and nor had the separate National Association of Local Government Officers and Employees. Other national centres for African workers were active: the African Trade Union Congress (ATUC) of 1962 was close to the Zimbabwe African People's Union (ZAPU) and to the ATUC, whilst the National African Federation of Unions (NAFU) was formed in 1965 by supporters of the Zimbabwe African National Union (ZANU) and was affiliated to the AATUF; also the Zimbabwe Federation of Labour (ZFL), supported by the African–American Labour Centre, the Zimbabwe Trade Union Congress (ZTUC) and the National African Trade Union Congress (NATUC). A number of International Trade Secretariats claimed affiliates in Zimbabwe.

7 CONFLICTS, ARMED FORCES AND COUPS

MAJOR CONFLICTS

REVOLT IN MADAGASCAR 1947–8

A revolt against French rule, centring on the east coast, was suppressed after much bloodshed.

EGYPT'S WARS WITH ISRAEL 1948–73

War of Independence 1948. As soon as Israel had been established as an independent Jewish state in May 1948, it was invaded by Egypt, Iraq, Lebanon, Jordan and Syria. After initial Arab gains, the Israelis counter-attacked successfully. An armistice was agreed between Israel and Egypt on 23 Feb 1949.

Sinai Campaign 1956. After secret negotiations with France and Britain, Israel attacked Egypt on 29 Oct 1956. Israeli forces overran most of Sinai and advanced to within 30 miles of the Suez Canal when they halted in response to an ultimatum by France and Britain (see SUEZ CRISIS). Israeli troops withdrew and were replaced by a UN peace-keeping force.

Six-Day War 1967. In May 1967 Egypt demanded the withdrawal of the UN peace-keeping force and signed a defence pact with Jordan. The Israelis decided on a pre-emptive strike and launched a devastating air attack on the Egyptian air-force on 5 June 1967. Israeli forces invaded Sinai and reached the Suez Canal. A cease-fire was agreed on 10 June.

Yom Kippur War 1973. Egyptian forces crossed the Suez Canal in well-planned surprise attack on 6 Oct 1973, Israel's Day of Atonement. Israel's Bar Lev defence line was overwhelmed as men and equipment were rushed across the canal under cover of Soviet-supplied surface-to-air· missiles, but the Egyptians proved unable to extend their bridgehead. In a daring counter-stroke, Israeli forces crossed to the west bank of the canal on 15 Oct 1973 through the gap between the Egyptian Second and Third Armies, and encircled the Third Army. A cease-fire became effective on 24 Oct.

MAU MAU REVOLT 1952–60

Violence by Mau Mau, an African secret society which aimed at driving white settlers out of Kenya, led the British government of Kenya to declare a state of emergency on 20 Oct 1952. Leading Kikuyu nationalists were arrested, and Jomo Kenyatta was given a seven-year prison sentence in Oct 1953. Assassinations and terrorist attacks on the farms of white settlers and on Africans who did not support Mau Mau were countered by a British military campaign in which the insurgents were driven into the remote mountain areas of western Kenya. Some 600 British and African troops died in the operations against Mau Mau. The state of emergency ended on 12 Jan 1960.

MOROCCAN REVOLT 1953–6

Morocco had been divided into French and Spanish spheres of influence as a result of a protectorate treaty between France and the Sultan signed at Fez on 30 Mar 1912 and a convention between France and Spain signed at Madrid on 27 Nov 1912. Anti-French nationalist activity developed in the 1950s and after a period of rioting and terrorism France recognised Morocco as an independent sovereign state on 2 Mar 1956. Spain followed suit on 7 Apr 1956.

WAR OF ALGERIAN INDEPENDENCE 1954–62

In 1954 the nationalist movement in Algeria, the Front de Libération Nationale (FLN), 'declared war' on France. Despite the employment of 400,000 troops with modern equipment and the use of torture, the French were unable to crush the rebellion, which gained in popular support. On 13 May 1958 criticism of army methods led the military in Algeria to refuse to recognise the government of France. General de Gaulle came to power in June 1958, and after further fighting the French voted in a referendum on 8 Jan 1961 to support his plan for self-determination for Algeria. A mutiny by the French army in Algeria led by Generals Challe and Salan on 22 Apr 1961 was suppressed. Despite terrorism by the French settlers belonging to the Organisation Armée Secrète (OAS) in Algeria, peace-talks were conducted between the Algerian nationalists and the French at Evian-les-Bains, and Algeria was granted its independence on 3 July 1962.

SUEZ CRISIS 1956

Following the decision by the United States and Britain to withdraw aid from Egypt's Aswan Dam project, Egypt announced the nationalisation of the Suez Canal on 26 July 1956. After secret talks with Britain and France, Israel invaded Sinai on 29 Oct 1956. When Egypt rejected a cease-fire ultimatum by France and Britain, their air-forces began to attack Egyptian air-bases on 31 Oct. On 5–6 Nov French and British troops moved into the Canal Zone by sea and air, but as a result of pressure from the United Nations and world opinion, they ended hostilities at midnight on 6–7 Nov. A UN emergency force took the place of the Franco-British forces.

FRANCO-TUNISIAN CONFLICT 1958–61

Tunisian support for anti-French operations by Algerian nationalists resulted in border incidents in 1958. French bombing of the border town of Sakhiet on 25 Feb 1958 led to evacuation of all French bases in Tunisia except Bizerta by June 1959. In fighting at Bizerta on 19–22 July 1961 800 Tunisians were killed. The base was returned to the Tunisians on 30 June 1962.

INDEPENDENCE STRUGGLES IN PORTUGAL'S AFRICAN COLONIES: MOZAMBIQUE, GUINEA AND ANGOLA 1960–76

Guerrilla activity in Portugal's African colonies grew during the 1960s. This became an increasing drain on Portugal's resources. Over half Portugal's annual budget went on defence, and its army in Africa numbering 135,000 in 1974 could only be maintained by unpopular conscription at home. Following the military coup which overthrew the Caetano regime in Portugal on 25 Apr 1974, the new government opened negotiations with the African nationalists. These led to the independence of Portuguese Guinea on 10 Sep 1974 and of Mozambique on 25 June 1975.

The situation in Angola was complicated by the presence of three rival liberation movements (MPLA, FNLA and UNITA). The Marxist MPLA took control of the capital Luanda in July 1975, and received tanks and artillery from the Soviet Union; from Oct 1975 over 15,000 Cuban soldiers began to arrive to support the MPLA. The FNLA and UNITA formed a joint military command, and when independence was formally proclaimed, on 11 Nov 1975, they established a rival government in Huambo. The UNITA–FNLA forces received aid from China and also from the United States until Congress stopped further appropriations. As full-scale civil war developed, the MPLA occupied northern Angola, driving the FNLA into Zaïre. UNITA forces were then attacked and Huambo fell in Feb 1976. South African troops had advanced into Angola but now began to withdraw, remaining to protect the Cunene hydro-electric scheme and refugee camps until March. The MPLA under Agostinho Neto was recognised as the government of Angola and became a member of the United Nations in Nov 1976, but the FNLA and UNITA continued to wage a sporadic guerrilla campaign.

CONFLICT IN THE CONGO 1960–7

The Congo (now Zaïre) was granted its independence by the Belgians on 30 June 1960, but it proved to be ill prepared for this step. There was widespread disorder, the army mutinied and on 11 July 1960 Moïse Tshombe proclaimed the rich mining province of Katanga an independent state and requested Belgian aid. Fearing for his country's independence, the Prime Minister of the Congo, Patrice

Lumumba, appealed to the United Nations for assistance. A peace-keeping force, which eventually grew to some 20,000 men, was established on 14 July 1960. After he had sought and received Soviet aid, Lumumba was dismissed by the President, Joseph Kasavubu, on 5 Sep 1960, but refused to resign. On 14 Sep the army leader, Col. Mobutu, took power. Lumumba was captured by Mobutu's troops on 1 Dec 1960, handed over to the Katangese and murdered in Feb 1961. For the next two years periods of armed conflict and negotiation between the central government, the Katangese secessionists and the United Nations failed to resolve the Congo's problems. Katanga's secession was not finally ended until Dec 1962 when a UN offensive against the province forced Moïse Tshombe into exile on 15 Jan 1963.

The last UN forces left the Congo on 30 June 1964. In an attempt to find a stable government Tshombe was recalled as Premier on 10 July 1964, but there was continued fighting. Rebels established a rival government in Stanleyville and held 2000 white hostages, but Belgian paratroops intervened on 24 Nov 1964 to free them. Following Kasavubu's dismissal of Tshombe in Oct 1965, Gen. Mobutu again took power in Nov. Violence continued until July 1967, when a revolt by mercenaries in the eastern provinces was suppressed.

EGYPT'S INVOLVEMENT IN THE YEMEN 1962–7

Following the death of the Imam of the Yemen in 1962, Egypt supported an armed uprising which resulted in a new regime. A civil war then developed in the Yemen in which some 70,000 Egyptian troops and republican forces fought against royalists supported with arms by Saudi Arabia. An agreement for a cease-fire was signed in Aug 1965 and Egypt withdrew her forces in 1967.

ERITREAN SECESSION FROM ETHIOPIA 1962–79

Eritrea, formerly an Italian colony, was made a federated state of the Ethiopian Empire in 1952 and fully integrated 10 years later. A secession movement grew up in the province and by 1976 there were some 15,000 guerrillas in arms. While the Ethiopian government was also engaged in fighting in the Ogaden, the guerrillas were able to take control of almost the whole of Eritrea, with the exception of Asmara and the Red Sea ports of Massawa and Assab. However, once the Somali-backed forces in the Ogaden had been defeated, Ethiopian troops, with Soviet and Cuban assistance, launched a major counter-offensive against the Eritrean guerrillas in May 1978. The guerrillas were forced to lift the siege of Asmara, and in Nov 1978 Ethiopian troops regained control of the 72-mile road linking Massawa and Asmara. The last big town in rebel hands, Keren, fell to government forces at the end of Nov 1978.

BORDER CONFLICT BETWEEN ALGERIA AND MOROCCO 1963

Serious border fighting took place between Algeria and Morocco in Oct 1963 in the Atlas Mountains area.

KENYA–SOMALI BORDER WAR 1963–7

The 1960 independence constitution of the Somali Democratic Republic contained a commitment to recover its 'lost territories', one of which was the Northern Frontier district of Kenya. Serious border clashes between the Kenyans and Somalis began in Mar 1963 and diplomatic relations were broken off in Dec. The conflict continued until the two countries agreed to end the fighting by the Declaration of Arusha on 28 Oct 1967.

CIVIL WAR IN THE SUDAN 1963–72

The Anyanya rebels demanding secession for southern Sudan began a campaign of guerrilla warfare in 1963. They were supported by the Israelis, who provided training and captured Soviet and Chinese weapons. The Sudanese government received help from Arab states, such as the United Arab Republic and Libya, and the Soviet Union. Peace talks between the government and the rebels began in Addis Ababa in Feb 1972. An agreement for a cease-fire and regional self-government for the southern provinces was reached on 28 Feb, and this was ratified on 27 Mar.

SOMALI–ETHIOPIAN CONFLICT 1964–78

The Somali Democratic Republic claims the Ogaden desert region in the south of Ethiopia, as well as parts of Kenya and the tiny state of Djibouti. Clashes between Ethiopia and the Somali Republic resulted in an inconclusive border war in 1964. The turmoil in Ethiopia after the downfall of Emperor Haile Selassie in 1974 led Somalia to foster a guerrilla movement in the Ogaden, the Western Somali Liberation Front. A Somali-backed offensive during 1977 gave the guerrillas control of the southern desert area. A new situation developed, however, when the Russians switched their support from Somalia to Ethiopia. In Nov 1977 President Barre of Somalia expelled the 6000 Russian military and civilian advisers from his country, withdrew all naval and military facilities and renounced his 1974 treaty of friendship with the Soviet Union. Massive quantities of Russian military equipment were transported to Ethiopia in preparation for a counter-offensive in the Ogaden. This offensive in 1978 restored Ethiopian control of the Ogaden region.

INSURGENCY IN SOUTHERN AFRICA 1965–79

In Rhodesia black nationalist guerrilla activity grew after Ian Smith's Unilateral Declaration of Independence on 11 Nov 1965. By the end of 1978 it was estimated that there were some 9000–15,000 guerrillas operating inside Rhodesia and martial law had been extended to three-quarters of the country. In Mar 1978 Ian Smith reached agreement with three leaders of African organisations inside Rhodesia, Bishop Muzorewa, the Revd Ndabaningi Sithole and Chief Chirau, but the 'internal settlement' did not bring the fighting to an end. The guerrilla campaign continued, conducted by the Zimbabwe People's Revolutionary Army (Zipra), the military wing of Joshua Nkomo's Zimbabwe African People's Union (ZAPU), and the Zimbabwe African National Liberation Army (ZANLA), the military wing of Robert Mugabe's Zimbabwe African National Union (ZANU). Rhodesian government forces carried out raids on guerrilla camps in Mozambique and Zambia.

Guerrilla warfare is also being conducted in Namibia (South West Africa). Namibia was mandated by the League of Nations to South Africa in 1920. South Africa was prepared to move towards independence for Namibia, but refused to recognise the South West Africa People's Organisation (SWAPO), which was designated as the 'sole authentic representative of the Namibian people' by the United Nations in 1973. Guerrilla warfare was stepped up by SWAPO in 1978 from bases in Angola and Zambia as South Africa organised pre-independence elections in Namibia.

CIVIL WAR IN CHAD 1965–79

Since 1965 there have been sporadic outbreaks of fighting inspired by the Chad National Liberation Front (Frolinat). Guerrillas backed by Libya opposed the government of Chad, which was provided with support by France. A cease-fire agreement was signed in Mar 1978 after talks between the government and the rebels at Sebha in Libya, but there was renewed fighting in 1979.

NIGERIAN CIVIL WAR 1967–70

Tribal rivalry in Nigeria led to a prolonged civil war when the Ibos of the Eastern Region attempted to form a break-away state. On 30 May 1967 the military governor of Eastern Nigeria, Col. Ojukwu, declared the region an independent sovereign country under the name of the Republic of Biafra. Troops of the Nigerian federal army attacked across the northern border of Biafra on 7 July 1967. On 20 May 1968 they captured Port Harcourt, but the Ibos continued to resist tenaciously. European nations became involved in the war as suppliers of arms, equipment and advisers, and in 1969 Count Carl-Gustav von Rosen, a Swedish pilot, formed a small but effective Biafran air-force, which carried out attacks on federal territory. Exhaustion and shortage of supplies finally led to the collapse of Biafran resistance after a four-pronged federal attack in Dec 1969. Col. Ojukwu flew into exile and the Biafran army surrendered on 15 Jan 1970.

TRIBAL WARFARE IN BURUNDI AND RWANDA 1972–3

In Apr 1972 guerrillas from the majority Hutu tribe in Burundi attacked the ruling Tutsi minority, killing between 5000 and 15,000. The Burundi armed forces, which were under Tutsi command, retaliated with help from troops from Zaïre and by the end of May the death toll had risen to between 50,000 and 100,000. There was renewed fighting between the Hutu and Tutsi in Rwanda in Feb 1973. In May 1973 Hutu rebels from Rwanda and Tanzania invaded

Burundi. In response Burundi troops crossed the Tanzanian border and killed 10 Tanzanians.

CONFLICT BETWEEN UGANDA AND TANZANIA 1972-9

On 17 Sep 1972 a 'People's Army' of some 1000 men supporting the ex-President of Uganda, Milton Obote, invaded Uganda from Tanzania and advanced on Kampala. However, they were repulsed by President Amin's forces and Ugandan aircraft bombed the Tanzanian towns of Bukoba and Mwanza. On 21 Sep the Somali Foreign Minister negotiated a cease-fire and a peace agreement was signed at Mogadishu on 5 Oct 1972. Spasmodic guerrilla warfare continued in the area west of Lake Victoria. More serious fighting flared up in Oct 1978 when Ugandan forces invaded Tanzania. Ugandan troops occupied some 700 square miles of Tanzanian territory but withdrew in Nov. Fighting continued on the border in 1979.

CONFLICT IN SPANISH SAHARA 1975-9

Spanish Sahara was claimed by Morocco and Mauritania. After the International Court of Justice at the Hague had ruled in favour of a plebiscite to settle the future of the territory in Oct 1975, King Hassan of Morocco called on 350,000 of his subjects to march unarmed into Spanish Sahara. They crossed the border on 6 Nov, but were recalled three days later. On 14 Nov Spain agreed to hand over Spanish Sahara to Morocco and Mauritania, and Spanish troops were evacuated in Jan 1976. However, in Dec 1975 Moroccan and Mauritanian troops clashed with guerrillas of the Algerian-backed Saharan liberation movement Polisario, and this conflict continues. French military aircraft have been in action in support of Mauritania against Polisario forces.

EGYPT–LIBYA BORDER CLASH 1977

After several years of strained relations, fighting broke out on the border between Egypt and Libya in July 1977. President Sadat of Egypt ordered a cease-fire on 24 July, which was observed by both sides.

CONFLICT IN ZAÏRE 1977-8

On 10 Mar 1977 Zaïre's Shaba province (formerly Katanga) was invaded from Angola by the Congolese Front de Libération Nationale. President Mobutu of Zaïre accused the Cubans of leading the invasion and suspended diplomatic relations with Cuba on 4 Apr. On 10 Apr 10 French transport aircraft airlifted 1500 Moroccan troops to Zaïre. They successfully aided the Zaïreans in repelling the invaders. In May 1978 a fresh invasion of Shaba by 2000 Katangan exiles took place. French and Belgian paratroopers were sent to Kolwezi to rescue white hostages on 19 May, and the invaders were dispersed.

THE MANPOWER OF AFRICAN ARMED FORCES

	1970	1972	1974	1976	1978 Army	1978 Navy	1978 Air-Force	1978 Paramilitary
Algeria	57,000	60,200	63,000	69,300	70,000	3,800	5,000	10,000
Angola	–	–	–	30,000	30,000	1,500	1,500	–
Benin	n.a.	n.a.	n.a.	1,650	2,100	–	150	1,000
Burundi	n.a.	n.a.	n.a.	n.a.	4,500[1]	–	–	2,000
Cameroon	4,350	4,350	5,500	5,600	5,500	300	300	7,000
Central African Republic	n.a.	n.a.	n.a.	n.a.	1,100	–	100	1,400
Chad	2,650	2,700	4,100	4,700	5,000	–	200	6,000
Congo	2,200	2,200	5,100	7,000	6,500	200	300	3,900
Egypt	213,000	325,000	323,000	342,000	350,000	20,000	25,000	50,000
Ethiopia	45,400	44,570	44,570	50,800	90,000	1,500	2,000	119,000
Gabon	n.a.	n.a.	n.a.	n.a.	950	100	200	1,600
Ghana	15,900	18,600	17,700	17,600	15,000	1,300	1,400	3,000
Guinea	5,400	6,100	5,500	5,850	8,000	350	500	8,000
Ivory Coast	4,500	3,500	3,450	4,100	4,500	250	200	3,000
Kenya	5,400	6,730	7,430	7,600	7,500	400	1,200	1,500
Liberia	4,150	4,150	5,170	5,220	5,250[1]	–	–	21,300
Libya	15,000	25,000	32,000	29,700	30,000	3,000	4,000	–
Madagascar	4,500	4,100	4,250	4,760	9,550	600	350	7,000
Malawi	1,150	1,150	1,600	2,300	2,400[1]	–	–	460
Mali	3,650	3,650	3,650	4,200	4,200[1]	–	–	5,700
Mauritania	1,530	1,530	1,800	4,750	12,000	300	150	6,000

(continued)

	1970	1972	1974	1976	1978			
					Army	Navy	Air-Force	Paramilitary
Morocco	50,000	53,500	56,000	73,000	81,000	2,000	6,000	30,000
Mozambique	–	–	–	–	20,000	700	500	1,800
Niger	2,100	2,100	2,100	2,100	2,000	–	50	–
Nigeria	163,500	274,000	210,000	230,000	221,000	4,500	6,000	–
Rwanda	2,750	2,750	4,000	3,750	3,750[1]	–	–	1,200
Senegal	5,850	5,900	5,900	5,950	6,000	350	200	1,600
Sierra Leone	1,600	1,600	1,650	2,145	2,200[1]	–	–	2,500
Somalia	12,000	13,500	23,050	25,000	50,000	500	1,000	29,500
South Africa	43,800	44,000	47,450	51,500	50,000	5,500	10,000	165,500
Sudan	27,450	36,300	43,600	52,600	50,000	600	1,500	3,500
Tanzania	7,900	11,000	14,600	14,600	25,000	700	1,000	36,400
Togo	1,250	1,250	1,250	2,250	2,400[1]	–	–	1,400
Tunisia	21,050	24,000	24,000	20,000	18,000	2,500	1,700	2,500
Uganda	6,700	12,600	21,000	21,000	20,000	–	1,000	–
Upper Volta	1,800	2,050	2,050	3,050	8,010[1]	–	–	1,850
Zaïre	38,250	50,000	50,000	43,400	30,000	400	3,000	35,000
Zambia	4,400	5,700	5,800	7,800	12,800	–	1,500	1,200
Zimbabwe	4,600	4,700	4,700	9,200	9,500	–	4,300	44,000

[1] All services form part of the army.
n.a. = no figures available.

COUPS, MUTINIES AND ASSASSINATIONS

1952	23 July	EGYPT. Coup by 'Free Officers' led by Gen. Neguib results in King Farouk's abdication. Neguib replaced by Nasser 14 Nov 1954.
1958	17 Nov	SUDAN. Military junta takes power, with Gen. Ibrahim Abboud as Prime Minister and Minister of Defence. Three further attempted military coups take place in 1959. Student demonstrations lead to the restoration of civilian rule 30 Oct 1964.
1960	13 Dec	ETHIOPIA. While Emperor Haile Selassie is in Brazil the Imperial Bodyguard under Brig. Gen. Mengistu Neway carries out a coup. It is suppressed by units of the regular army.
1962	21 Jan	TOGO. Unsuccessful attempt to assassinate President Olympio.
	1 Aug	GHANA. Unsuccessful attempt to assassinate President Nkrumah.
	17 Dec	SENEGAL. Attempted coup by the Prime Minister, Mamadou Dia, to forestall a censure motion by the National Assembly. Paratroop commanders support President Senghor and Dia and his followers are arrested.
1963	13 Jan	TOGO. President Olympio assassinated during an army coup. The army installs a civilian government under Olympio's political rival, Nicholas Grunitzky.
	15 Aug	CONGO (ex-French). President Youlou forced to resign and the army oversees handing over of power to Alphonse Massemba-Débat.
	23 Oct	DAHOMEY. During a political crisis caused by the arrest of trade union leaders, President Maga stands down and Col. Soglo, army chief-of-staff, assumes power. He returns the country to civilian rule in Jan 1964.
1964	2 Jan	GHANA. Unsuccessful attempt to assassinate President Nkrumah.
	12 Jan	ZANZIBAR. Popular armed insurrection drives the Sultan into exile and Sheikh Karume becomes President.
	20 Jan	TANGANYIKA. Army mutiny over pay and conditions put down with the help of British troops.

23 Jan   UGANDA. Mutiny at army barracks at Jinja suppressed with the help of British troops.

23 Jan   KENYA. British troops restore order after a mutiny among Kenyan forces at Lanet.

18 Feb   GABON. Group of young lieutenants carry out a coup against President Léon M'Ba and begin to form a new government under the former Foreign Minister, Jean Aubame. Two days later the revolt is suppressed by the intervention of French troops.

1965 19 June   ALGERIA. President Ben Bella overthrown by Col. Boumédienne, army chief-of-staff.

18 Oct   BURUNDI. Army mutineers attack the King's palace and wounded the Prime Minister, Léopold Biha. Martial law declared on 20 Oct 1965.

25 Nov   CONGO (ex-Belgian). Gen. Mobutu deposes President Kasavubu and becomes President in his place.

29 Nov   DAHOMEY. Col. Soglo forces the resignation of the President and Prime Minister. An interim government set up under Tahirou Congacou, but Col. Soglo again takes power on 22 Dec 1965, when politicians fail to agree on the composition of a new government.

1966 1 Jan   CENTRAL AFRICAN REPUBLIC. Col. Bokassa, army commander-in-chief, ousts President Dacko and takes power.

4 Jan   UPPER VOLTA. Lt-Col. Lamizana deposes President Maurice Yameogo after conflict between political factions and installs a military government.

15 Jan   NIGERIA. Young army officers led by Maj. Nzeogwu carry out a coup. The Nigerian cabinet requests Maj.-Gen. Ironsi, the army commander, to take over the government. In a fresh coup on 29 July 1966 Lt-Col. Gowon takes power.

24 Feb   GHANA. Military coup overthrows President Nkrumah while he is in Peking. A government formed by Maj.-Gen. Ankrah and Police Commissioner Harlley.

24 May   UGANDA. Armed expulsion of the Kabaka of Buganda by the Prime Minister.

30 May   CONGO (ex-Belgian). Unsuccessful coup against Gen. Mobutu.

June CONGO (ex-French). Abortive coup by discontented army units.

8 July BURUNDI. King Mwambutsa IV, absent in Europe, is deposed by his son, Crown Prince Ndizeye, who becomes King Ntare V. He himself is deposed by his premier, Capt. Michel Micombero, on 28 Nov 1966 and a republic is proclaimed.

26 Oct CONGO (ex-Belgian). Prime Minister Gen. Mulamba ousted and President Mobutu assumes the office of Prime Minister as well as head of state.

1967 13 Jan TOGO. Successful coup by Lt-Col. Eyadéma, army chief-of-staff, ousts President Grunitzky.

8 Feb SIERRA LEONE. Failure of attempted military coup.

23 Mar SIERRA LEONE. Following disputed elections, Sir Albert Margai's government overthrown by army under Lt-Col. Juxon-Smith.

17 Apr GHANA. Abortive coup led by Lt Arthur; leaders of coup publicly executed 9 May 1967.

5 July CONGO (ex-Belgian). Rising by mercenaries against President Mobutu put down by Congolese army.

14 Dec ALGERIA. Unsuccessful coup by Col. Zbiri, who had been dismissed as army chief-of-staff earlier in the week.

17 Dec DAHOMEY. President Soglo overthrown by junior army officers. Government dissolved and a revolutionary military committee set up. On 18 Dec 1967 Maurice Kouandeté appointed President.

1968 18 Apr SIERRA LEONE. Juxon-Smith's military junta overthrown in a 'sergeants' coup'. Civilian rule under Siaka Stevens restored 26 Apr 1968.

26 Aug CHAD. At request of President Tombalbaye, French parachute troops flown in to help government put down rebellion.

4 Sep CONGO (ex-French). President Massemba-Débat resigns, after fighting in Brazzaville. On 6 Sep a provisional government formed under Capt. Raoul, who is succeeded as President by Maj. N'Gouabi.

19 Nov MALI. President Keita overthrown in a coup led by Lt. Moussa Traoré.

1969 5 Mar EQUATORIAL GUINEA. Unsuccessful attempt to seize power by Foreign Minister, Atanasio Ndongo.

10 Mar GUINEA. Unsuccessful attempt to overthrow President Sekou Touré.

25 May SUDAN. Government overthrown in left-wing military coup and National Revolutionary Council formed under Col. Jaafar al-Nemery.

1 Sep LIBYA. King Idris deposed by military junta led by Col. Gaddafi, who proclaimes a Socialist Arab Republic.

15 Oct SOMALIA. President Abdelrashid Ali Shermarke assassinated; army and police commanders seize power and set up a Revolutionary Council.

Nov CONGO (ex-French). Alleged coup attempt by supporters of ex-President Youlou.

10 Dec DAHOMEY. President Zinsou overthrown in military coup.

19 Dec UGANDA. President Obote wounded in assassination attempt.

1970 27 Mar SUDAN. Unsuccessful attempt to assassinate President Nemery.

1971 25 Jan UGANDA. President Obote overthrown by Gen. Amin.

22 Mar SIERRA LEONE. Abortive army coup, after which Prime Minister Stevens signs a mutual defence treaty with Guinea and Guinean forces enter Sierra Leone at his request on 28 Mar 1971.

5 May SOMALIA. Revolutionary Council announces failure of coup.

31 May MADAGASCAR. President Tsiranana announces failure of plot against his government.

5 July BURUNDI. Unsuccessful attempt to overthrow government.

10 July MOROCCO. Attempt to overthrow King Hassan fails.

11 July UGANDA. Abortive coup against Gen. Amin by troops in north-east Uganda.

19 July SUDAN. President Nemery overthrown in left-wing coup but restored in counter-coup on 22 July 1971.

1972 13 Jan GHANA. Government of Dr Busia overthrown by Lt-Col. Acheampong, who establishes a military National Redemption Council to rule by decree.

| 22 Feb | CONGO (ex-French). Unsuccessful left-wing coup. |

22 Feb   CONGO (ex-French). Unsuccessful left-wing coup.

23 Feb   DAHOMEY. Abortive coup by mutinous army units from Ouidah.

7 Apr   TANZANIA. Sheikh Karume, First Vice-President, assassinated.

18 May   MADAGASCAR. Following fighting between students and security forces, President Tsirinana relinquishes executive power to army commander, Maj.-Gen. Ramanantsoa.

16 Aug   MOROCCO. In an attempted coup, rebel aircraft attack King Hassan's aircraft, Rabat airport and the royal palace; Gen. Oufkir, Minister of Defence and leader of coup, commits suicide.

26 Oct   DAHOMEY. Following military coup, Maj. Mathieu Kerekou, deputy commander of armed forces, becomes President and Defence Minister.

1973   5 July   RWANDA. Maj.-Gen. Habyarimana seizes power from President Kayibanda in a bloodless coup.

1974   7 Jan   LESOTHO. Failure of attempted coup.

8 Feb   UPPER VOLTA. Successful army coup.

26 Feb   ETHIOPIA. Dissident troops take over Asmara, and Emperor Haile Selassie's government resigns next day.

24 Mar   UGANDA. Attempted army mutiny fails.

15 Apr   NIGER. President Hamani Diori overthrown in military coup; Lt-Col. Seyni Kountché becomes head of state.

1975   11 Feb   MADAGASCAR. President Ratsimandrava assassinated after six days in office.

13 Apr   CHAD. President Tombalbaye killed in army coup, Gen. Félix Malloum takes power.

29 July   NIGERIA. Gen. Gowon ousted by Brig. Murtala Mohamed while attending OAU summit meeting.

18 Dec   MOZAMBIQUE. Revolt by dissident soldiers and police crushed by Frelimo government.

1976   13 Feb   NIGERIA. Gen. Mohamed killed in an unsuccessful coup. Army chief-of-staff, Lt. Gen. Obasanjo, takes power. Leader of coup, Col. Dumka, executed by firing squad 15 May 1976.

15 Mar   NIGER. Unsuccessful coup led by Maj. Bayere; eight leaders of coup executed in May.

11 June   UGANDA. Unsuccessful attempt to assassinate President Amin.

2 July   SUDAN. Unsuccessful attempt to assassinate President Nemery.

2 Nov   BURUNDI. President Micombero's government overthrown by the army in a bloodless coup.

1977 16 Jan   BENIN. Unsuccessful coup attempt by group of mercenaries.

3 Feb   ETHIOPIA. Brig.-Gen. Teferi Benti, Chairman of Military Council, killed and Lt-Col. Mengistu Haile Mariam succeeds him.

18 Mar   CONGO (ex-French). President N'Gouabi assassinated. Col. Yhombi-Opango elected head of state 3 Apr 1977. Former President Massemba-Débat executed as one of the assassins.

1 Apr   CHAD. Attempted coup crushed by security forces.

27 May   ANGOLA. Unsuccessful coup attempt by followers of pro-Soviet Nito Alves.

5 June   SEYCHELLES. President Mancham overthrown by ex-Premier Albert René in a bloodless coup.

1979 12 Feb   CHAD. Attempt by Prime Minister, Hissène Habré, to oust President Malloum leads to bitter fighting between their forces.

1980 Apr   LIBERIA. Successful coup against the government of President Tolbert led by Master-Sgt Doe. Tolbert and many of his cabinet killed.

Nov   GUINEA-BISSAU. Successful coup deposed Government of President Luis Cabral. A Revolutionary Council was established under Joâo Bernardo Viera.

8 FOREIGN AFFAIRS AND TREATIES

1945	10 May	Arab League formed. Present members: Algeria, Bahrain, Djibouti, Egypt, Iraq, Jordan, Kuwait, Lebanon, Libya, Mauritania, Morocco, Oman, Palestine, Qatar, Saudi Arabia, Somalia, Sudan, Syria, Tunisia, United Arab Emirates, Yemen Arab Republic and People's Democratic Republic of the Yemen
1950	17 June	Collective Security Pact signed in Alexandria by EGYPT, SAUDI ARABIA, SYRIA, LEBANON and YEMEN
1951	9 Nov	Mutual defence assistance agreement between UNITED STATES and SOUTH AFRICA
1952	1, 3 July	Exchange of notes between ETHIOPIA and UNITED KINGDOM on provision of facilities for British military aircraft
1953	11, 13 Mar	Exchange of notes between ETHIOPIA and UNITED KINGDOM on provision of facilities for British military aircraft.
	29 July	20-year agreement on military bases between LIBYA and UNITED KINGDOM
1954	14 May	Agreement between ETHIOPIA and UNITED STATES on military bases
	9 Sep	Agreement between LIBYA and UNITED STATES on air bases
	Oct	Treaty between EGYPT and UNITED KINGDOM for withdrawal of British forces from the Canal Zone
1955	4 July	Simonstown naval co-operation agreement between SOUTH AFRICA and UNITED KINGDOM (revised Jan 1967 and ended 17 June 1975)
	27 Sep	Armaments agreement between EGYPT and CZECHO-SLOVAKIA
1957	Jan	Treaty of friendship between TUNISIA and LIBYA

1958	1 Feb	EGYPT entered into a union with SYRIA, forming the United Arab Republic (dissolved in 1961).
1959	9 Apr	Treaty of friendship between ISRAEL and LIBERIA
	8 July	Defence agreement between LIBERIA and UNITED STATES
1960	22 June	Defence agreement between FRANCE and SENEGAL
	27 June	Defence agreement between FRANCE and MADAGASCAR
	13 Aug	Defence agreement between FRANCE and CENTRAL AFRICAN REPUBLIC
1960	15 Aug	Defence agreement between FRANCE and CHAD
	15 Aug	Defence agreement between FRANCE and CONGO (ex-French)
	17 Aug	Defence agreement between FRANCE and GABON
	13 Nov	Defence agreement between FRANCE and CAMEROON
	Nov	Defence agreement between UNITED KINGDOM and NIGERIA (abrogated 21 Jan 1962)
1961	24 Apr	Defence agreement between FRANCE and IVORY COAST
	24 Apr	Defence agreement between FRANCE and DAHOMEY
	24 Apr	Defence agreement between FRANCE and UPPER VOLTA
	24 Apr	Defence agreement between FRANCE and NIGER
	19 June	Defence agreement between FRANCE and MAURITANIA
	18 Aug	Treaty of friendship between GHANA and CHINA
	31 Aug	Treaty of friendship and mutual assistance between ISRAEL and MADAGASCAR
1962	18 Mar	Evian agreement between FRANCE and ALGERIA
1963	May	Organisation of African Unity formed in Addis Ababa
	10 July	Defence agreement between FRANCE and TOGO
	July	Defence agreement between KENYA and ETHIOPIA
1964	3 Mar	Defence agreement between UGANDA and UNITED KINGDOM
	6 Mar	Defence agreement between KENYA and UNITED KINGDOM
1965	20 Feb	Treaty of friendship between TANZANIA and CHINA
	24 Aug	Yemen cease-fire agreement signed by EGYPT and SAUDI ARABIA

1966	4 Nov	Defence agreement between EGYPT and SYRIA
1967	30 May	Defence pact between EGYPT and JORDAN (joined by IRAQ 4 June 1967)
	30 Aug	Agreement on the Yemen between EGYPT and SAUDI ARABIA
	28 Oct	Declaration of Arusha by KENYA and SOMALIA ending border war
1968	4 Feb	Union of Central African States formed by CHAD, CONGO (ex-French) and CENTRAL AFRICAN REPUBLIC
	12 Mar	Defence agreement between MAURITIUS and UNITED KINGDOM
	5 Sep	Agreement between ETHIOPIA and SOMALIA to end subversive activity
1969	15 Jan	Treaty of co-operation between ALGERIA and MOROCCO
	10 Apr	Treaty of solidarity between ALGERIA and LIBYA
	13 Dec	Agreement between LIBYA and UNITED KINGDOM for British withdrawal from Libyan bases
1970	6 May	Agreement on naval base at Dar es Salaam between CHINA and TANZANIA
	9 June	Treaty between KENYA and ETHIOPIA delimiting their border
	5 Nov	Agreement on political federation between EGYPT, LIBYA and SUDAN (joined by IRAQ 26 Nov 1970)
1971	16 Mar	Agreement for united military command between EGYPT and SYRIA
	26 May	Mutual defence treaty between SIERRA LEONE and GUINEA
	27 Mar	15-year treaty of friendship between EGYPT and SOVIET UNION (abrogated by Egypt 15 Mar 1976)
	20 Aug	Agreement for Federation of Arab Republics between EGYPT, SYRIA and LIBYA
	9 Oct	Aid agreement between ETHIOPIA and CHINA
1972	27 Mar	Peace agreement between SUDANESE GOVERNMENT and ANYANYA REBELS
	28 June	Mutual defence and trade agreements between UGANDA and SUDAN
	5 Oct	Peace treaty between UGANDA and TANZANIA

1973	3 Mar	Treaty of co-operation and mutual assistance between NIGERIA and MALI
	4 June	Agreement between FRANCE and MADAGASCAR ending French military presence
	11 Nov	Agreement on cease-fire line between ISRAEL and EGYPT
1974	14–18 Jan	Trade and economic and technical co-operation treaties between CHINA and MADAGASCAR
	18 Jan	Agreement between EGYPT and ISRAEL on disengagement of forces on Suez Canal
	13–15 Feb	Agreement on technical and economic co-operation between FRANCE and LIBYA
	Feb	Co-operation agreement between FRANCE and CAMEROON
	29 Mar	Co-operation agreement between FRANCE and SENEGAL
	12–14 June	Declaration of co-operation and friendship between EGYPT and UNITED STATES
	2–5 July	Aid pact between EGYPT and WEST GERMANY
	11 July	Friendship and co-operation treaty and technical agreement between SOMALIA and SOVIET UNION (renounced by the former Nov 1977)
	26 Aug	Independence agreement between PORTUGAL and PORTUGUESE GUINEA
	5 Sep	Economic and technical co-operation agreement between TOGO and CHINA
	7 Sep	Lusaka agreement between PORTUGAL and FRELIMO for independence of Mozambique
	27 Nov	Independence agreement between PORTUGAL and SAÓ TOME and PRINCIPE
1975	15 Jan	Agreement on Angolan independence between PORTUGAL and ANGOLAN LIBERATION MOVEMENTS
	4 Sep	Agreement between ISRAEL and EGYPT signed in Geneva for Israeli withdrawal in Sinai and establishment of buffer zone
	Dec	Defence agreement between ALGERIA and LIBYA
1976	20 Apr	Military aid protocol between EGYPT and CHINA
	19 July	Defence agreement between EGYPT and SUDAN

	10 Oct	Treaty of friendship between ANGOLA and SOVIET UNION
	21 Dec	Agreement of formation of unified political command between EGYPT and SYRIA
1977	Jan	Defence agreement between EGYPT and SUDAN
	31 Mar	Treaty of friendship between MOZAMBIQUE and SOVIET UNION
	6 May	Co-operation pacts between ETHIOPIA and SOVIET UNION
1979	Sep–Nov	Lancaster House agreement on future of Zimbabwe between UNITED KINGDOM and ZIMBABWE

9 POPULATION AND ETHNIC GROUPS

The United Nations Population Division estimated the population of Africa in 1978 to be about 435 millions while the World Bank gave a figure of 449 millions. Both figures are tentative owing to the lack of accurate population data for the continent. Many African states do not have a precise idea of their population size. Certain states have never taken a census and in many others official population figures are based on sample surveys. There have been fairly accurate census records for some states – for example, Mauritius and Ghana. However, many of the census returns that have been produced are of questionable value as an accurate return. A good example is the various census returns in Nigeria, which have produced figures which are highly questionable.

Africa's population is growing at a rapid rate, somewhat in excess of 2.6 per cent per annum. It is also a very young population, with about half the total below the age of 20 years. 80 per cent of Africans live in rural areas, but urban growth is very rapid both by natural growth and by movement from the countryside to the towns. The UN estimates that in 1980 one in five of the population was living in towns of 20,000 or more persons. The largest city in Africa is Cairo, with about 8 million inhabitants; other large urban centres are Alexandria, Casablanca, Lagos, Algiers and Johannesburg, which includes the African township of Soweto with a population estimated to be well in excess of 1 million.

Density of population in rural areas varies greatly. Countries bordering desert or Sahelian regions (e.g. Libya, Namibia, Mauritania, Somalia) have relatively low population densities. The areas with the greatest density of population are some of the islands (Mauritius, Zanzibar) and the Nile valley, Rwanda and Burundi, and regions of southern Nigeria.

In the tables that follow, C = 'census'. Other figures are estimates.

AFRICA

Year	Total population (millions)	Growth rate	
1940	158	1925–50	45%
1950	175		
1960	260	1950–75	100%
1970	357		
1975	410	estimated	
1978	435	annual rate	
1980	460	of increase	
1985	552 (projection)	1975–80	2.7%
2000	800 (projection)		

ALGERIA

Year	Total population	Muslims	Non-Muslims	Urban (per cent)	Algiers
1948C	8,681,000	7,679,000	922,000		
1954C	9,529,000	8,449,000	984,000	26.9	449,299
1960C	10,853,000	9,760,000	1,093,000		
1966C	12,101,000[1]				897,352
1974	16,275,000			52	
1978	18,500,000				2,000,000

[1] Includes 268,800 registered Algerian migrants in France, although c. 70,000 Algerians were also resident there. The census of 1966 did not distinguish between Muslims and non-Muslims.
Between 1960 and 1962 about 900,000 *colons* (i.e. European settlers) left Algeria.

ANGOLA

Year	Total population	Europeans	
1945	3,788,000		
1950	4,140,000	78,820	
1960C	4,840,700	172,000	
1965	5,150,000		c. 600,000 refugees
1970C	5,645,100	300,000	in Zaïre.
1975	6,761,000		exodus of c. 300,000
1978	7.180,000		Europeans.

In 1960 11 per cent of the population was urban. In 1972 the population of Luanda was estimated at 400,000.

BENIN (formerly DAHOMEY)

Year	Total population	Urban (%)	Cotonou	Porto Novo
1945	1,458,000			
1950	1,538,000			
1960[1]	1,934,000	10		
1965	2,300,000	12		
1970	2,710,000	12.6		
1972			120,000	85,000
1974	3,029,000	13.5		
1977			175,000	100,000
1978	3,300,000			

About 55 per cent of the population belongs to the Fon ethnic group.
[1] 1961C 2,640,000.

BOTSWANA (formerly BECHUANALAND)

Year	Total population	
1946C	296,883	
1950	310,000	
1956C	320,675	
1964C	543,105	(Bamangwato ethnic group 199,782)
1971C	630,379	
1976	693,000	
1978	749,000	(Gaberone 20,000)

BURUNDI

Year	Total population	Bujumbura
1959C	2,213,300	
1965C	3,210,000	71,000
1971	3,615,000	
1976	3,820,000	157,000
1978	4,070,000	

About 84 per cent of the population belongs
to the Hutu, and 14 per cent to the Tutsi, ethnic
group. It is estimated that in 1972 100,000
Hutu were killed.

CAMEROON

Year	Total population	French Cameroons	British Cameroons
1950	3,558,000	2,500,000	797,000
1955	3,955,000	3,073,000	1,084,000
1960	4,700,000		
1970	5,836,000		
1975	6,539,000		
1976C	7,663,240		

Population of principal towns in 1975: Doula 485,000, Yaoundé 274,400.

CAPE VERDE ISLANDS

Year	Total population
1950C	147,328
1960C	201,549
1970C	272,071
1978	330,000

CENTRAL AFRICAN REPUBLIC
(formerly UBANGI-CHARI)

Year	Total population	Bangui
1946	1,060,000	
1951	1,092,000	
1960	1,227,000	100,000
1965C	2,088,000	
1968	2,255,000	
1971	1,637,000	187,000
1978	1,910,000	

CHAD

Year	Total population
1946	1,901,000
1951	2,241,000
1961	2,675,000
1970	3,640,000
1978	4,280,000

About 46 per cent of the population is of Arab type.

COMORO ISLANDS

Year	Total population	
1945	150,000	
1950	168,890	
1958C	175,552	
1966C	248,517	
1970	275,227	
1978	330,000	(Mayotte 40,000)

CONGO (formerly MIDDLE CONGO)

Year	Total population	
1946	651,000	
1951	684,000	
1961	773,000	
1970	900,000	
1974C	1,300,120	(Brazzaville 289,700)
1978	1,450,000	

About 47 per cent of the population belongs to the Bakongo ethnic group.

DJIBOUTI (formerly FRENCH SOMALILAND, then FRENCH TERRITORY OF THE AFARS AND ISSAS)

Year	Total population	Djibouti town
1952	61,000	
1963	88,000	
1967	125,000	60,000
1976	220,000	100,000

EGYPT

Year	Total population	Cairo
1947C	19,021,000	
1950	20,461,000	
1960C	25,832,000	3,346,000
1966C	30,075,000	
1976C	38,228,000	
1978	40,230,000	8,000,000

Annual growth rate 2.3 per cent.

EQUATORIAL GUINEA

Year	Total population	
1950	170,582	(Fernando Po 33,980)
1960C	245,989	(Fernando Po and Annobón 62,612)
1968	300,000	
1978	325,000	

In 1970–8, about one-third of the population of the mainland region fled into neighbouring countries.

ETHIOPIA

Year	Total population	
1945		(Eritrea 600,000)
1950	12,000,000	
1961	21,800,000	
1971	25,248,000	
1975	27,946,000	
1978	30,000,000	(Addis Ababa 1,000,000)

Drought and famine in the early 1970s are estimated to have killed 400,000.

About 40 per cent of the population belongs to the Oromo and 30 per cent to the Amhara–Tigre social group.

GABON

Year	Total population	
1946	382,000	
1951	407,389	
1961C	448,564	
1965	463,000	
1970[1]	500,000	
1978	538,000	(Libreville 270,000)

[1] 1972C 1,027,000.

THE GAMBIA

Year	Total population	
1944	241,135	
1951C	279,686	
1963C	315,486	
1973C	494,279	(Banjul 39,476)
1977	546,000	

GHANA (formerly GOLD COAST)

Year	Total population	
1942	3,959,500	
1948C	4,412,000	(Ashanti 877,000, Northern Territories, 1,154,000)
1960C	6,727,000	(Accra 337,000–$c.$ 10% of population foreign-born)
1970C	8,559,300	(Accra–Tema 738,000)
1978	10,970,000	

About 28 per cent of the population belongs to the Ashanti ethnic group.

GUINEA

Year	Total population	Conakry
1945	2,125,000	
1950	2,250,000	
1955C	2,570,000	
1960	2,726,000	
1967C	3,780,000	167,000
1972	4,108,000[1]	
1978	4,760,000	600,000

[1] Plus $c.$ 1,000,000 refugees. 1972C 5,143,000.

About 500,000 people left the country between 1958 and 1968.

About 30 per cent of the population belong to the Malinke, and 28 per cent to the Fulani, ethnic group.

GUINEA-BISSAU

Year	Total population
1940	351,000
1950C	510,700
1960C	544,184
1970C	487,400
1978	553,500

IVORY COAST

Year	Total population	Abidjan
1945	4,056,000	
1950	2,170,000	69,000
1961	3,300,000	180,000
1965	3,835,000	300,000
1970	4,310,000	
1975C	6,671,000	
1978	7,300,000	1,000,000

Annual growth rate 2.6 per cent.
About 19 per cent of the population belongs to the Baoulé ethnic group.

KENYA

Year	Total population	African	Asian	European	Nairobi
1948C	5,406,000	5,000,000	98,000	29,600	110,000
1962C	8,636,000	8,366,000	176,613	55,759	270,000
1969C	10,942,000	10,735,000	139,030	40,593	478,000
1973	12,482,000				
1978	14,650,000				650,000

Annual growth rate 3.3 per cent.
About 19 per cent of the population belongs to the Kikuyu ethnic group, 14 per cent to the Luo, and 11 per cent to the Kamba.

LESOTHO (formerly BASUTOLAND)

Year	Total population	
1946C	563,850	
1956C	641,670	
1966C	969,630	(nearly 120,000 working in South Africa)
1976C	1,213,960	(Maseru 20,000)

About 95 per cent of the population belongs to the Sotho ethnic group.

LIBERIA

Year	Total population	Monrovia
1950	under 1,000,000	42,000
1962C	1,016,400	81,000
1974C	1,501,400	172,000
1978	1,830,000	200,000

Annual growth rate 2.5 per cent.
About 21 per cent of the population belongs to the Kpellé, and 16 per cent to the Bassa, ethnic group.

LIBYA

Year	Total population	
1945	1,000,000	
1954C	1,091,800	
1964C	1,564,000	
1970	1,840,000	
1973C	2,259,000	
1978	2,620,000	(Tripoli 600,000)

Annual growth rate 3.1 per cent.

MADAGASCAR

Year	Total population	
1945	4,000,000	
1951	4,369,000	
1958	5,070,000	
1963	5,862,000	
1971C	7,653,000	(incl. 50,000 French citizens)
1975	8,835,000	(Antananarivo 439,000)

Annual growth rate 3 per cent.
About 25 per cent of the population belongs to the Hova ethnic group.

MALAWI (formerly NYASALAND)

Year	Africans	Europeans	Asians
1945C	2,049,450	1,948	2,804
1954	2,494,830	5,128	7,795
1956C	2,900,000	8,900	12,200
1966C	4,020,720	7,395	11,299
1970	4,130,000		
1977C	5,310,000		

Annual growth rate 2.5 per cent.
About 28 per cent of the population belongs to the Chewa, and 14 per cent to the Yao, ethnic group.

MALI (formerly SOUDAN)

Year	Total population	Bamako
1945	3,480,000	
1959	4,200,000	130,000
1967	4,700.000	182,000
1976C	6,308,000	400,000

Annual growth rate 2.5 per cent.
About 31 per cent of the population belongs to the Bambara ethnic group.

MAURITANIA

Year	Total population	
1945	497,000	
1952	560,000	
1958C	655,650	(Nouakchott founded 1957)
1964	1,200,000	
1976C	1,420,000	(Nouakchott 134,380; nomadic population over 500,000)

About 82 per cent of the population are Moors, and about 13 per cent belong to the Tukulor–Fulani ethnic group.

MAURITIUS

Year	Total population	
1946	425,770	
1953C	540,700	(Indians 67%, Euro-Africans 29%, Chinese 3%)
1962C	700,269	
1972C	851,335	
1976	867,880	(Port Louis 141,343)

Annual growth rate 1.5 per cent.

MOROCCO

Year	Total population	
1950	8,953,000	(Tangier 100,000; Jews 250,000; Europeans 590,000)
1955	10,113,000	
1960	11,626,000	(Jews 162,000, Europeans 170,000)
1965	13,325,000	
1971C	15,379,259	
1978	19,150,000	(Rabat 700,000, Casablanca 1,371,000; urban population 35%)

Annual growth rate 3 per cent.

MOZAMBIQUE

Year	Total population	Europeans	Maputo (formerly Lourenço Marques)
1945	5,000,000	31,221	
1950C	5,732,000	48,213	48,000
1955	6,117,000	67,798	
1960C	6,603,000	97,240	178,000
1970C	8,223,000	150,000	354,000
1973		200,000	
1975	9,320,000		
1978	9,890,000		900,000

Most Europeans returned to Portugal 1974–6.
Annual growth rate 2.3 per cent.

NAMIBIA (SOUTH WEST AFRICA)

Year	Total population	Whites	
1946C	352,075	37,858	
1951C	417,768	49,524	
1960C	526,004	73,464	
1970C	746,328	90,658	(Ovambos 342,455)
1977	908,000	105,000	(Windhoek 70,000)

Annual growth rate 1960–70 3.7 per cent.

NIGER

Year	Total population	Niamey
1946	2,000,000	
1951C	2,160,000	
1960C	3,090,000	30,000
1965	3,510,000	
1970	4,020,000	
1978	4,992,000	130,000

Annual growth rate 2.8 per cent.
About 46 per cent of the population belongs to the Hausa ethnic group.

NIGERIA

Year	Total population	North	East	West	Lagos
1945	20,000,000				
1952–3C[1]	31,500,000	16,840,000	7,218,000	6,087,000	272,000
1962[2]	45,332,000	22,027,000	12,332,000	8,157,000	450,000
1963C[3]	55,670,000	29,808,000		10,265,000	665,000
1970	55,070,000				1,100,000
1973C[2]					
1978[4]	68,450,000				2,700,000

About 29 per cent of the population belongs to the Hausa–Fulani ethnic group, 20 per cent to the Yoruba and 17 per cent to the Igbo.

[1] Possibly 10 per cent in error.
[2] Census declared void.
[3] Figures not widely accepted; UN figure for 1963 46.3 million.
[4] UN Population Division estimate; the World Bank gave a figure for 1976 of 77.1 million.

RWANDA

Year	Total population	Kigali
1935	1,680,000	
1955	2,300,000	
1963	2,500,000	
1970	3,590,000	
1975	4,233,000	15,000
1978C	4,820,000	60,000

Annual growth rate 2.9 per cent.

About 95 per cent of the population belong to the Hutu, and 4 per cent to the Tutsi, ethnic group.

ST HELENA, ASCENSION ISLAND, TRISTAN DA CUNHA

Year	St. Helena	Ascension	Tristan
1945	4,700		
1951C	4,748	174	267 (1950C)
1961C	4,648	336	281 (1960C)[1]
1973C	5,159	1,231	271 (1969C)
1976C	5,147	1,058	314 (1977)

[1] Island evacuated 1961–3.

SÃO TOMÉ AND PRINCIPE

Year	Total population	Principe
1941	60,490	
1950C	60,159	
1960C	63,676	4,574
1970C	73,631	4,599
1978	83,000	

Annual growth rate 1.2 per cent.

SENEGAL

Year	Total population	Dakar
1945	1,895,000	
1949	1,992,000	
1951	2,093,000	250,000
1960C	3,110,000	375,000
1965	3,490,000	
1970	3,775,000	600,000
1976C	5,085,300	
1978	5,350,000	800,000 (urban population 32 %)

Annual growth rate 1970–8 2.2 per cent.

About 37 per cent of the population belongs to the Wolof ethnic group, 24 per cent to the Fulani–Tukulor and 16 per cent to the Serer.

SEYCHELLES

Year	Total population	
1945	34,419	
1950	36,000	
1955	39,000	
1960	42,000	
1966	46,700	
1971C	52,650	(Mahé 23,000)
1978	63,300	(c. 28,000 Seychellois living abroad)

SIERRA LEONE

Year	Total population	Freetown
1948C	1,860,000	
1951	2,005,000	85,000
1963	2,183,000	125,000
1970	2,550,000	
1974C	3,003,000	274,000
1978[1]	2,980,000	300,000

[1] UN estimate.

Annual growth rate 2.5 per cent.

About 45 per cent of the population belongs to the Temne, and 36 per cent to the Mendi, ethnic group.

SOMALIA

Year	Total population	Mogadishu
1950	1,886,000	78,000
1960	2,010,000	
1970	2,790,000	
1972	2,941,000	
1978	3,440,000	400,000

Annual growth rate 2.8 per cent.
About 97 per cent of the population belongs to the Somali ethnic group.

SOUTH AFRICA

Year	Total population	Black	White	Coloured	Asian
1946C	11,415,925	7,830,559	2,372,044	928,062	285,260
1951C	12,671,452	8,560,083	2,641,689	1,103,016	366,604
1960C	16,002,797	10,927,922	3,088,492	1,509,258	477,125
1970C	21,448,169	15,057,952	3,751,328	2,018,453	620,436
1976	26,227,000	18,700,000	4,320,000	2,434,000	764,000

Annual growth rate for the Black and Coloured population, 3 per cent; for the White c. 1 per cent.
Urban population: Coloured and Asian, well over 80 per cent; Black, near to 40 per cent.

POPULATION OF MAJOR CITIES IN 1970

	Black	White	Coloured	Asian
Cape Town	107,000	378,000	598,000	11,200
Johannesburg[1]	809,000	501,000	82,000	39,000
Durban	224,000	257,000	43,000	317,000

[1] This figure is in all probability a considerable underestimate. Soweto has a black population of well over 1 million.

SPANISH WEST AFRICA

SPANISH SAHARA

	Total	Saharans	Spaniards
1950	13,627	12,287[1]	1,340
1960	23,793	18,489[1]	5,304
1970	76,425	59,777	16,648[2]

[1] The figures for Saharans are very low estimates and in all probability inaccurate.

[2] The large increase in Spaniards is accounted for by the presence of Spanish troops.

IFNI

Year	Total population
1950	35,000
1960	49,889
1964	51,517

SUDAN

Year	Total population
1945	7,500,000
1951	8,764,000 (Khartoum 71,000, Omdurman 130,000)
1956C	10,260,000
1968	14,770,000
1978	16,720,000 (Khartoum 400,000)

Annual growth rate 3.2 per cent.
Urban population 20 per cent.
About 51 per cent of the population are Arabs, and about 23 per cent belong to the Nilotic ethnic group.

SWAZILAND

Year	Total population
1946	187,997
1956	240,511
1960	316,000
1966C	395,264
1976C	527,791[1]

[1] Includes c. 30,000 migrant workers in South Africa.

Annual growth rate 2.9 per cent.

TANZANIA (formerly TANGANYIKA, and including ZANZIBAR from 1964)

Year	Total population	Asians	
1948C	7,410,000	46,254	(Europeans 11,300)
1952C		59,739	
1957C	8,665,000	75,983	
1967C	12,231,000	84,600	(Dar es Salaam 250,000)
1975	15,600,000		
1978C	17,551,900		(Zanzibar 475,665, Dar es Salaam 400,000)

Annual growth rate 3.1 per cent.

TOGO

Year	Total population	Lomé
1950	990,000	33,000
1960	1,440,000	
1970C	1,955,900	140,000
1978	2,440,000	230,000

Annual growth rate 2.9 per cent.
About 44 per cent of the population belongs to the Ewé, and 23 per cent to the Kabré, ethnic group.

TUNISIA

Year	Total population	Europeans	Tunis	
1946C	3,231,000	240,000	364,000	
1956	3,943,000	255,000		(urban population 30%)
1966C	4,533,000		469,000	
1975C	5,788,200			
1978	6,200,000		800,000	

UGANDA

Year	Total population	Asians	Kampala
1948C	4,958,000	35,215	
1959C	6,536,000	71,399	60,000
1963	7,200,000		
1970C	9,548,000	74,300	330,700
1974	11,171,000	88,000	
1978	12,430,000		

About 30,000 Asians were forced to leave 1972–3.
Annual growth rate 3 per cent.
About 16 per cent of the population belongs to the Ganda, and 15 per cent to the Nilotic, ethnic group.

UPPER VOLTA

Year	Total population	Ouagadougou
1949	3,069,000	
1960	4,340,000	
1966		78,000
1970	5,380,000	
1978	6,520,000	140,000

Annual growth rate 2.3 per cent.
About 50 per cent of the population belongs to the Mossi ethnic group.

ZAÏRE (formerly BELGIAN CONGO, then REPUBLIC OF THE CONGO)

Year	Total population	Europeans	Kinshasa (formerly Leopoldville)	
1945	10,000,000	33,786	40,000	
1951	11,662,000	69,200	200,000	
1955			325,000	
1959	13,540,000	110,000		
1965			1,000,000	
1970C	21,637,800			
1978	26,460,000		2,000,000	(urban population 30%)

Annual growth rate 2.6 per cent.
About 34 per cent of the population belongs to the Kongo, and 9 per cent to the Luba, ethnic group.

ZAMBIA (formerly NORTHERN RHODESIA)

Year	Total population	Europeans	Lusaka	
1941C	1,381,000		20,000	
1946C	1,656,800	21,919		
1951C	1,930,000	37,221	80,000	
1956C		66,000	170,000	
1961C	2,480,000	76,000		
1969C	4,056,000	58,000		
1972	4,515,000	58,000		
1978	5,510,000		430,000	(urban population 37%)

Annual growth rate 3.1 per cent.
About 15 per cent of the population belongs to the Bemba ethnic group, 12 per cent to the Tonga and 3 per cent to the Lozi.

ZANZIBAR

Year	Total population	Asians/Arabs	
1948C	264,162	59,771	
1958C[1]	299,111	70,000	(urban population 37.9%)
1967C	354,360		
1978C	475,665		

[1] 1958C did not distinguish ethnic groups.

ZIMBABWE (formerly SOUTHERN RHODESIA; RHODESIA; ZIMBABWE–RHODESIA)

Year	Total population	Europeans	Coloured/Asian	Harare (Salisbury)
1946C	1,777,000	82,382	7,501	
1951C	2,146,000	136,017	10,283	
1956C	3,640,000	178,000		183,000
1958		207,000		
1961C	3,857,000	221,504	17,812	
1963				315,400
1969C	5,090,000	228,580	24,118	
1977	6,820,000	263,000	33,300	600,000

Annual growth rate 3.5 per cent.

About 60 per cent of the population belongs to the Shona, and 14 per cent to the Ndebele, ethnic group.

10 BASIC ECONOMIC STATISTICS

Product	Country	World status	Total production (recent estimate, '000 tonnes)
MINERAL PRODUCTION			
Antimony ore	South Africa	1st	16,305
Asbestos	South Africa	3rd	355
	Zimbabwe	4th	165
Bauxite	Guinea	2nd	11,316
Chrome	South Africa	1st	906
	Zimbabwe	5th	295
Coal	South Africa	8th	75,732
Copper	Zambia	4th	850
	Zaïre	6th	445
	South Africa	11th	197
Crude petroleum	Nigeria	8th	102,660
	Libya	9th	92,772
	Algeria	14th	50,100
	Gabon	24th	11,388
	Egypt	29th	9,286
	Angola	33rd	6,276
Diamonds	Zaïre	1st	12,810 ⎫
	South Africa	3rd	7,295 ⎪
	Botswana	4th	2,414 ⎬ '000 carats
	Ghana	5th	2,328 ⎪
	Namibia	6th	1,740 ⎪
	Sierra Leone	7th	1,650 ⎭
Gold	South Africa	1st	713,400 ⎫
	Zimbabwe	7th	17,000 ⎬ kilos
	Ghana	9th	16,295 ⎭
Iron ore	Liberia	9th	18,474
	South Africa	12th	9,803
	Mauritania	14th	5,642
	Angola	19th	3,503
Lead	Namibia	17th	42
Manganese	South Africa	2nd	2,006 ⎫ tonnes
	Gabon	3rd	1,115 ⎭

(continued)

Product	Country	World status	Total production (recent estimate, '000 tonnes)	
	Ghana	8th	199 ⎫	tonnes
	Zaïre	9th	160 ⎬	
	Morocco	11th	105 ⎭	
Mercury	Algeria	3rd	1.5	
Natural gas	Algeria	13th	9,533,000	
Nickel ore	South Africa	7th	22.4	
	Botswana	12th	12.6	
	Zimbabwe	13th	12.0	
Phosphate rock	Morocco	3rd	14,119	
	Tunisia	4th	3,512	
	Western Sahara	6th	3,300	
	South Africa	7th	1,824	
	Senegal	8th	1,600	
	Togo	12th	1,100	
Silver	South Africa	15th	88 ⎫	tonnes
	Morocco	16th	85 ⎬	
	Zaïre	18th	77	
Tin concentrates	Zaïre	9th	4.0	
	Nigeria	10th	3.7	
	South Africa	12th	2.7	
Tungsten ore	Rwanda	15th	500 ⎫	
Uranium	Niger	5th	1,200 ⎬ tonnes	
	Gabon	6th	800	
Varadium ore	South Africa	1st	10,971	
	Namibia	6th	562 ⎭	
Zinc	Zaïre	14th	80	
	South Africa	19th	77	
AGRICULTURE				
Apples	South Africa	21st	310	
Bananas	Burundi	12th	915	
	Tanzania	15th	770	
Barley	Morocco	15th	2,862	
Cacao	Ghana	1st	320	
	Ivory Coast	2nd	240	
	Nigeria	4th	180	
	Cameroon	5th	90	
Cassava	Nigeria	3rd	10,800	
	Zaïre	4th	9,832	
	Tanzania	7th	5,100	
	Mozambique	8th	2,400	
	Ghana	10th	1,800	
	Angola	11th	1,600	
	Madagascar	13th	1,348	
	Uganda	15th	1,000	

(continued)

Product	Country	World status	Total production (recent estimate, '000 tonnes)
Coconuts	Mozambique	9th	410
	Tanzania	10th	307
	Ghana	11th	300
Coffee	Ivory Coast	3rd	305
	Uganda	5th	211
	Ethiopia	7th	170
	Cameroon	10th	93
	Madagascar	11th	89
	Kenya	14th	80
	Angola	16th	72
Cotton	Sudan	14th	114
Cotton seed	Egypt	8th	680
	Sudan	15th	208
Dates	Egypt	2nd	419
	Algeria	6th	185
	Sudan	7th	105
	Morocco	8th	102
Grapefruit	South Africa	5th	85
Grapes	South Africa	12th	1,150
	Algeria	19th	680
Groundnuts	Senegal	4th	1,192
(in shell)	Sudan	5th	980
	Nigeria	6th	170
	Zaïre	11th	289
	Mali	12th	258
	Uganda	13th	220
	Cameroon	14th	179
	Malawi	15th	169
	South Africa	17th	153
Maize	South Africa	8th	7,312
Millet	Nigeria	4th	3,200
	Niger	5th	1,195
Natural rubber	Nigeria	6th	85
	Liberia	7th	73
	Zaïre	8th	36
	Ivory Coast	12th	19
	Cameroon	14th	16
Olive oil	Tunisia	5th	132
Oranges	Egypt	8th	900
	South Africa	11th	640
	Morocco	12th	566
Palm oil	Nigeria	2nd	510
	Ivory Coast	4th	176
	Zaïre	6th	155
Pineapples	Ivory Coast	8th	240

(continued)

Product	Country	World status	Total production (recent estimate, '000 tonnes)
	South Africa	10th	190
Rice	Egypt	15th	2,530
Sorghum	Nigeria	3rd	3,680
	Sudan	5th	1,800
Sugar cane	South Africa	11th	19,221
Tea	Kenya	7th	62
	Malawi	11th	28
	Uganda	13th	21
Tobacco	Zimbabwe	16th	85
Tomatoes	Egypt	6th	1,230
Cattle	Ethiopia	10th	25,963 ⎫
	Sudan	13th	15,395 ⎪
	Tanzania	15th	14,362 ⎪
	South Africa	21st	12,700 ⎪
	Nigeria	22nd	11,300 ⎪
Goats	Nigeria	3rd	23,000 ⎪
	Ethiopia	5th	17,064 ⎬ '000
	Sudan	10th	10,105 ⎪
	Somalia	12th	8,000 ⎪
Sheep	South Africa	9th	31,001 ⎪
	Ethiopia	12th	23,065 ⎪
	Morocco	16th	16,800 ⎪
	Sudan	19th	15,262 ⎭
Wool (greasy)	South Africa	5th	103
Wool (clean)	South Africa	5th	52
Fish catches	South Africa	14th	1,314
Whale catches	South Africa	3rd	1,707

MANUFACTURING

Product	Country	World status	Total production (recent estimate, '000 tonnes)
Cheese	Egypt	10th	228
Mutton, lamb and goat	South Africa	10th	167
Wheat flour	Egypt	10th	2,880
Wine	Algeria	10th	6,100 ⎫ '000
	South Africa	11th	5,900 ⎭ hectolitres
Raw sugar	South Africa	12th	2,042
Cotton yarn	Egypt	12th	181
Timber (broad-leaf)	Nigeria	6th	65.4 ⎫
	Tanzania	8th	33.8 ⎪ million
	Sudan	12th	22.2 ⎬ cu metres
	Ethiopia	14th	21.3 ⎪
	Uganda	20th	14.7 ⎭
Wood pulp (chemical)	South Africa	15th	601
Aluminium	Ghana	18th	151

(continued)

Product	Country	World status	Total production *(recent estimate, '000 tonnes)*
Copper (smelted)	Zambia	5th	706
	Zaïre	7th	408
	South Africa	13th	159
Copper (refined)	Zambia	4th	695
Crude steel	South Africa	18th	7,140
Pig iron (ferro-alloy)	South Africa	17th	6,636
Tin	Nigeria	15th	3.8
Zinc	South Africa	21st	66
	Zaïre	24th	61
Kerosene and jet fuel	Egypt	17th	1,540

Source: Geographical Digest 1978 (George Philip).

GROSS DOMESTIC PRODUCT AND VALUE OF TRADE

Country	GDP 1975 US$ million	GDP 1975 US$ per capita	Imports c.i.f. (value in million US$) 1948	1958	1968	1976	Exports f.o.b. (value in million US$) 1948	1958	1968	1976
Algeria	11,561	710	482	1,139	815	5,312	420	488	830	5,163
Angola	1,645	294	49	130	303	625[1]	60	128	271	1,227[1]
Benin[2]	336	111	10	21	50	150[3]	12	18	22	46[3]
Botswana	276	424	(Included in South African total)				(Included in South African total)			
Burundi	224	67	(under Zaïre)				(under Zaïre)			
Cameroon[4]	1,868	303	42	107	187	609	36	115	189	511
Central African Republic	205	127	(under Congo)	19	36	69[3]	(under Congo)	16	36	52
Chad	270	74	(under Congo)	28	34	132[3]	(under Congo)	25	28	37[1]
Congo	283	238	53[5]	58	84	177	50[5]	14	49	182
Djibouti	104	1,100	17	24	35	104[1]	9	16	4	20[1]
Egypt	9,273	260	674	667	666	3,808[6]	607	478	622	1,522
Equatorial Guinea	76	267								
Ethiopia	2,678	98	45	75	173	353	33	63	106	278
Gabon	1,545	2,972	(under Congo)	35	64	701	(under Congo)	39	124	898
Gambia	46	101	9	11	22	74	9	12	13	35
Ghana	2,214	257	127	237	308	805[3]	202	263	307	760[3]
Guinea	320	82								
Guinea-Bissau	127	359	7	8	18	37	5	7	3	6[3]
Ivory Coast[2]	3,073	644	34[7]	109	307	1,296	42[7]	150	425	1,620
Kenya[8]	3,139	234	155[9]	170	321	941	105[9]	93	175	656
Lesotho	69	74	(Included in South African total)				(Included in South African total)			
Liberia	545	334	9	38	107	399	16	54	168	476
Libya	12,284	5,236	22	97	645	3,950	12	14	1,876	8,438
Madagascar	899	133	78	126	170	363[3]	50	96	116	291[3]
Malawi	637	129	(under Rhodesia)	–	70	205	(under Rhodesia)	20	48	148
Mali[2]	275	54	(under Senegal)	(under Senegal)	34	150	(under Senegal)	(under Senegal)	11	97
Mauritania[2]	293	232	(under Senegal)	(under Senegal)	36	180	(under Senegal)	(under Senegal)	72	178
Morocco	7,375	426	389	393	549	2,618	178	345	450	1,262
Mozambique	1,872	228	71	115	234	300	40	71	155	202[3]

(continued)

Country	GDP 1975 US$ million	GDP 1975 US$ per capita	Imports c.i.f. (value in million US$) 1948	1958	1968	1976	Exports f.o.b. (value in million US$) 1948	1958	1968	1976
Niger[2]	363	90	3	11	42	99[3]	6	18	29	85[3]
Nigeria	13,881	223	169	466	541	8,199	252	380	591	10,565
Rhodesia[10]	3,386	555	240[11]	-	260	541[12]	210[11]	138	246	650[12]
Rwanda	309	75	(under Zaïre)		22	103	(under Zaïre)		15	81
Senegal[2,13]	1,163	294	115	208	180	576[3]	84	137	151	461[3]
Sierra Leone	591	222	20	67	91	153	22	55	96	112
Somalia	249	89	9	31	48	162[2]	5	21	30	85
South Africa[10,14]	35,290	1,353	1,424	1,555	2,632	6,751	557	1,096	2,109	4,776
South West Africa			(Included in South African total)				(Included in South African total)			
Sudan	1,832	117	92	170	258	980	99	125	233	554
Swaziland	113	270	(Included in South African total)				(Included in South African total)			
Tanzania[8]	2,506	170	92	109	214	566	71	135	227	459
Togo	418	197	7	18	47	174[3]	10	15	39	126[3]
Tunisia	3,533	626	179	155	217	1,529	61	153	158	789
Uganda[8]	1,323	135	(under Kenya)	76	123	80	(under Kenya)	130	186	360
Upper Volta[2]	456	77	(under Ivory Coast)	9	41	144	(under Ivory Coast)	5	21	53
Zaïre[15]	3,533	146	191	362	310	824	245	406	505	930
Zambia	2,804	590	(under Rhodesia)	-	455	780	(under Rhodesia)	209	762	1,046

[1] Latest figure 1974.
[2] 1948–58 excluding trade with countries of former French West Africa.
[3] Latest figure 1975.
[4] 1948–58 East Cameroon only.
[5] Includes Cameroon, Central African Republic and Chad.
[6] Excludes crude petroleum imported without stated value.
[7] Includes data for Upper Volta.
[8] Excludes trade between Kenya, Uganda and Tanzania.
[9] Includes data for Uganda.
[10] Imports f.o.b.
[11] Includes Malawi and Zambia.
[12] Latest figure 1973.
[13] 1948–58 Including data for Mauritania and Mali.
[14] Figures adjusted to approximate trade of present customs area.
[15] 1948–58 including data for Burundi and Rwanda.

Sources: *UN Statistical Year book 1977; Geographical Digest 1978, (George Philip).*

AID RECEIVED AND MAIN TRADING PARTNERS

Country	Aid (US$ million)			Main trading partners (in percentage terms 1975)				
	From centrally planned economies (1976 or most recent available)	From developed market economies (1974–6 annual averages)	From multilateral institutions					
Algeria	265	112.0	17.3	USA 26.8	FR Ger. 19.0	France 14.8	Italy 11.4	UK 4.0
Angola	2	5.0	1.0 (1974)	USA 38.3	Portugal 26.9	Canada 7.7	Japan 5.7	FR Ger. 4.1
Benin	46[1]	25.1	21.1	France 24.3	China 11.2	Nigeria 11.0	Niger 6.9	Japan 6.7
Botswana		36.4	10.0 (1974)					
Burundi	20[1]	23.7	19.4	USA 45.5	FR Ger. 21.3	France 6.3	Belg./Lux. 5.9	Neth. 3.6
Cameroon	75[2]	66.8	34.3	France 26.8	Neth. 21.4	USSR 10.5	FR Ger. 7.4	Gabon 4.8
Central African Republic	6[1]	25.9	18.6	France 42.0	Belg./Lux. 9.4	USA 8.3	Italy 7.7	Chad 5.4
Chad	9[3]	36.4	28.0 (1974)	Zaire 5.8	Nigeria 4.6	Congo 3.7	France 3.3	Cent. Afr. Rep. 1.7
Congo	14[2]	35.1	18.8	France 27.0	Italy 26.1	USA 13.1	UK 6.7	Brazil 6.1
Djibouti		30.2	0.4					
Egypt	7	261.2	81.7	USSR 43.2	Czech. 7.4	GDR 5.9	Romania 4.6	Italy 4.5
Equatorial Guinea	11[1]	—	1.0					
Ethiopia	1[3]	75.3	60.9	USA 19.5	Saudi Arabia 13.3	Djibouti 11.7	Egypt 8.6	Japan 8.4

(continued)

Country	Aid (US$ million)				Main trading partners (in percentage terms 1975)				
	From centrally planned economies (1976 or most recent available)	From developed market economies (1974–6 annual averages)	From multilateral institutions						
Gabon	25	30.2	2.4		France 38.8	USA 27.3	UK 8.3	FR Ger. 6.0	Italy 4.9
Gambia	17	4.2	4.7		UK 38.7	Neth 19.8	Portugal 13.9	Italy 11.7	France 8.5
Ghana	65[4]	54.7	21.3		UK 15.3	USA 12.8	Neth. 11.4	FR Ger. 9.0	Japan 7.8
Guinea	1[3]	5.5	4.0						
Guinea-Bissau	17	6.6	4.7						
Ivory Coast		66.3	30.2		France 27.1	Neth. 10.4	USA 10.2	FR Ger. 8.8	Italy 6.6
Kenya	71[1]	113.7	21.7		UK 13.2	FR Ger. 11.3	USA 4.9	Neth. 4.3	Italy 3.4
Lesotho		15.1	12.3						
Liberia	1[4]	13.0	9.6		USA 22.0	FR Ger. 21.5	Italy 13.0	Neth. 9.8	France 8.1
Libya	27	5.8	3.8		Italy 21.9	USA 21.9	FR Ger. 19.5	Spain 5.1	Bahamas 4.4
Madagascar	55	31.6	38.6	(1974)	France 35.3	USA 20.6	Réunion 8.1	Japan 5.9	FR Ger. 4.6
Malawi		41.5	15.1		UK 39.6	USA 7.3	Rhodesia 6.9	Neth. 6.5	Zambia 6.1
Mali	2[3]	56.4	49.4	(1974)	France 26.6	China 17.2	Ivory Coast 15.2	Senegal 10.5	Italy 1.3
Mauritania	37[4]	18.7	23.6	(1973)	UK 15.3	France 11.8	Spain 10.1	Japan 9.7	FR Ger. 8.6

(continued)

Country	Aid (US$ million)			Main trading partners (in percentage terms 1975)				
	From centrally planned economies (1976 or most recent available)	From developed market economies (1974–6 annual averages)	From multilateral institutions					
Morocco	34	133.3	17.0	France 21.7	Italy 7.5	Poland 7.0	Belg./Lux. 6.7	UK 6.7
Mozambique	59[3]	15.4	5.5	Portugal 23.8	USA 13.7	S. Africa CU 8.1	Japan 4.5	India 4.6
Niger	54[4]	81.0	49.8	France 63.7	Nigeria 21.9	USA 2.6	Benin 2.4	Upper Volta 2.1
Nigeria	156	56.8	15.4	USA 29.0	UK 14.1	Neth. 11.3	France 10.9	Neth. Antilles 7.4
Rhodesia		3.9	0.1					
Rwanda	1[2]	47.3	22.1	Belg./Lux. 16.7	UK 3.6	Malaysia 2.3	USA 1.9	FR Ger. 1.3
Senegal	1[4]	75.8	42.0	France 31.5	Mauritania 8.4	Mali 5.1	Neth. 4.7	UK 4.5
Sierra Leone	48[1]	7.3	6.8 (1974)	UK 63.1	Neth. 15.4	USA 5.7	Japan 4.9	FR Ger. 4.5
Somalia	62[3]	16.9	44.0 (1973)	Saudi Arabia 57.0	Italy 16.3	Yemen 7.7	Oman 3.8	USSR 2.7
Sudan	62[3]	49.3	68.3	France 14.4	China 7.8	Egypt 7.0	Italy 6.5	FR Ger. 5.6
Swaziland		10.8	7.4					
Tanzania	4[3]	195.7	48.4	UK 13.8	FR Ger. 9.4	USA 6.6	India 5.9	China 4.4

(continued)

Country	Aid (US$ million)			Main trading partners (in percentage terms 1975)				
	From centrally planned economies (1976 or most recent available)	From developed market economies (1974–6 annual averages)	From multilateral institutions					
Togo	1[3]	22.3	17.3	France 39.3	Neth. 32.4	FR Ger. 10.4	Belg/Lux. 6.4	Mali 2.2
Tunisia	115	129.3	27.8	France 19.1	Italy 17.0	Greece 14.1	USA 10.3	FR Ger. 7.6
Uganda	30[1]	6.9	11.6	USA 24.4	UK 20.2	Japan 8.0	FR Ger. 6.1	France 4.1
Upper Volta	60[4]	54.5	34.0	Ivory Coast 48.1	France 18.8	Italy 6.6	UK 6.4	Togo 5.2
Zaïre	115[2]	152.0	42.9 (1974)	Angola 23.0	Belg./Lux. 19.5	Italy 15.0	Tanzania 10.2	France 6.7
Zambia	51[4]	58.4[4]	12.4	UK 22.5	Japan 17.6	FR Ger. 14.2	Italy 12.9	France 8.4

[1] 1954–72 cumulative total.
[2] 1973.
[3] 1975.
[4] 1974.

Source: UN Statistical Yearbook 1977.

11 BIOGRAPHIES

Abbas, Ferhat (1899–), Born Constantine; educ. local *lycée* and Algiers Univ.; pharmacist. President of Algerian Muslim Students' Union. Involved in municipal politics; founded and edited weekly journal *L'Entente* 1933–9. Signatory of the Manifeste du Peuples Algérien 1943. Founded Union Démocratique du Manifeste Algérien 1945. Deputy in French National Assembly 1946–7. Founder and editor of *La République Algérienne* 1954. Joined FLN 1955; based in Switzerland 1956–8. President of provisional government of Algeria in exile 1958–61. President of the National Assembly of independent Algeria 1962–4. Detained 1964–5.

Abboud, Ferik Ibrahim (1900–), Sudanese army officer and politician. Educ. local schools and Gordon Memorial College, Khartoum. Commissioned in Egyptian army 1918–25 as military engineer; fought with British in North African campaign during Second World War. Principal Staff Officer, Sudan Defence Force 1952; C-in-C Sudanese army 1956. Led military coup against government and became Prime Minister 1958–64. Regime overthrown by a civilian coup 1964.

Acheampong, Ignatius Kutu (1931–79), Ghanaian solider and head of state. Born Kumasi; educ. RC schools; teacher in commercial college 1949–52. Joined army 1953; commissioned 1959; military training in UK and USA; served in UN Congo operations 1962–3. Following 1966 coup served National Liberation Council as chairman of Western Regional administration. Acting head 1st Brigade Ghanaian army 1971; led coup overthrowing Busia government 1972. Chairman of National Redemption Council 1972; Chairman Supreme Military Council and head of state 1972–8. Deposed 1978; executed 1979.

Adoula, Cyril (1921–78), Zaïrean politician. Born Leopoldville; educ. RC Schools; employed in commerce and Banque Centrale as clerk. A trade-union activist in the 1950s and secretary of Fédération Générale du Travail du Congo. Founder-member of Patrice Lumumba's Mouvement National Congolais 1958. Elected senator for Equatorial Province in May 1960; Minister of Interior 1960; delegate to UN 1961; Prime Minister 1961–4. Ambassador to Belgium and the EEC and then the USA 1964–6.

Afrifa, Akwasi. A. (1936–79), Ghanaian soldier and politician. Born near Kumasi; educ. Adisadel College. Joined army 1956; trained Sandhurst 1957; commissioned 1960. Served twice with UN Congo operation 1961–2. One of the leaders of 1966 coup which overthrew President Nkrumah. Member National Liberation Council and Chairman 1969. In detention 1972–3. Executed for corrupt practices 1979.

Aguiyi-Ironsi, Johnson (1925–66), Nigerian soldier and head of state. Served in British colonial army in West Africa from 1942; officer-training in Britain 1948; commissioned 1949. Commander of Nigerian contingent in UN Congo operation 1960; C-in-C of UN forces in Congo 1963. Appointed Commander in Chief of Nigerian army 1965. Assumed power as head of state following coup of January 1966. Killed in the second coup, in July 1966.

Akuffo, Frederick William Kwasi (1937–79), Ghanaian soldier and head of state. Born Eastern Region, Ghana; educ. Presbyterian schools to 1955; civil servant 1955–7. In 1957 enlisted in army; selected for officer-training in UK 1958–60; commissioned 1960; served with UN emergency force in Congo 1962; Commander 2nd Infantry Brigade Group of Ghanaian army 1972; army commander and member of Supreme Military Council in Acheampong government, 1975; Chief of Defence Staff 1976–8. Head of state 1978–9. Overthrown in a junior officers coup led by Flight-Lt Rawlings and then executed for corrupt practices 1979.

Ahidjo, Ahmadou (1924–), first President of Cameroon. Born Garona, Cameroon; educ. secondary school Yaoundé; radio operator in post office 1941. Member Cameroon territorial assembly 1947–58. Representative in Assembly of French Union 1953; Vice-Premier and Minister of Interior 1957–8; Prime Minister of autonomous French Cameroons 1958–60. President of Cameroon Republic since 1960.

Amin, Idi (1925–), Ugandan soldier and former head of state. Born a Kakwa, from West Nile province, Uganda. Joined King's African Rifles 1946; corporal 1949; fought with British in 'Mau Mau' campaign in Kenya; commissioned 1961; battalion commander 1963; deputy commander Uganda army 1965; commander 1968. Seized power in Uganda from Obote's civilian government Jan 1971. During his presidency, 1971–9, introduced a reign of terror and bloodshed resulting in deaths of several hundred thousand Ugandans. Overthrown following Tanzanian invasion 1979. Fled country and took refuge in Saudi Arabia.

Ankrah, Joseph Arthur (1925–), Ghanaian soldier. Educ. Wesleyan School, Accra. Military service in Second World War with Gold Coast Regiment; commissioned 1947; brigadier in Ghanaian army and in UN operations in Congo

1960–1. Deputy Chief of Defence Staff but dismissed from army by President Nkrumah 1965. Chairman of National Liberation Council and Chief of Defence Staff following coup against Nkrumah 1966–9.

Awolowo, Chief Obafeni (1909–   ), Nigerian nationalist leader and politician. A Yoruba, born Ijebu, southern Nigeria; educ. Protestant schools; teacher 1928–9; trader, trade-union organiser, and journalist 1934–44. Gained degree by private study 1944; studied law in London 1944–7; solicitor and advocate of Nigerian Supreme Court 1947–51. Helped found and led Action Group 1950; Minister of Local Government in Western Region 1951–4; Premier Western Region 1954–9. Leader of opposition in federal parliament 1960–2; imprisoned 1962–6. Released from prison after military coup of 1966. Federal Commissioner for Finance 1967–71. Chancellor of Univ. of Ife 1967; returned to private legal practice 1971. Author of several books on politics. Leader of Unity Party of Nigeria and its unsuccessful candidate in presidential elections 1979.

Azikiwe, Benjamin Mhamdi (1904–   ), Nigerian nationalist leader and the country's first President. An Ibo, born Zenguru, northern Nigeria, son of an army clerk; educ. mission schools; government clerk 1921–5; studied at two univs in the USA, where he remained to teach 1925–34. Returned to West Africa 1934; active in nationalist politics and as founder and editor of various newspapers, including the *West African Pilot* 1934–47. Executive member of Nigerian Youth Movement 1934–41. President of National Council of Nigeria and Cameroon 1944; member Nigerian Legislative Council 1947–51. Elected member Western Region House of Assembly 1952–3, of Eastern Region House 1954–9; Premier Eastern Region 1954–9. Governor-General of Nigeria 1960–3 and President of the Republic 1963–6.

Bakary, Djibo (1922–   ), Niger politician. Educ. William Ponty School, Dakar; teacher in Niger 1941. Founder secretary of Niger-section of the Rassemblement Democratique Africain, the PPN. Split with RDA and formed the UDN 1951. Mayor of Niamey 1956. Opposed de Gaulle's proposals in the referendum of 1958. The UDN was crushingly defeated and then dissolved by the government in 1959. Bakary went into exile.

Balewa, Sir Abubakar Tafawa (1912–66), Nigerian politician. A Muslim born in Northern Nigeria; teacher and education officer 1930s–40s. Member Nigerian Legislative Council 1947. Helped found Northern People's Congress 1951. Federal Minister of Works 1952–4; Minister of Trade 1954; Chief Minister 1957–9; Federal Prime Minister 1959; knighted 1960. Federal Prime Minister of independent Nigeria 1960–6. Killed in first military coup 1966.

Banda, Hastings Kamazu (1906–   ), first President of Malawi. Born Kasungu district, Nyasaland; educ. in Nyasaland and South Africa; went to USA to study medicine 1927–37; medical practitioner in UK 1939–53 and Ghana 1954–8. Returned to Nyasaland as President-General of African National Congress 1958. Imprisoned 1959–60. Leader Malawi Congress Party 1961; Minister of Natural Resources and Local Government 1961–3; Prime Minister of Nyasaland 1963–4 and of independent Malawi 1964–6. President since 1966.

Bello, Sir Ahmadu (1910–66), one of the leaders of Northern Nigeria. Educ. Katsina College; teacher 1931; appointed Sardauna of Sokoto 1938. Leader of Northern People's Congress 1951. Minister in Northern Region government 1952; Prime Minister Northern Region 1954. Killed in first military coup Jan. 1966.

Ben Bella, Ahmed (1919–   ). Born near Oran, son of a trader; served in French army during Second World War. Joined Parti Populaire Algérien 1945; member of its military wing, the Organisation Secrète, 1948. Imprisoned 1950; escaped 1952. One of the organisers of the Front de Libération Nationale 1954 and the armed revolt against French rule. Captured and imprisoned by French 1956–62. Prime Minister of Algeria 1962–6. Deposed by Boumédienne's military coup 1965 and placed under house arrest until 1979.

Benjeddid, Chadli (1929–   ), Algerian head of state. Educ. in Arab and French-speaking schools. Active in politics and a member of the Mouvement pour le Triomphe des Libertés Démocratiques. Joined war of independence 1955; became a battalion commander of the FLN; arrested by the French 1961. Commander of a military region in independent Algeria 1963. Took part in the coup of 1965 which removed Ben Bella from office; member of the Revolutionary Council which ruled Algeria. Co-ordinator of the armed forces 1978. President of Algeria 1979.

Biko, Steve (1947–77), South African nationalist leader. Born Eastern Cape, son of a government clerk; expelled from Lovedale College because of his brother's involvement in the illegal nationalist body Poqo, he studied at an RC boarding school, and then at Natal University. One of the founders of the Black Consciousness movement and President of the South African Student's Organisation established in 1969. An organiser of the Black Community Programme, he was banned by the South African government following the Durban strikes of 1973. He was arrested, and died as a result of police brutality.

Binaisa, Godfrey (1920–   ), Ugandan politician. A Buganda, born near Kampala; educ. King's College, Budo; studied law, London Univ. 1953–6. Member of Milton Obote's Uganda People's Congress. Appointed Attorney-General 1962; resigned office following disagreements with Obote over policies 1967. Chairman Uganda Law Society 1968. In exile during much of Amin regime. President of Uganda 1979–80.

Blundell, Sir Michael (1907–   ). Born London; emigrated to Kenya as farmer 1937. War service 1939–45. Member Legislative Council 1948–58, 1961–3. Minister of Agriculture 1955–9, 1961–2. Leader of New Kenya Party 1959–63.

Bokassa, Jean Bédel (1921–   ), army officer and former head of state of Central African Republic. Educ. mission schools in Bangui and Brazzaville. Joined French army 1939; became a sergeant and eventually commissioned in 1956; C-in-C army of Central African Republic 1963. Led coup to depose President Dacko. President 1966–76. Proclaimed himself Emperor of Central African Empire 1976. Deposed by a coup 1979. Exiled in Ivory Coast.

Bongo, Omar, formerly *Albert Bernard* (1935–   ), Gabonese politician. Educ. commercial college, Brazzaville. Civil servant in President's Office. Head, Ministry of Information and Tourism 1963; head, Ministry of National Defence 1964–5; Vice-President Gabon 1967; President of Gabon since 1967 and Prime Minister 1968–76. Secretary-General of Parti Démocratique Gabonais 1968.

Botha, Pieter Willem (1916–   ), South African politician. Educ. Univ. of Orange Free State. Deputy Minister of Interior 1958–61; Minister of Community Development, Public Works and Coloured Affairs 1961–6; Minister of Defence 1965 and of National Security 1978. Leader of National Party in Cape Province 1966; Prime Minister of South Africa 1978.

Boumédienne, Houari (1925–78), Algerian nationalist leader and politician. Born near Bône; educ. in Tunis and Cairo. Served in French army. Joined Front de Libération Nationale in 1955 in war against French; FLN commander in Wilaya area 1955–7; Chief of Staff FLN 1960–2. Chief of Staff, Algerian army 1962–5; Minister of Defence 1962; and First Vice-Premier 1963–5. Led coup which overthrew President Ben Bella 1965. President of Algeria 1965–78.

Bourguiba, Habib Ben Ali (1903–   ), Tunisian politician and President. Educ. in Tunis; studied in France 1924–30. Member of Destour Party 1921, but split away from it to form the Neo-Destour Party, 1934; imprisoned by French 1934–6, 1938–43. Lived outside Tunisia 1946–9. Returned to Tunisia and again imprisoned by French 1952–4. Prime Minister of Tunisia 1956–7; President of republic of Tunisia since 1957.

Busia, Kofi (1913–78), Ghanaian politician and academic. Born Ashanti; educ. Oxford and London Univs; one of the first African assistant administrative officers appointed by British in Gold Coast 1942; lecturer, and later professor, Univ. College of Ghana 1948. Elected to Legislative Council 1951. A leader of the National Liberation Movement 1954–9; in exile 1959–66. Returned to Ghana as adviser to National Liberation Council after coup which deposed Nkrumah 1966. Founder and leader of Progress Party, which won general election 1969. Prime Minister of Ghana 1969–72. His government was overthrown by a military coup led by Lt-Col. Acheampong and he went into exile 1972. Held various academic posts; died in Oxford.

Buthelezi, Chief Mangosuthu Gatsha (1928–), South African politician. Born into Zulu royal family; educ. Fort Hare Univ. College. Government interpreter 1951–7; head of Buthelezi tribe 1953; elected leader Zulu Territorial Authority 1970. Rejected plan of South African Government to make Zululand into a 'bantustan'. Prime Minister of Kwazulu 1972; leader Black Unity Front 1976–7, and Inkatha Movement 1977.

Cabral, Amilcar (1924–73), Guinean nationalist leader. Born Bafatu, Portuguese Guinea; educ. in Bissau and at Lisbon Univ. as agronomist and hydraulic engineer. Civil servant in Portuguese Guinea and Angola 1956. Founded the nationalist PAIGC in Portuguese Guinea 1956; led war against the Portuguese from 1963 until his murder 10 years later.

Cabral, Luiz (1931–), Guinean nationalist leader. Born 1931, brother of Amilcar Cabral; educ. in Portuguese Guinea; clerk, accountant and trade union organiser 1953–60. Member PAIGC; fled into exile 1960. Active in struggle for independence of Guinea. President of Republic of Guinea Bissau 1973–80 when he was overthrown in a coup.

Chipembere, Henry M. (1931–75), Malawian nationalist leader. Born Nyasaland; educ. there and at Fort Hare Univ. College. Secretary-General of the African National Congress (Nyasaland) and later the Malawi Congress Party. Elected to Legislative Council 1955. Detained for nationalist activity 1959–60. Minister of Local Government in Nyasaland government 1963; Minister of Education 1964. Resigned from the government of newly independent Malawi in protest against the increasingly autocratic rule of Prime Minister Banda. Organised an abortive revolt in Malawi 1964–5. Exiled in Tanzania and the USA, where he worked mainly as a teacher 1965–75.

Dacko, David (1930–), first President of the Central African Republic. Born Bouchia, Ubangi-Chari; educ. Brazzaville; teacher and leader of teachers' union. Elected to territorial assembly 1957; Minister of Agriculture 1957–8; Minister.of Administrative Affairs 1958; Minister of Interior 1958–9; Prime Minister 1959–60. President of Central African Republic 1960–6. Deposed by military coup led by Bokassa 1966; imprisoned 1969–76. Appointed an adviser to President Bokassa 1976, but helped to overthrow him 1979. President 1979.

Daddah, Mohtar Ould (1924–), first President of Mauritania. Born into a prominent Berber family; educ. St Louis, Senegal, and Paris. Interpreter and lawer. Elected to territorial assembly 1957; Vice-President to Executive Council

1957; Prime Minister 1959–61. President of Republic of Mauritania 1961–78. Deposed by coup 1978. Chairman OAU 1971–2.

Danquah, Joseph Boakye (1895–1965), Ghanaian nationalist leader and politician. Born Kwawu; educated locally and at London Univ.; lawyer. Returned to Ghana and founded *Times of West Africa* in 1931 and was active in the Gold Coast Youth Movement. One of the leaders of the United Gold Coast Convention (UGCC) 1947, which campaigned for self-government for the Gold Coast. The UGCC was eclipsed by Nkrumah's Convention People's Party, and with the introduction of self-government in 1951 Danquah led the opposition to the CPP. Imprisoned by Nkrumah's regime 1961–2, 1964–5. Died in prison.

Dia, Mamadou (1910–   ), Senegalese politician. Educ. William Ponty School, Dakar, and in Paris; teacher and journalist. Councillor for Senegal 1946–52; helped form Bloc Démocratique Sénégalaise 1948. Grand Councillor for French West Africa and deputy in French National Assembly 1952. Vice-President Senegalese Council of Ministers 1957; President of Senegal 1958–60. Vice-President of Mali Federation 1959–60. Prime Minister of Senegal 1960–2. Imprisoned 1963–74. Political rights restored 1976.

Diori, Hamani (1916–   ), first President of the Republic of Niger. Born near Niamey; educ. locally, in Dahomey and at the William Ponty School, Dakar; teacher in Niger 1936–8; instructor in language school for colonial administrators 1938–46. Helped form Niger branch of Rassemblement Démocratique Africain 1946. Represented Niger in French National Assembly 1946–51, 1956–7. Head of Government Council in Niger 1958–60; President of Niger 1960–74. Chairman of West African Economic Community 1973. Ousted from presidency by coup and imprisoned 1974.

Dlamani, Prince Makhosini J. (1914–   ), Swazi politician. Educ. locally and in South Africa; teacher 1940–7. Active in local politics and as rural-development officer. Leader of royalist Imbokadvo party 1964. Prime Minister of Swaziland 1967–76.

Du Bois, William Edward Burghardt (1868–1963), pan-Africanist leader. Born Massachusetts, USA; educ. Harvard Univ. (PhD 1895); univ. teacher. Founder member of National Association for the Advancement of Colored People, 1909. Participated in pan-African conferences from 1900. In later life joined Communist Party of USA. Moved to Ghana and became a citizen of that country 1963.

Eyadéma, Gnassingbe, formerly *Étienne* (1937–   ), Togolese soldier and head of state. Born northern Togo. Served in French army 1953–61; commissioned in Togolese army 1963; Chief of Staff 1965. Led military coup 1967; President and Minister of Defence since 1967.

Gadaffi, Mu'ammar Mohamed al- (1938–), President of Libya since 1969 and staunch Muslim. Expelled from school for political activity but joined army and studied at Military Academy, Benghazi, 1965. Commissioned in Libyan army. Organised coup which overthrew King Idris 1969. Head of state, Chairman of Revolutionary Command Council and C-in-C armed forces since 1969.

Gizenga, Antoine (1925–), Zaïrean politician. Educ. RC mission schools. Helped found Parti Solidaire Africain in Kwango-Kwilu 1959. Deputy Prime Minister in Lumumba's coalition government 1960. Established breakaway pro-Lumumba regime in Stanleyville 1960–1. Resumed office as Vice-Premier of Congo 1960–2. Imprisoned 1962–5. Exile in USSR 1966.

Gowon, Yakubu (1934–), Nigerian army officer and former head of state. Born in what is now Benue-Plateau state; educ. Zaria and Royal Military Academy, Sandhurst. Commissioned into Nigerian army 1960; served with UN emergency force in Congo 1960–1; Adjutant-General Nigerian army 1963; Chief of Staff 1966. Head of Federal Military Government and C-in-C July 1966–75. Deposed 1975. Exile in UK, where he studied at Warwick Univ. 1976–80.

Graaf, Sir de Villiers, Bart (1913–), South African politician. Educ. at univs in South Africa, UK and Netherlands. Military service in Second World War. Elected United Party MP 1948; party leader 1956–77. Member of New Republic Party 1977.

Grunitzky, Nicolas (1913–), Togolese politician. Born in central Togo; educ. in France as an engineer. Returned to Togo 1937. Deputy in French National Assembly 1951–6. Formed Parti Togolais du Progrès and was Prime Minister 1956–8. Exiled in Dahomey 1962–3. President of Togo 1963–7; overthrown by military coup and went into exile in France 1967.

Haile Selassie I (1892–1975), Emperor of Ethiopia. Born into royal family, a cousin of Emperor Memelik II. Governor of Harar province 1910; regent and head of government 1916–28. Became Emperor 1930. Exiled following Italian invasion of Ethiopia 1936–41. Leading figure in Organisation of African Unity which had its headquarters in Addis Ababa. Overthrown by a military coup 1974 and died the next year while in detention.

Hassan II (1924–), King of Morocco. Born Rabat, elder son of King Mohamed V. From 1945 adviser to his father, with whom he went into exile 1953–5. At Moroccan independence became C-in-C army 1956; Prime Minister and Minister of Defence 1960. Designated heir 1957; succeeded to throne on death of his father 1961. Chairman OAU 1972.

Houphouët-Boigny, Félix (1905–), President of Ivory Coast. Son of a Baoulé chief; educ. in Bingerville and Senegal; medical assistant and planter 1925–40. President of Syndicat Agricole Africain 1944. Founded Parti Démocratique de la Côte d'Ivoire 1945; deputy in French National Assembly 1946–59; Mayor of Abidjan 1956; minister of French governments 1956–9. Prime Minister of Ivory Coast 1959; President since 1960.

Huggins, Godfrey, later *Lord Malvern* (1883–1971), Southern Rhodesian politician. Born in UK; medical practitioner. Emigrated to Southern Rhodesia 1911; member of Legislative Council 1924. Leader of Reform Party 1931. Prime Minister and Minister of Native Affairs 1933–53. Advocate of Central African Federation and its Prime Minister 1953–6. Created Lord Malvern 1955.

Hussein, Abdirizak Hadji (1924–), Somali politician. Son of a poor trader; educ. Koranic school and Al-Azhar Univ. Cairo 1953. Joined Somali Youth League 1944; President of SYL 1956. Founded Greater Somalia League 1958. MP 1959; held various ministries in government 1960–4; Prime Minister 1964–7. Imprisoned 1969–73. Somali Permanent Representative at UN 1974.

Idris I (1890–), former King of Libya. Succeeded to head of Senussi order in 1916. Recognised by Britain as Amir of Cyrenaica 1949. Became King of Libya on the territory's independence 1950. Deposed 1969 and later sentenced to death *in absentia*. Exiled in Egypt.

Ileo, Songoamba, formerly *Joseph* (1921–), Zaïrean politician. Educ. mission school; accountant. Co-founder with Patrice Lumumba of Mouvement National Congolais 1958, but joined Abako in 1959. Prime Minister 1960–1; Minister of Information and also in charge of Katangese affairs 1961–4. Member of Political Bureau of Zaïre government 1975.

Ironsi: see *Aguiyi-Ironsi*.

Jawara, Sir Dauda Kairaba (1924–), President of the Gambia. Born McCarthy Island; educ. locally at Achimota School, in Ghana and at Edinburgh Univ.; veterinary officer 1954–60. Leader of People's Progressive Party 1960; elected to Legislative Council and Minister of Education 1960–2; Chief Minister 1962 and Prime Minister 1963–70; President of the Gambia since 1970.

Jonathan, Chief Leabua (1914–), Lesotho politician. Educ. mission schools; worked in South African mines 1930s. Involved in Basutoland local politics from 1937 onwards; member Basutoland National Council 1956; founded Basutoland National Party 1959; member of Legislative Council 1960–4; Prime Minister of Lesotho since 1965. First black prime minister to make an official visit to South Africa.

Kapwepwe, Simon Mwanza (1922–80), Zambian nationalist leader and politician. Educ. mission schools; teacher 1945–51; helped found Northern Rhodesian African National Congress 1946; studied in India 1951–5. Treasurer of ANC 1956–8. Helped form Zambia National Independence Party (UNIP); treasurer UNIP 1960–7. Detained 1959. Held various ministries in Zambian governments 1964–71, including vice-presidency 1967–70. Resigned from UNIP government to form United Progress Party 1971; UPP banned and Kapwepwe detained 1972–3. Rejoined UNIP 1977.

Karume, Sheikh Abeid (1905–72), Zanzibari politician. Born on island of Zanzibar; sailor. Active in local politics 1940s–50s; town councillor 1954; founder-member Afro-Shirazi party 1957; Minister of Health and Administration 1959. Following coup which deposed the Sultan of Zanzibar became President of Revolutionary Council 1964. With union of Zanzibar and Tanganyika became First Vice-President of Tanzania 1964–72. Assassinated 1972.

Kasavubu, Joseph Ileo (1910–69), first President of Zaïre. Born Kongo region of Belgian Congo; educ. seminary 1928–39; teacher 1940; colonial civil service 1942. President of Abako 1955; Mayor of Leopoldville 1957. President of Republic of Congo 1960, 1961–5.

Kaunda, Kenneth David (1924–), Zambian nationalist leader and politician. Born Northern Rhodesia; educ. mission schools; teacher and welfare assistant, farmer. Secretary-General African National Congress 1953; formed Zambian National Congress 1958. Imprisoned for political activity 1959–60. Founder and leader of United National Independence Party 1960. Chief Minister Northern Rhodesia 1962–4; Prime Minister and then President of Zambia from 1964.

Kawawa, Rashidi M. (1929–), Tanzanian politician. Educ. at secondary school in Tabora. Founder member of TANU 1954; President of Tanganyika Federation of Labour 1950s; member of Legislative Council 1957. Various ministerial appointments 1960–2; Prime Minister 1962; Vice-President 1962–4; Second Vice-President 1964–72; Prime Minister and Second Vice-President 1972–7; Minister of Defence and National Service 1977.

Kayibanda, Grégoire (1924–), Rwandan politician. A Hutu; educ. RC mission schools; teacher 1949 and school inspector 1953; editor of a RC newspaper. Founded Mouvement Coopératif de Ruanda in 1952, and the Mouvement Social Hutu in 1957, which became Parmehutu. Head of provisional government 1960; Prime Minister 1961; President of Rwanda 1962–3. Deposed by military coup 1963.

Keita, Modibo (1915–77), Mali politician. Born near Bamako; educ. William Ponty School, Dakar. Helped found Rassemblement Démocratique Africain in

Soudan 1946. Elected to territorial assembly 1948; deputy in French National Assembly 1956. President of Mali Federation 1959–60; President of Mali 1960–8. Imprisoned 1968–77.

Kenyatta, Jomo (1891–1978), first President of Kenya, Born in Kikuyuland; educ. mission school and London School of Economics; interpreter and employee of Nairobi municipal government 1920s. General Secretary of Kikuyu Central Association. Studied and worked mainly in the UK 1931–46; author of *Facing Mount Kenya* 1938. Returned to Kenya 1946; President of Kenya African Union 1947. Imprisoned and restricted during the 'Mau Mau' emergency 1952–61. President *in absentia* of Kenya African National Union 1960. Elected to Legislative Assembly 1962; Prime Minister 1963–4; President of Kenya 1964–78.

Kerekou, Mathieu (1933–   ), Benin soldier and politician. Born in northern Dahomey, son of a soldier; educ. army schools; served in French army. Commissioned in Dahomey army 1961; Commander of army 1966. Took part in military coup 1967; Vice-President of Military Revolutionary Council 1967–8; led military coup 1972; President and Prime Minister from 1972.

Khama, Sir Seretse (1921–80), Botswana head of state. Educ. Fort Hare Univ. College, South Africa, and in the UK; lawyer. Heir of Ngwato chieftainship; banned from Bechuanaland 1950–6 because of his marriage to a white woman. Founded Bechuanaland Democratic Party 1962. Elected to Legislative Assembly 1965. President of Republic of Botswana 1966–80.

Kountché, Seyni (1931–   ), Niger soldier and head of state. Joined French army 1949; sergeant 1957; military training school in France 1957–9; joined Niger army 1961; officer-training France 1965–6. Chief of Staff Niger army 1973–4; Led coup against President Diori 1974. President of Niger 1974.

Lamizana, Sangoulé (1916–   ), Upper Volta soldier and head of state. Joined French army 1936; served in Second World War and in Indochina. Chief of Staff army of Upper Volta 1961; led coup which deposed President Yameogo 1966. President of Upper Volta 1966.

Limann, Hilla (1934–   ), Ghanaian diplomat and head of state. Educ. Tamale, and univs in London and Paris; teacher and educationalist. Ghanaian diplomat to United Nations 1969–79. Leader of the People's National Party and successful presidential candidate in elections of 1979. President of Ghana 1979–81.

Lumumba, Patrice (1925–61), first Prime Minister of the Congo (now Zaïre). Born Kasai province; educ. RC and Protestant schools; post-office clerk; director of a brewery 1957. Helped form Mouvement National Congolais 1958; attended independence conference in Brussels 1960. Prime Minister of Congo Republic June–Sep. 1960; advocate of a centralised government for Congo. Arrested by army and handed over to Katanga secessionists, by whom he was murdered Feb 1961.

Luthuli, Chief Albert (1898–1967), nationalist leader in South Africa. Born in Southern Rhodesia of South African parents; educ. mission schools Natal; teacher. Inherited minor Zulu chieftainship 1935. Joined African National Congress 1946 and became president of Natal branch. Led passive resistance in Defiance Campaign against apartheid and as a result deposed from his chieftainship by South African government 1952. President ANC 1952 until it was declared an illegal organisation 1960. Repeatedly 'banned' by the government after 1952. Defendant in Treason Trial and imprisoned 1956–7. Awarded Nobel Prize for Peace 1961.

Machel, Samora M. (1933–   ), Mozambique nationalist leader and politician. Born Southern Mozambique; trained as medical assistant. Joined Frelimo 1963; active in guerrilla war against Portuguese 1964–74. Leader of Frelimo after death of Mondlane 1969. President of Republic of Mozambique 1975.

Macias Nguema, Francisco (1922–79), first President of Equatorial Guinea. Educ. RC mission schools; coffee-planter and colonial civil servant 1944–63. Entered politics 1963. Vice-President Administrative Council 1964–8. President and Minister of Defence of Republic of Equatorial Guinea 1968. His 10 years of arbitrary and harsh rule were ended by a coup and his execution 1979.

Maga, Hubert (1916–   ), first President of Dahomey (now Benin). Born northern Dahomey; educ. locally and at the William Ponty School, Dakar. Deputy in French National Assembly 1951–8. Formed Groupe Ethnique du Nord and the Mouvement Démocratique Dahoméen 1956. Prime Minister of Dahomey 1959–60; President 1960–3. First leader of three-man Presidential Council 1970–2. Deposed and imprisoned by military in coup 1972.

Malan, Daniel François (1874–1959), South African politician. Born western Cape Colony; educ. South Africa and the Netherlands; minister in Dutch Reformed Church. Member of National Party 1914; editor *Die Burger* 1915; Minister of Interior 1924; helped re-form National Party 1933. Prime Minister 1948–54 and led government which introduced policy of apartheid in South Africa.

Malvern, Lord: see *Huggins*.

Mancham, James Richard (1929–   ), first President of the Seychelles. Educ. London and Paris; lawyer in Seychelles and member of Legislative Council 1961.

Founded Seychelles Democratic Party 1964. Chief Minister 1970–5; President, Republic of the Seychelles 1976–7. Deposed by coup 1977.

Mandela, Nelson Rolihlahla (1918–), South African nationalist leader. Born in Transkei; educ. Fort Hare Univ. College 1938–40; lawyer 1942. Joined African National Congress and helped found Congress Youth League 1944. 'Banned' by South African government 1953–5; defendant in Treason Trial 1956–61. Leader of underground militant organisation Mkhonto we Sizwe 1961–4. Arrested and sentenced to life imprisonment on Robben Island 1964.

Mangope, Chief Lucas L. M. (1927–), first President of Bophuthatswana 'bantustan'. Civil servant and teacher; succeeded his father as chief. Vice-Chairman Tswana Territorial Authority 1961–8. Chief Minister of Bophuthat-swana 1972–7; President of 'independent' state 1977.

Margai, Sir Albert Michael (1910–), Sierra Leone politician, brother of Milton Margai. Son of a Mende trader; educ. RC schools; nurse and pharmacist; studied law in London 1944–7. Member Legislative Council 1951; Minister of Education, Welfare and Local Government 1951–7. Member of Sierra Leone People's Party 1951–8. Helped found People's National Party 1958. Minister of Finance 1962–4; Prime Minister 1964–7. Exile in London 1968.

Margai, Sir Milton A. S. (1895–1964), Sierra Leone nationalist leader and politician. Born in southern Sierra Leone, son of a Mende trader and brother of Albert Margai; educ. mission schools, Fourah Bay College and in UK; medical practitioner. Member Protectorate Assembly 1940; Elected to Legislative Council 1951. Helped found Sierra Leone People's Party 1951. Chief Minister 1954–8; Prime Minister 1958–64.

Mariam, Mengistu Haile (1937–), Ethiopian soldier and head of state. A Wolamo; educ. primary school and military academy; joined army and became major. Member of the Armed Forces Co-ordinating Committee (Dergue), which helped overthrow Emperor Haile Selassie 1974; head of Executive Committee of Dergue; head of state 1977.

Massemba-Débat, Alphonse (1921–), Congo politician. Educ. locally; teacher in Chad 1940–7; secretary of Association of Chad évolués 1945–7. Returned to Middle Congo 1947. Member of Congo Assembly 1959–63; Minister of Planning 1961; Head of provisional government and Minister of Defence 1963. President of Republic of Congo 1963–8. Arrested 1969.

Matanzima, Chief Kaiser D. (1915–), South African politician. A Xhosa; educ. Lovedale Mission and Fort Hare Univ. College; lawyer. Member of United Transkeian Territorial Council 1942–56; Chief of Transkei Territorial Authority

1961, and Chief Minister 1963. Prime Minister of 'independent' bantustan Republic of Transkei since 1976.

Matthews, Zachariah K. (1901–68), South African academic and political leader. Born in Kimberley; educ. Fort Hare Univ. College, Yale, London School of Economics; lawyer. Principal of Adams College, Natal, 1925. Professor of African Studies and later Acting Principal of Fort Hare 1936 onwards. An organiser of the All-African Convention 1935. Joined African National Congress 1942. Defendant in the Treason Trial 1956–9; imprisoned 1960. Botswana ambassador to the United States in the 1960s and at the UN 1966–8.

M'Ba, Léon (1902–67), Gabon politician. Born Libreville; educ. RC school; accountant, journalist and administrator. Elected as Rassemblement Démocratique Africain member to Gabon Assembly 1952; Mayor of Libreville 1956; head of government 1957–60. First President of Gabon 1960–7.

Mboya, Thomas (Tom) Joseph (1930–69), Kenyan trade-union leader and politician. A Luo born in western Kenya; educ. RC mission school and Ruskin College, Oxford. Municipal employee 1951. Treasurer Kenya African Union 1953. Founder of Nairobi People's Convention; Secretary-General Kenya Federation of Labour 1955; Member of Legislative Council and then of Kenyan Parliament 1957–69. Founder member of Kenya African National Union and its Secretary-General 1960–9. Minister of Labour 1962; Minister of Justice and Constitutional Affairs 1963; Minister for Economic Planning and Development 1964. Assassinated 1969.

Messali, Hadj (Hadj Abd-el-Kadar) (1898–1974), Algerian nationalist leader. Soldier in French army in First World War; factory worker in France and an early member of the French Communist Party. Founded Étoile Nord-Africaine in Paris 1925, and also the nationalist newspaper *El Ouma* ('The National'). Imprisoned by French 1933–4, 1935, 1937–9, 1940–5. Founded Union Nationale de Musulmans Nord-Africains (1935), which was banned, and then the Parti du Peuple Algérien (1937). Imprisoned again 1945–7.

Micombero, Michel (1940–), Burundi army officer and former head of state. Educ. Bujumbura and at École Royale Militaire, Brussels, 1960–2. C-in-C Burundi army 1962; Minister of Defence 1965–6. Prime Minister 1966. Led coup which overthrew monarchy and in consequence became President 1966. Deposed and imprisoned by military coup 1976.

Mobutu, Sese Seko (1930–), Zaïrean soldier and politician. Born Equator province; educ. local primary and secondary schools. Sergeant-major in *Force publique* 1949–56. Member Mouvement National Congolais 1958; attended pre-independence talks in Brussels 1959–60; Chief of Staff Congolese army 1960.

Took over government in name of army 1960; C-in-C army 1962; Prime Minister and Minister of Defence 1965–6; President of Congo, now Zaïre 1965. Founded Mouvement Populaire de la Revolution, 1967.

Mohamed V (1909–61), King of Morocco. Became Sultan of Morocco 1927. Supported Moroccan independence but deposed by French 1953; exile in Comoros and Madagascar 1954–5; returned to Morocco 1955. King of independent Morocco 1956; head of government 1960–1.

Mohamed, Murtala Ramal (1937–76), Nigerian soldier and head of state. A Muslim Hausa from northern Nigeria. Trained at Sandhurst and the Royal School of Signals in Britain. Commissioned in Nigerian army; served in UN Congo operations 1960; commander Nigerian 2nd Battalion at start of Biafra war. Inspector of Signals 1968; federal Commissioner of Communications 1974. Became head of state when General Gowon was deposed in 1975. Assassinated 1976.

Moi, Daniel T. Arap (1924–   ), Kenyan politician. Born north-west Kenya; educ. mission and government schools; teacher 1949–57. Member of Legislative Council 1957–63; Chairman Kenya African Democratic Union 1960–1; Minister of Education 1961–2; Minister of Local Government 1962–4; member of House of Representatives 1963; Minister of Home Affairs 1964–8; Vice-President of Kenya 1967–78; President 1978.

Mondlane, Eduardo (1920–69), Mozambiquan nationalist leader. Born Gaza district; educ. mission school and univs in South Africa, Lisbon and the USA. Sociologist with research post in USA and for UN. Returned to Mozambique 1961 and helped form Frelimo 1962. Launched guerrilla war against Portuguese 1964. Murdered in Dar es Salaam 1969.

Moshoeshoe II (Constantine Bereng Seciso) (1938–   ), King of Lesotho. Educ. Roma College and Oxford. King 1960; went into exile for nine months 1970. Head of state again 1970.

Mugabe, Robert Gabriel (1928–   ), Zimbabwean politician. A Zezeru; educ. local RC mission schools; teacher in Southern Rhodesia 1952, Northern Rhodesia 1955, and Ghana 1958–60. Returned to Southern Rhodesia 1960 and became publicity secretary of the National Democratic Party 1960. Deputy Secretary-General Zimbabwe African People's Union 1961; helped form Zimbabwe African National Union 1963. Imprisoned 1962 and 1963 and detained by Smith regime 1964–74. Released 1974 and went into exile; leader of Zimbabwe Liberation Army. Joint leader with Joshua Nkomo of Patriotic Front in guerrilla war 1976–9. His Zimbabwe African National Union – Popular Front party won the pre-independence elections of 1980 and he became Prime Minister of Zimbabwe.

Mutesa II (*Edward Frederick*; '*King Freddie*') (1924–69), first President of Uganda. A member of Buganda royal family; educ. Makerere College and Cambridge Univ. Became Kabaka (king) of Buganda 1940. Opposed the development of Uganda as a centralised state and was deported by British authorities 1953–5. Co-operated with Obote's ruling party at independence and appointed president of Uganda 1963–6. Obote seized complete power 1966 and Mutesa went into exile in London, where he died.

Muzorewa, Abel T. (1925–), Zimbabwean churchman and politician. Educ. Methodist schools and at theological college USA 1958–63; ordained 1963; bishop of United Methodist Church in Southern Rhodesia 1968. Founder President African National Council 1971; mobilised African opinion against proposed Rhodesia settlement 1971–2; member of Executive Council of the transitional government in Zimbabwe–Rhodesia 1978–80.

Nasser, Gamal Abdul (1918–70), Egyptian army officer and nationalist leader. Born Alexandria, son of a postal official; educ. Cairo and Alexandria. Joined Egyptian army 1937; fought in Arab–Israeli war 1948–9. Member of 'Free Officers' movement 1948 and president of its executive committee 1950. A leader of the military coup which deposed King Farouk 1952. Member Revolutionary Command Council 1952–4; Deputy Prime Minister and Minister of Interior 1953–4. Took over power from Gen. Neguib to become President of Egypt 1954–70.

Neguib, Mohamed (1901–79), Egyptian soldier and head of state. Joined Egyptian army; fought in Arab–Israeli war 1948–9. As a major-general he was the senior officer in the 'Free Officers' movement which overthrew the monarchy 1952. Prime Minister 1952–3; President and Prime Minister 1953–4. Under house arrest from 1954.

Nemery, Jaafar Mohamed al-(1930–), Sudanese army officer and head of state. Born Omdurman; educ. Sudan Military College. Army officer in Southern Sudan 1959–63; in charge Shendi district 1966–9; led military coup 1969. Chairman Revolutionary Command Council and Prime Minister 1969–71; President 1971.

Neto, Antonio Agostinho (1922–79), Angolan nationalist leader. Son of a Methodist pastor; educ. Methodist school Luanda and studied medicine at univs in Portugal. Returned to Angola to work in colonial medical service. Joined MPLA; imprisoned four times 1952–60 and in Cape Verde Islands 1960–2. Escaped to Congo (ex-Belgian). President of MPLA and its leader in guerrilla war against Portuguese 1962–74. First President of Republic of Angola 1974–9.

N'Gouabi, Marien (1938–77), Congolese soldier and head of state. Joined army 1962; commander Brazzaville paratroop battalion; Chief of General Staff 1968.

Seized power from President Massamba-Débat and became head of National Revolutionary Council 1968. President until assassinated 1977.

Nkomo, Joshua M. N. (1971–   ) Zimbabwean nationalist leader. Educ. Adams College, Natal, and Univ. of South Africa. General Secretary of Rhodesian Railway African Employees Association 1951. Chairman Bulawayo branch, African National Congress 1951; President ANC 1957–60. In exile 1959–60. President National Democratic Party 1960. When NDP was banned helped form and became President of Zimbabwe African Peoples Union; imprisoned 1964–74; joint leader of African National Council 1976; joint leader, with Robert Mugabe, of Patriotic Front in guerrilla war 1976–9. His Zimbabwe African People's Union–Popular Front party won 20 seats in the pre-independence elections; Minister of Home Affairs 1980–1.

Nkrumah, Kwame (1909–72), nationalist leader and first President of Ghana. Born Western Gold Coast; educ. local RC school, Achimota College, Lincoln and Pennsylvania Univs USA 1935–45; studied law London 1945–7. Co-chairman Fifth Pan-African Congress, Manchester 1945. Returned to Gold Coast as General Secretary of United Gold Coast Convention. Broke with UGCC and formed Convention People's Party 1949. Imprisoned 1950–1; elected to parliament and released from prison to become 'leader of government business' 1951; Prime Minister 1952–7. Prime Minister of Republic of Ghana 1957–60; President 1960–6. Deposed by military coup while on visit to Peking 1966. Exile in Guinea, where Sekou Touré made him titular co-President.

Nkumbula, Harry M. (1916–   ), Zambian nationalist leader. Educ. local schools; teacher 1934; studied at Makerere College and London School of Economics 1946–50. President of Northern Rhodesia African National Congress 1951; imprisoned 1955. Supported a moderate constitution but lost support of Kaunda, who left the ANC to form UNIP 1958. Member of coalition government with Kaunda 1962–4. A leader of opposition to UNIP 1965–72; restricted 1970 but rejoined UNIP 1973.

Nujoma, Sam (1929–   ), Namibian nationalist leader. Educ. mission schools; railway worker and clerk to 1959. Founder SWAPO 1959; arrested same year. Went into exile 1960; presented Namibian case at UN; returned to Namibia but expelled from country 1966. Leader of SWAPO's armed struggle against South Africa's continued occupation of Namibia from 1966.

Nyerere, Julius K. (1922–   ), Tanzanian nationalist leader and politician. Born north-west Tanganyika; educ. Tabora, Makerere College 1943–5 and Edinburgh Univ. 1949–52; secondary-school teacher 1945–49, 1952–3. Secretary of Tanganyika African Association 1953; temporary nominated member of Tanganyika Legislative Council. Founder member and President of TANU

1954; full-time organiser of TANU 1955. Nominated member Legislative Council 1957, but resigned. Elected to Legislative Council 1958; Chief Minister 1960–1; Prime Minister 1961–2; President of Tanzania 1964. Introduced Arusha Declaration 1967.

Obasanjo, Olusegun (1937–), Nigerian army officer and former head of state. A Yoruba, born Abeokuta. Joined army 1958; trained at military colleges in UK and India; a military engineer. Served with Nigerian unit in UN Congo peace-keeping force 1960; military commander in Federal forces during Biafran war 1967–70. Federal Commissioner of Works and Housing 1975; Chief of Staff 1975; head of state 1975–9.

Obote, A. Milton (1924–), Ugandan nationalist leader. Born Lango district, north-east Uganda; educ. mission schools and Makerere College; worked as labourer, clerk and salesman in Kenya 1950–7. Founder member of Kenya African Union. Member Uganda National Congress 1952–60; elected to Legislative Council 1957. Helped form Uganda People's Congress 1960; leader of opposition in Ugandan parliament 1961–2; Prime Minister 1962–71; President of Uganda 1966–71. Deposed by military coup led by Gen. Amin. Exile in Tanzania 1971–9. Regained presidency 1980.

Odinga, Ajuma Oginga (1911–), Kenyan politician. A Luo; educ. Alliance High School, Kenya, and Makerere College; school-teacher; active in local politics 1947–57. Elected Legislative Council 1957; Vice-President Kenya African National Union 1960–6; Minister of Home Affairs 1963–4; Vice-President of Kenya 1964–6; resigned office to form Kenya People's Union 1966, which was banned by government 1969. Imprisoned 1969–71, 1977. Rejoined KANU 1971.

Ojukwu, Chukwenmeka O. (1933–), Nigerian army officer and politician. An Ibo; educ. Lagos and Oxford Univ. Joined Nigerian army 1957; attended military college UK; served in UN peace-keeping force in Congo 1962; Lieutenant-colonel 1963. Military governor Eastern Nigeria 1966; proclaimed Eastern Region the independent Republic of Biafra 1967; President of Biafra and leader in war with federal Nigeria 1967–70. On collapse of Biafra fled to Ivory Coast 1970.

Olympio, Sylvanus (1902–63), Togolese politician and head of state. Born Lomé; studied at London School of Economics; district manager of United Africa Company. President of Togolese Assembly 1946; leader Togolese government 1958–60; President of Republic of Togo 1960–3. Killed in military coup 1963.

Pereira, Aristides Maria (1924–), Cape Verde politician. Educ. Senegal; radio telegraphist. Founded PAIGC with Amilcar Cabral (q.v.) 1956; exile in Guinea

1960. Leader of PAIGC war council in guerrilla war with Portugal 1965–74. President of Republic of Cape Verde 1975.

Ramanantsoa, Gabriel (1906–), Malagasy soldier and politician. Educ. Antananarivo, at military colleges in Madagascar and France. Joined French army 1931; served North Africa, Paris, Indochina 1931–55. C-in-C Malagasy army 1960–72. President 1972–5.

Ramgoolam, Sir Seewoosagur (1906–), Mauritian politician. Educ. Mauritius and London Univ.; practised as medical doctor in Mauritius. Member Legislative Council 1940–8, and Executive Council 1948. Ministerial Secretary to the Treasury 1958–60; Chief Minister and Minister of Finance 1961. Prime Minister 1965; Chairman OAU 1977–8.

Ratsiraka, Didier (1936–), Malagasy naval officer and former head of state. Educ. in Madagascar and at French naval college; naval posts 1963–70. Minister of Foreign Affairs 1972–5; President Supreme Revolutionary Council 1975; President of Republic 1976.

Rawlings, Jerry (1948–), Ghanaian air-force officer and former head of state. Educ. Achimota College and Univ. of Ghana; commissioned in air-force. Led abortive coup and imprisoned 1979; escaped from prison and staged successful coup a few months later. Headed Armed Forces Revolutionary Council. Head of state but returned power to an elected president in 1979. Retired from air-force 1979. Seized power again in military coup early 1982.

René, France Albert (1935–), Second President of Seychelles. Educ. Switzerland and UK; lawyer 1957. Founded and led Seychelles People's United Party 1964; member of Legislative and National Assembly 1965–77; Minister of Works 1975–7 and Prime Minister 1976–7. Seized power and became President 1977.

Roberto, Holden (1925–), Angolan nationalist leader. Born São Salvador, northern Angola; educ. at mission schools in Belgian Congo. Formed União das Populações de Angola (1954), which joined other nationalist groups in 1963 to become the Frente Nacional de Libertação de Angola (FNLA). Led FNLA in guerrilla war with Portugal 1963–74. Continued war against the government of Angola following the withdrawal of Portuguese forces in 1975.

Sadat, Mohamed Anwar El (1918–81), Egyptian head of state. Educ. military college; joined army 1938. Member of 'Free Officers' movement 1948, and the Revolutionary Command Council after army coup 1952. Minister of State 1955–6; Vice-Chairman National Assembly 1957–61; Speaker United Arab Republic Assembly 1961–9; Vice-President 1964–6, 1969–70. Interim President

1969–70; President of Egypt since 1970. Negotiated peace terms with Israel 1977–9. Assassinated 1981.

Santos, José Eduardo dos (1942–   ), second President of Angola. Born Luanda; educ. Moscow (petroleum engineering) and Lisbon (medicine). An early member of the MPLA and organiser of its medical services during the guerrilla war against the Portuguese 1964–74. At independence became Foreign Minister and First Deputy Prime Minister, Planning Minister and head of the National Planning Commission 1976–7. President on death of Agostinho Neto (q.v.) 1979.

Savimbi, Jonas (1934–   ), Angolan politician. Born Central Angola; educ. Angola and Switzerland. Leader of Popular Union of Angola (UPA) and Foreign Minister in the Angolan government-in-exile 1962–4. Formed Union for the Total Independence of Angola (UNITA) 1966 and fought against the Portuguese until 1974. When Angola became independent the UNITA forces continued a civil war from bases in the south-east of the country.

Senghor, Léopold Sédar (1906–   ), poet and first President of Senegal. Born Joal, Senegal; educ. RC schools Dakar, and Univ. of Paris; teacher in France 1935–9. Joined French army 1939; prisoner-of-war 1940–2; member of Resistance 1942–4. Helped found Bloc Africain 1945 and the journal *La Présence Africaine* in Paris 1947. Deputy for Senegal in French National Assembly 1946–58; formed Bloc Démocratique Sénégalaise 1948. University teacher 1948–58. Formed Union Progressiste Sénégalaise 1958. President of Federal Assembly, Mali Federation 1959; President of Senegal 1960. A distinguished poet in French.

Shagari, Alhaji Shehu Usman A. (1925–   ), Nigerian head of state. Born in northern Nigeria; educ. there and became school-teacher. Member of the federal parliament 1954–8; Federal Minister of Economic Development 1959–60; Minister of Establishments 1960–2, of Internal Affairs 1962–5, of Works 1965–6. State Commissioner for Education, Sokoto province, 1968–70; Federal Commissioner for Economic Development and Reconstruction 1968–70, and Finance 1971–5. Member of the Constituent Assembly 1977. Successful presidential candidate for the National Party of Nigeria in the elections of 1979. President of Nigeria 1979.

Siad Barre, Mohamed (1919–   ), Somali soldier and head of state. Educ. locally and at military academy in Italy. Police officer in British and Italian trust administrations 1941–50. Joined Somali army as colonel 1960. President following army coup 1969.

Sisulu, Walter M. U. (1912–   ), South African nationalist leader. Born Transkei; educ. mission schools. Joined African National Congress Youth

League 1944; organised Defiance Campaign to oppose apartheid 1952; restricted by government 1952–6; defendant in Treason Trial 1956–61. Imprisoned 1962; escaped to Bechuanaland but returned to South Africa; recaptured and sentenced to life imprisonment on Robben Island 1964; transferred to mainland, 1982.

Sithole, Ndabaningi (1920–). Zimbabwean nationalist leader. Educ. Waddilove Institute, Southern Rhodesia; teacher 1941–53; studied theology in USA 1953–6 and ordained as Congregational clergyman 1958. Wrote *African Nationalism* 1959. President African Teachers' Association 1959–60; treasurer National Democratic Party 1960. With Joshua Nkomo founded Zimbabwe African People's Union 1962; split with Nkomo and helped formed Zimbabwe African National Union 1963; imprisoned by Smith regime 1964–75; exile in Zambia 1975–7 as leader of African National Council; formed his own faction of the ANC; negotiated with Smith regime and became a member of the Executive Council of the transitional government in Zimbabwe–Rhodesia 1978–80.

Smith, Ian Douglas (1919–), white Rhodesian politician. Born Southern Rhodesia; educ. Gwelo and Rhodes Univ., South Africa. Served with Royal Air Force in Second World War; farmer. Member of Southern Rhodesian Legislative Assembly 1948; member of Federal Parliament, 1953, becoming Chief Whip for United Federal Party. Helped found Rhodesia Front 1962. Prime Minister 1964–78. Declared Southern Rhodesia independent of UK 1965 (UDI). Forced by guerrilla war and external pressure to negotiate an internal settlement with certain African nationalists 1978. Member of Executive Council of the transitional government in Zimbabwe–Rhodesia 1978–80.

Smuts, Jan Christian (1870–1950), South African politician. Born Western Cape Colony; educ. Stellenbosch and Cambridge Univs 1889–94; lawyer 1895. Moved to Transvaal 1896; State Attorney of Transvaal 1898–1900. General commanding Boer troops in Cape 1901–2. Helped form an Afrikaner party, Het Volk, in Transvaal 1906; Minister of Interior and Education in Transvaal Colony 1907–9; Transvaal delegate to National Convention 1909. South African Minister for Mines, Interior, Defence, Finance 1910–19. Commanded forces in South West African campaign 1914–15; East Africa 1916–17. Member Imperial War Cabinet in UK 1917–18. Prime Minister, Minister of Defence, Native Affairs 1919–24; leader of white opposition in South African parliament 1924–33; Deputy Prime Minister, Minister of Justice in United Party government 1933–9; Prime Minister, Minister of Defence, External Affairs 1939–48. Defeated by National Party in general election 1948.

Sobhuza II (1899–), King of Swaziland. Educ. Lovedale College, South Africa. Installed as King 1921. Head of state of independent Swaziland 1968; assumed full executive and legislative powers 1973.

Sobukwe, Robert M. (1924–77), South African nationalist leader. Born Cape Province; educ. mission schools, Fort Hare Univ. College. President Students' Representative Council 1949; member African National Congress Youth League. Became teacher but dismissed for his part in the Defiance Campaign against apartheid 1952. Univ. teacher 1953–60. Helped found Pan-African Congress and became its president 1959. An organiser of anti-'pass-law' demonstrations 1960. Banned and imprisoned 1960–9. Released from prison but restricted to Kimberley 1969–77.

Stevens, Siaka Probyn (1905–   ), Sierra Leone head of state. Born in northern Sierra Leone; educ. Freetown; railwayman and miner. Founded Mineworkers Union 1943; appointed representative in Protectorate Assembly 1943. Studied at Ruskin College, Oxford, 1945. Helped found Sierra Leone People's Party 1951. Member of Protectorate Assembly; Minister of Lands, Labour, Mines; member Government Executive Council 1953. Attended independence conference London 1960. Founded All People's Congress Party 1960; Mayor of Freetown. Invited to be Prime Minister but forced into exile by army 1967; returned to Sierra Leone as Prime Minister 1968. President 1971.

Strijdom, Johannes Gerhardus (1893–1958), South African politician. Born Cape Province; educ. South African univs; lawyer and farmer. Elected to South African parliament 1929; Minister of Lands and Irrigation 1948; Prime Minister 1954–8.

Tambo, Oliver (1917–   ), South African Nationalist leader. Born Pondoland; educ. mission schools and Fort Hare Univ. College; teacher 1942–7; lawyer 1952. Joined African National Congress Youth League 1944; member of ANC executive 1949; Secretary-General 1955. Defendant in Treason Trial 1956–7. Deputy President ANC 1959; went into exile from South Africa 1960; President of ANC in exile 1977.

Thuku, Harry (1895–1970), Kenyan nationalist. Born Kiambu; educ. mission school. Founded East African Association 1921; arrested and imprisoned 1922–30. Leader Kikuyu Central Association 1930–5; founded Kikuyu Provincial Association 1935. Strongly opposed 'Mau Mau' but out of mainstream politics and earning his living as a farmer after the mid-1940s.

Todd, Reginald Stephen Garfield (1908–   ), white Rhodesian politician. Born in New Zealand; educ. New Zealand and South Africa. Came to Southern Rhodesia as a missionary 1934. Member Southern Rhodesian Legislative Assembly 1946. President United Rhodesia Party and Prime Minister of Federation of Rhodesia and Nyasaland 1953–8. Helped form multi-racial Central Africa Party 1959 and then the New Africa Party 1961. Returned to farming 1962. Opponent of Smith regime; restricted and imprisoned 1965–6, 1972–6. Associated with Joshua Nkomo in the elections of 1980.

Toiva Ja Toiva, Herman (1924–), Namibian nationalist leader. Born Ovamboland; educ. mission school. Served in South African forces in Second World War. Miner of Rand; moved to Cape Town and involved in nationalist politics; expelled from South Africa 1957. Founder member of South West Africa People's Organization (SWAPO) 1959 and its Northern Region secretary. Arrested 1966; sentenced to life imprisonment 1968.

Tolbert, William Richard (1913–80), President of Liberia. Educ. Liberia College, Monrovia; civil servant 1935–43. Member House of Representatives 1943–51; Vice-President 1951–71; President 1971–80. President of Baptist World Alliance 1965–6. Assassinated in the 1980 army coup.

Tombalbaye, N'Garta, formerly *François*, (1918–75), Chad politician. Born in Chad and educ. locally; teacher; trade-union organiser. Helped organise the Chad branch of the Rassemblement Démocratique Africain (RDA) in 1947. Member of the territorial assembly 1952, and also of the General Council of West Africa 1957. Prime Minister of Chad 1959–62; President 1962–75. Killed in a military coup in Apr 1975.

Touré, Ahmad Sekou (1922–), first President of Guinea. Educ. koranic school and Conakry 1936–40. Commercial worker and trade-union organiser 1945–7. Helped form Union Cégétiste des Syndicats de Guinée; attended the Confédération Générale des Travailleurs (CGT) Congress in Paris 1947; imprisoned by French 1947. Helped found Rassemblement Démocratique Africain in Guinea 1946 and Secretary-General of that branch 1952; Secretary-General CGT in Guinea 1952; organised general strike 1953. Member territorial assembly 1953; Mayor of Conakry 1955. Deputy in French National Assembly 1956. Founded Union Générale des Travailleurs d'Afrique Noir 1957. Vice-President Governor's Council 1957. Secured overwhelming *non* vote in de Gaulle's referendum 1958 and Guinea became independent. President since 1958.

Traoré, Moussa (1936–), Mali politician. Born Kayes; educ. cadets' college, Kati, and in France. Non-commissioned officer in French army. Senior officer in Mali army 1964. President of Mali following coup 1968.

Tshombe, Moïse (1919–69), Congolese politician. Born Katanga (Shaba) province, had close links with Lunda royal family; educ. mission schools; businessman. Helped found Confédération des Associations du Katanga (Conakat) 1957. President of secessionist Katanga province 1960–3. Exile from Congo 1963–4 but returned as President 1964–5. Went into exile a year after Mobutu's coup, 1966, and sentenced to death *in absentia* by Kinshasa high court 1967. In same year he was kidnapped to Algiers, where he died in prison.

Tsirinana, Philibert (1912–   ), first President of Madagascar. Born northern Madagascar; educ. locally and in France 1946–50. Organised Social Democratic Party. Member of Representative Assembly 1956; deputy to French National Assembly 1957. Deputy President of Madagascar 1958; President 1959–72. Overthrown by military coup 1972.

Tubman, William V. S. (1895–1971), Liberian President. Born Maryland, south-east Liberia, a member of the Americo-Liberian elite; educ. Methodist seminary; teacher 1913–17; lawyer and Methodist preacher. True Whig Party member of Senate 1922–30; Deputy President Supreme Court 1937–44. President of Liberia 1944–71.

Verwoerd, Hendrik Frensch (1901–66), South African politician. Born Nether-lands but taken as a baby to South Africa; educ. South Africa, Netherlands and Germany; Professor of Psychology and later Sociology, Stellenbosch Univ. 1927. Founder and editor of *Die Transvaaler* 1937. Appointed to Senate by National Party after its victory in general elections 1948. As Minister of Bantu Affairs he introduced the apartheid legislation 1950–8. Prime Minister 1958–66. Strong advocate of a South African republic and withdrawal from Commonwealth – both achieved in 1961. Crushed African opposition 1960–4. Assassinated in parliament by a mentally deranged man 1966.

Vorster, Balthazar Johannes (1915–   ), South African politician. Born Cape Province; educ. Stellenbosch Univ.; lawyer. Interned for pro-Nazi sympathies during Second World War. National Party MP 1953; Deputy Minister of Education 1958; Minister of Justice 1961–6; Prime Minister 1966–78. President of South Africa 1978, but resigned following 'Muldergate' scandal 1979.

Welensky, Sir Roland (Roy) (1907–   ), white Rhodesian politician. Born Southern Rhodesia; educ. locally; railway worker from age 14; boxing champion. Leader Railway Worker's Union in Northern Rhodesia 1933. Member Northern Rhodesian Legislative Council 1938–53; founded Northern Rhodesia Labour Party 1941; chairman unofficial opposition in Legislative Council 1947–53. A strong advocate of a federation in Central Africa, he attended the Victoria Falls Conference in 1951. Elected to Federal Parliament; Deputy Prime Minister 1953; Prime Minister and Minister of Transport of Federation of Rhodesia and Nyasaland 1953–63. Retired from politics 1964.

Whitehead, Edgar C. F. (1905–71), Southern Rhodesian politician. Born and educ. UK; emigrated to Southern Rhodesia 1928; civil servant 1928–30; farmer 1930–9; elected to parliament 1939; war service 1940–5. Southern Rhodesian High Commissioner in London 1945–6; Minister of Finance 1946–53. Retired to farming 1953–7. Representative of Federation of Rhodesia and Nyasaland in USA 1957–8; Prime Minister 1958–62.

Yameogo, Maurice (1921–   ), first President of Upper Volta. A Mossi; educ. locally; civil servant and trade-union leader. Elected to territorial assembly 1946; member Grand Council of French West Africa 1948. Vice-President Upper Volta section of Confédération Français du Travailleurs Chrétiens and activist in the local branch of the Rassemblement Démocratique Africain 1954. Founded the Mouvement Démocratique Voltaique 1957. Minister of Agriculture in coalition government 1957–8; Minister of the Interior 1958; President of Upper Volta 1958–66. Deposed by military coup 1966; imprisoned 1966–70; went into exile in Ivory Coast.

Youlou, Abbé Fulbert (1917–72), first President of the Congo Republic. Born near Brazzaville; educ. at seminaries in Cameroon and Gabon; ordained an RC priest in 1946. Mayor of Brazzaville 1957. Formed Union Démocratique de la Défence du Interêts Africains, opposed to the local socialist party, the MSA. Elected to territorial assembly 1957; Minister of Agriculture 1957–8; Prime Minister 1958–9; President of Congo 1959–63. A general strike and widespread unrest in the country forced him to resign and to go into exile in Spain in 1963.

BIBLIOGRAPHY

Africa South of the Sahara (London: Europa Publications, annually from 1971).

Africa Year Book and Who's Who (London: Africa Journal, annually from 1976).

Baum, Edward, and Gagliano, Felix, *Chief Executives in Black Africa and South East Asia* (Athens, Ohio: Ohio University Centre for International Studies, 1976).

Caldwell, John C., and Okonjo, Chukuka, *The Population of Tropical Africa* (London: Longman, 1968).

Caldwell, John C. (ed.), *Population Growth and Socio-economic Change in West Africa* (New York: Columbia University Press, 1975).

Colonial Office Lists (London, annually from 1945).

Constitutions of African States, prepared by the Secretariat of the Asian–African Legal Consultative Committee, New Delhi (Dobbs Ferry, NY: Oceana, 1972), 2 vols.

Cook, Chris, and Paxton, John, *Commonwealth Political Facts* (London: Macmillan, 1979).

Hailey, Lord, *An African Survey* (Oxford University Press, 1938; rev. ed. 1956).

Henige, David P., *Colonial Governors from the Fifteenth Century to the Present* (Madison, Wis.: University of Wisconsin Press, 1971).

Legum, Colin (ed.), *Africa Handbook*, rev. edn (Harmondsworth: Penguin, 1969).

Legum, Colin, and Drysdale, John (eds), *Africa Contemporary Record* (London: Rex Collings, annually from 1967–8).

Morrison, D. G., Mitchell, R. C., Paden, J. N., and Stevenson, H. M., *Black Africa: A Contemporary Handbook* (New York: Free Press, 1972).

New African Yearbook (London: IPC, 1978, 1979).

Ominde, S. H., and Ejiogu, C. N. (eds), *Population Growth and Economic Development in Africa* (London: Heinemann, 1972).

Paxton, John (ed.), *The Statesman's Year-Book* (London: Macmillan, annually from 1945).

Potgieter, D. J. (chief ed.), *Standard Encyclopaedia of Southern Africa* (Cape Town, 1971).

UN Demographic Yearbook (New York: United Nations, annually).

UN Statistical Yearbook (Paris: UNESCO, annually from 1963).

Whitaker's Almanack (London, annually from 1945).

World Statistics in Brief: UN Statistical Pocketbook (New York: United Nations, 1977).

INDEX

DATE DUE
